Signs of Agni Yoga
SUPERMUNDANE
Vol. II

SUPERMUNDANE

THE INNER LIFE

II

1938

Agni Yoga Society
319 West 107th Street
New York NY 10025
www.agniyoga.org

© 1994 by the Agni Yoga Society.
Published 1994.

Reprinted 2017. Updated July 2020.
Translated from Russian by the Agni Yoga Society.

SUPERMUNDANE

The Inner Life

290. Urusvati knows how much We value the many aspects of wisdom. Wisdom accepts goodness, regardless of its source. Wisdom condemns evil, regardless of its source. Do not take wisdom for granted; it is quite rare. Many people perish because they judge good and evil according to their personal concepts. They expect good only from one particular source, and fear an evil that is often only a ghost of their own imagining.

You know how capricious are the scales of good and evil. In an earthly sense no one can predict where good or evil may originate. We have seen thieves who became saints, and pillars of the church who committed evil deeds. It is folly to be limited by one's preconceptions.

Broad-mindedness is based on tolerance. Wisdom will say, "Let justice be done," yet will not dictate the verdict, for wisdom understands the complexity of the conditions required for justice. Wisdom will sense the right time and will not force events. Wisdom realizes that every event involves all nations.

Circumstances may appear one way on the surface, but the true, deeper meaning may be entirely different. Sometimes the predestined is manifested in an unexpected guise. Thus one becomes used to the idea that Justice has many faces.

People judge in accordance with their habits, but the law of justice is forged in the three worlds and may be considered supermundane. Acceleration and retardation of events depend on many cosmic causes.

Often an insignificant earthly happening is a reflection of great events in the far-off worlds. There should be a harmonious, mutual understanding if one wants wisdom to transform the reality of everyday life.

The Thinker liked to emphasize that although the earthly pilgrim goes his own way, there are countless ways above.

291. Urusvati knows that people underestimate the influence of cosmic currents, and assume that a more refined organism is less susceptible to them. But the saying, "The Burden of this World," was known in remote antiquity. Simply, it states that this burden is carried by the most refined and most elevated ones, who resound intensely to the currents of space. They suffer greatly who sense distant earthquakes and the shock of cosmic currents that exceed the speed of light. The study of such currents has not yet been developed, and people stumble upon obscure evidence only by accident. But physicians should remember that cosmic currents influence many diseases.

People produce strong poisons within themselves, and exhale them in their fits of hatred. The legend about poisonous breath has a true basis. The roar of crowds does shatter space, and the breath of malice pollutes the atmosphere for a long time. It is particularly timely to remind you about this during the days of Armageddon.

People protect themselves from poisonous gases by wearing gas masks. But they should provide themselves with one more mask—the protective mask of pure thought—for only thought can shield one from the poisonous breath. People should admit that there is such poison, and remember that thought has the power to resist the most harmful vibrations.

Only thought can produce the antidote. These

words should not be taken as symbolic. Thought produces a substance that attracts the helping forces from space. We have spoken about resistance to evil. Precise, clear, and disciplined thought is a powerful aid, and also a powerful antidote. So-called immunity is the result of thought. If you remember Us you will intensify your thoughts and they will acquire a new power. Think about Us. Think about reality and face the terrors of Armageddon.

The Thinker consoled His disciples, saying, "An Invisible Messenger is ready to contact you. Allow Him to reach you."

292. Urusvati knows how the information about the Brotherhood has been distorted. Mediums invent strange fables, and there are even more harmful fabrications. There are certain types who can be called semi-mediums, who obtain only fragmentary impressions of the Subtle World, and then attribute them to the life of the White Brotherhood.

You have heard about the false Olympus, which was built by thought-forms in the lower astral spheres. Fragmentary details of this Olympus are perceived by the mediums, but they know little about the thought-forms of the Subtle World and are always ready to attribute these ephemeral temples, solemn processions, and ostentatious garments to Our Towers. Those who have little knowledge of the conditions of the Subtle World can therefore become misled.

Ordinarily, earthly people are unable to imagine the subtle strata. They do not realize that multitudes of subtle entities can move among them, penetrate their dense bodies, and can even create their own entire cities. People think that thought-forms are only a fairy-tale, not realizing that their earthly existence leaves its mark in this way on the Cosmic Life.

How harmful are extremes! On the one hand, some deny the "hereafter" completely, whereas others put their faith in absurd images, forced upon them by religions in order to frighten them! It is wrong to remain in the grip of these limitations. People forget that only unprejudiced knowledge will help them to approach the Truth.

Let us discuss two ideas that are usually misunderstood. First, people assume that if clairaudience can be manifested under ordinary conditions, it will be even stronger when the currents are intensified. However, highly intensified currents can interfere with clairaudience, for when the currents are crossed they form a kind of shell that is impenetrable to thought-transmission.

Second, when We recommend vigilance, We mean it to be applied in all aspects of life. People think that vigilance is necessary only at times of great importance, but in fact it is required in even the most insignificant daily actions. It is impossible to separate the outward details from the essential, therefore events should not be evaluated by their appearance. All conditions should be calmly considered and one must learn from their diversity. Try to apply Our Vigilance, the vigilance that prevails in Our Tower.

The Thinker never tired of reminding His disciples about the importance of paying attention to every step and to every mental transmission. He said, "It is not for us to judge what is important and what is unimportant. Therefore, let us be vigilant!"

293. Urusvati knows that people more readily understand any advice when it is explained by analogies from the practice of medicine. For example, one can cite the case of a patient who is instructed to fully inhale a certain medicinal vapor, but because he distrusts the physician he only inhales half a dose, and the desired result is not obtained. Similarly, when people do not strive fully toward the Source of Ultimate Good, the results are lamentable. Disbelief, laziness, or ignorance will lead to the same sad end.

People should remember that their undisciplined striving causes suffering to their Guides, who receive poisonous stings, so to speak. We must point out that a considerable degree of the burden comes not so much from direct hostility as from undisciplined striving. We especially stress harmony in thought transmission, and the need for each one to concentrate his entire consciousness.

In the same way, the Thinker exhorted His disciples, "Perhaps you can find an even higher degree of concentration. Search your hearts! No one can say that he has exhausted his striving to the utmost degree. Let us express our aspiration to its maximum, and then we shall declare it to the whole world."

294. Urusvati knows how strong are the accumulations of human thought on objects, and that man himself creates good and bad things and places. Many leaders chose new locations so as to avoid the bad accumulations of previous dwellings. Some did this consciously because they knew the truth, but others simply had an unexplainable feeling that prompted them to live in a new, unsullied environment.

The time will come when people will learn to recognize the chemical compounds to be found in various strata. They will not then attribute manifestations to magic or conjurations, but will realize that man himself is a kind of magician at every moment of his life. Great power is given to a man who knows how to create the formulas of good and evil. We must not regard such people as magicians, but understand that the weaving of good or evil continues at every hour. Let us encourage the weavers of good and pity the weavers of evil, who will one day bitterly regret the dark shrouds they have woven.

Most people do not have the slightest idea of this, and those who do quickly forget. It is not an easy task to dissolve these dark stratifications. As you know, every substance emits and even harbors its own germs. People easily accept the idea that certain objects can be infectious and even poisonous, but refuse to understand that it is their own thoughts that permeate the objects. Indeed, people have a low opinion of the potency of their own thoughts! Likewise, few realize that by surrounding themselves with poisonous objects they put barriers between themselves and the Higher Realms. We suffocate in a polluted atmosphere. It would be wonderful if medical authorities would apply to the mental realm the same improvements they make to sanitary conditions!

Sometimes the Thinker advised a newcomer to wash his hands, because an evil thought could have settled on them.

295. Urusvati knows that profound similarities underlie all the moral Teachings of the ages. And how else could it be? The Law is one. There may be details that vary according to local life, or differences of language, but the foundations are changeless. Of course, it should be understood that We refer to real foundations and not to imagined ones.

For example, We say that the illusion of so-called peace is worse than actual war. People who are full of hatred may assure you that they live in peace, but they are liars. Such a lie is not easy to wash away; it continues to exist in the Subtle World. People should consider whether they have the right to pollute the subtle worlds, but they seldom think about their responsibility to the Universe. The continuity of life is not taught in the schools. There are few, if any, courses taught that reveal the grandeur of human life, and the teacher is rare who is capable of impressing upon students the dangers of false concepts. Yet all the Teachings testify to the Great Reality of true peace.

It is hard to accept human indifference to reality. People are fond of the untruths that mask the ulcers of corruption, and they refuse to understand that a lie created by them remains with them.

Speaking about false concepts, one should not relate them to only a few significant events. It should be remembered that man's entire life is filled with petty but characteristic falsehoods. So much false courage, so much false devotion, so much false diligence is manifested throughout the world!

It is deplorable to see how such make-believe concepts can lead to demoralization and mass lies. People put these lies into the very foundation of life, and there can be no evolution based on lies. Such lies produced by the make-believe mentality are sheer perversion, and should not be mistaken for *Maya*, which expresses the relativity of concepts.

Courage and fearlessness can truly protect one from all evil attacks, but the courage must be real and true. The borderline between the real and the false is subtle, and only from a distance is it possible to evaluate precisely where the corrupting process starts. It must be understood that only the real will bring lofty results.

The Thinker pointed out that the disciples must test their fearlessness. When the Teacher observed that a disciple was afraid of something, He placed him at once face to face with what had frightened him.

The same trial was also used in the schools of Sparta. There, the expression of the eyes was watched in order to confirm the disciple's courage. Thus We also watch the motion of the spirit, and rejoice when We perceive true courage.

Fear of scarecrows in this earthly life only shows an unpreparedness for life in the Subtle World, where one is also confronted with frightening images. But the courageous do not even notice them! Only fear breeds ghosts.

Such was the teaching of Pythagoras.

296. Urusvati knows that the heavens continually change. During a single earthly life one can observe many manifestations that cannot be explained by today's science, and even imperfect telescopes can show us that the infinite life is infinitely complex.

People improve their telescopes, but the results are insignificant compared with the astronomical scale. Only by combining telescopic observations with clairvoyance will it be possible to focus upon planetary movements that are beyond the capacity of the telescope.

The question may be asked how one can reconcile astrology with these unexplained movements of heavenly bodies. The fact is that once astrology is understood to be based on the chemism of the stars, it will be seen that each heavenly body has an influence upon Earth, and an experienced astronomer will take into account the special influences caused by the various positions of the heavenly bodies. In the same way, astrology should make use of telescopes and accept clairvoyance. In fact, all fields of knowledge should be synthesized and applied.

Scientists often bring the faculty of intuition into their research. This intuition may already dwell within or may be newly born in the depths of the consciousness. Either way, it should be heeded, for it is hard to discern the boundary between intuition and clairvoyance, and one should not limit the process of thinking to the physical abilities. Even during ordinary telescopic observation it must be remembered that the human eye works in diverse ways, and We can assure you that man sees things differently each day.

We can properly observe the heavenly bodies only by utilizing these methods. From an early age, young people should be taught that the complex process of learning is a broad synthesis of all knowledge. Those teachers who begin with methods that limit thinking are in error.

Ages ago the Thinker was concerned with the broadening of thought, for constraint of thought is unacceptable in philosophy.

297. Urusvati knows the meaning of labor. It is an intensification of psychic energy that can be understood in many ways. Some think of it as prayer, others joy, and still others ascension. People can create a natural discipline out of labor. The rhythm of labor is a form of *pranayama*, and can be made into a natural discipline. It is wrong to assume, as many people do, that routine work is repellent. The experienced worker is a master of his task and perfects every detail.

It is significant that people often sing or talk while performing their tasks, as if to encourage themselves. They may also murmur in a manner somewhat between thought and word, unaware of the fact that they are uttering a sound. Their rhythmic whisperings should be studied. They not only reveal one's character, but also demonstrate the degree to which psychic energy is manifested in all labor.

The whisperings may have nothing to do with the

work itself. The intensified energy of work may be evoking forgotten memories from the Chalice, and the murmuring may be revealing new tales. Such experiences should be investigated, for they may indicate accumulations from former lives.

During work a person may also whisper numbers, or letters, or an unfamiliar name. Any such manifestation has great significance, and the work itself acquires a majestic meaning. We can testify to this by Our own experience.

The Thinker often listened carefully to such accompaniments to people's labor.

298. Urusvati knows that We encourage mastery in all fields of work. Everyone should strive to perfect his art and his work. Even if these attempts are not always successful, they will nevertheless help one to achieve a new level of concentration.

While on Our Path We always implemented the betterment of arts and crafts; We taught new chemical combinations; We encouraged ceramics and carving. We even taught people how to preserve their food. I speak of all this so that you will understand the variety of approaches to evolution.

Let each one help where he can; no opportunities are insignificant. Where there is true striving, help is more easily granted. We try all the ways.

There is innate talent in every child. Children can recollect experiences in the Subtle World. Adults often do not understand their children, and impose games upon them according to their own tastes instead of observing the children's natural inclinations. Children are fond of toys, not so much for the toys themselves as for the possibilities for creativity that are inherent in them. A child loves to take a toy apart so that he can put it together and use it in his own way. In this activity children are not influenced by outside impressions, and often produce things that they could not have seen at all in their present life. These creative impulses are brought from the Subtle World, and have great significance.

We encourage the revealing of such accumulations, but you can imagine how We must struggle against family prejudice! Only one family in a thousand pays attention to a child's true nature.

We devote much energy in trying to give guidance to families. We affirm full rights for women, but as soon as these rights are pronounced there is barbaric opposition. Any country that approaches the idea of equal rights will lead in the quality of work. Remember, I said that from little rays will be made a sun. It takes time to manifest quality, and co-workers will come from among the young ones.

The Thinker would often ask children what they would like to do in life. Many answered that they did not know, but others spoke of their long-standing desires. To those the Thinker would say, "What seems impossible today may become possible tomorrow."

299. Urusvati has observed that some localities can have different names at different times. There has been a rumor that We deliberately changed the name of Our Abode, but this is not true. In fact We simply allowed the changes in name that would normally occur due to differences in language.

Generally We do not rely on names or rituals, but are concerned with the essentials. Urusvati knows that the essence of Our work, Our goal, is the transformation of consciousness. Like sculptors, We work on the coarse aspects of human consciousness and try to mold it into something beautiful.

We do not mind being accused of pointless repetition. First of all, it is not true. We do not repeat, but only refine and ennoble concepts that have not yet been assimilated. Physicians treat wounds until healthy new tissue is formed. They do not refuse to help, they show great patience, and are ever ready to take abuse from impatient sufferers! They know that certain treatments require extended amounts of time, and that patients do not understand the process of healing.

We know that a transformation of consciousness cannot take place at once. We do not refuse to provide a remedy, but when given it must be accepted in full measure. Do not be surprised when you meet with misunderstanding and ingratitude, which indicates that the consciousness of the one you help has still not been awakened. How often a person understands his tasks in the Subtle World, yet when incarnated in the flesh is once more as though turned to stone!

The Thinker spoke often about hearts of stone.

300. Urusvati knows that there are many stony hearts. Let us see what the Thinker had in mind when He made this severe statement. He was referring not so much to cruelty as to an inner stagnation, when the heart feels neither heat nor cold. Such hearts cannot be called evil, because they know not either good or evil.

Unfortunately, these hearts exist in great numbers, but are not easily recognized. They show no evident symptoms, though they are in a state almost identical to the recognizable condition known as coma, in which the organism is neither alive nor dead, nothing is remembered, and the subtle body is immobile and as numb as the rest of the organism. In this condition man ceases to be really human. Stone-like hearts are similar, and so numerous that they are a great burden to the world, and impede evolution.

To resist evolution is to oppose the inevitable and commit a dreadful crime. It is amazing that after millions of years of existence humanity fails to understand that the process of evolution takes place in all the kingdoms of nature. It can be clearly shown that outlived forms are dying away and new outlines of life are coming into existence.

Please understand that the spirals of evolution can be accelerated only if senseless human opposition ceases. People do not always know how to create, but they do indeed know how to oppose, and ugliness, discord, and calamities come into being.

We are now witnessing the disappearance of entire countries, but does this always happen in the name of evolution? Indeed not. People often either become like stone or attempt to sink into the old ruts, but Nature does not permit delay.

The Thinker used to say, "Oh, seafarer, do not sail with a cargo of stony hearts. With such a cargo you will never reach your destination."

301. Urusvati knows how even the greatest heroic deeds can be misunderstood. Are there many people who can look at the actions of others without prejudice? Picture a stranger making his way with great difficulty in rain and hail, and mud up to his knees. People watch him from the windows and laugh, wondering why he didn't stay home in the storm.

Compare those who sneer and laugh with those few who sympathize and wonder what the traveler's goal might be. Perhaps he is on his way to save a neighbor, or is a physician hastening to give help, or even a messenger bringing salvation to an entire nation. Those who serve Good will look for the good in others, but one rarely comes across such people! Most people usually look for the bad in others, and thus suspect every stranger to be a vagrant or a thief, not realizing that to accuse the innocent is an indelible crime.

People fear being cursed, but in fact bring curses upon themselves whenever they commit an injustice. Try an experiment; send the purest man to perform important work or a heroic deed, then see how he will be slandered. The majority will criticize without considering his task, and only a few, who are themselves persecuted, will think about the aim of the *podvig*. This lack of good will is a major obstacle to the progress of evolution.

Generally people do not consider who might have sent the messenger, or who may be harmed by their evil tongues. Some will argue that their slander is quite harmless, not realizing that anything unclean lessens purity.

We have been compelled more than once to take special measures for the purification of space. But such discharges of energy cause shocks so strong that they have consequences in the Subtle World. Such arrows cannot be sent forth frequently. We are very concerned about those unwise people whose actions boomerang.

The Thinker carefully watched the pilgrims and used to ask if He could be of help to them. When He was warned that they might be vagrants, He whispered, "Who knows, they may be from Beyond." When their poor attire was pointed out to Him, He smiled and said, "Pilgrims are not used to luxury." And when He was told that true heroes do not come from the lower classes, He became indignant and pointed out that the time would come when the common people would produce great things.

The Thinker directed attention to the people.

302. Urusvati knows that at times when the currents of space are in such opposition that the pulse of life is suspended, even many of those who are clearly alive are threatened by death. This danger is even greater when people are ill or suffer from a state of nervous stress.

The circumstances are complex and We indicate caution, but Our advice is seldom accepted. People think of caution as inertia, not realizing that even during days of great strain We would never advise inaction. We compensate for the collision of currents with the most intensified activity. This may not always be evident, but We are not concerned about outward manifestations. The Teacher must direct His inner energy and thus help to withstand the tension.

Can there be caution without vigilance? Even watchfulness can be of two kinds. A person is usually interested only in his immediate surroundings, and it is only when We exclaim, "Watch out!" that he will begin to look around. True alertness must encompass everything.

Can anyone be certain that there is anything that does not affect him? Can anyone affirm that nature manifests itself in the same way in all ages? Can anyone argue that human thinking has not changed over thousands of years? Even within this century thinking and language have changed.

It is evident that during periods of extraordinary tension the events of life are accelerated, and an especially keen vigilance is needed during these times. How can people acquire such vigilance? It is not the bold and daring ones but the plodding thinkers who fail to recognize the need for caution based on vigilance. They will reproach Us, unmindful of the fact that it is within everyone's power to be watchful.

The Thinker used to ask, "Have I failed to observe something important? Has something irreparable happened? May my eyes acquire the power to observe!"

303. Urusvati knows that the foundations of life should be expressed in every human action. It is not enough just to read and discuss fundamental truths; they must permeate one's life so that they need not be mentioned at all. For this one must learn to distinguish the different levels of thought.

Just as there are three worlds, there are also three levels of thought. Man can think simultaneously on all three levels. For instance, he can be absorbed in mundane thinking, which includes empirical reasoning. Behind this functions his subtle thought, and in the depths of his consciousness a fiery spark may radiate. At times these three layers can merge harmoniously into one, and there results a powerful projection of thought. But, as a rule, people exhibit only discord in their consciousness. Sometimes their earthly reasoning produces seemingly attractive ideas, but their subtle thinking will reject these ideas, knowing their true origin. For them, the fiery sparks may not ignite at all.

One can see how it is possible for the discordant consciousness to be influenced by these three impulses. What kind of power can be achieved with such disharmony? There is an ancient fairy tale about a man within whom lived an angel and a demon. Both whispered their instructions, but only when the fiery spark was kindled by love did the demon leave him.

It is instructive to observe how the three levels of thought replace one another. An earthly thought is not necessarily inferior to a subtle one. There are cases when earthly thought led people to lofty actions, whereas the subtle thought crept its way upon an outlived path. Of course, the fiery divine spark is always faultless, but it must be kindled.

We watch the process of human thinking and rejoice when the three strata are united in harmony. You must realize that these three layers of consciousness are only crude distinctions, and that in reality there are many more subdivisions. But let us now consider only the fundamental three, so as not to complicate the observations.

The Thinker instructed his disciples to strictly control their thoughts and to harmonize them. He called such harmony of thought music.

304. Urusvati knows how karma affects each nation. Some countries appear to be under a kind of curse. The history of these countries can offer a partial explanation, but there may be other causes that were not recorded on the pages of history.

There are many combinations of personal, family, and national karma. One may ask if it is possible that an injustice committed against one person could affect a whole country. Indeed, it can, especially since many who are involved with one another reincarnate in the same country. Such conditions increase the responsibility of mankind. People acknowledge that physical characteristics are transmitted through the generations; it is regrettable that they are not aware that karmic traits can also be transmitted.

Urusvati is right in thinking that it is desirable to be reincarnated into different ethnic groups. This idea must be assimilated so that people will not attempt to cling to their own kind while in the Subtle World and deprive themselves of new tests and experiences.

Communication in the Subtle World is mental, and there is no need for different languages. It is wonderful to be able to think in one's own language and at the same time be understood by those from other countries. There is no need to impress thoughts on others; on the contrary, the more natural the flow of thoughts, the more easily they are understood. Such communication is supermundane, but it must be realized here upon Earth so that the adjustment to the Subtle World will be less difficult.

During ordinary sleep one's psychic energy is strengthened by earthly currents, yet when passing into the Subtle World the consciousness may be interrupted. Thus it is advisable to assimilate certain ideas while still in the physical body. Upon transition, most people fall into a deep sleep and, while in this condition, lose their memory of many things. The accumulations remain sealed in the Chalice, and often the assistance of another person from outside is needed for removal of these seals. I am not speaking of those who pass into the Subtle World in full consciousness. In order not to lose consciousness, the most important thing is to remember and strengthen throughout one's life the decision to maintain consciousness during the transition. This consciousness is the treasure which we carry along with us.

In the Subtle World, those who have lost consciousness cannot be seen by Us, for they are covered by an impenetrable substance. They can be seen at the moment of awakening, but their sleep should not be disturbed prematurely.

The Thinker was concerned about the preservation of consciousness. Prompted by his inner awareness, He often repeated, "I will not lose my consciousness." Certainly, consciousness is needed in the Supermundane. The consciousness loses its earthly aspect, and can be transformed into spiritual knowledge. The clearer the earthly consciousness, the quicker the awakening of the spirit. While on Earth we can only sense the laws of karma, but in a state of spiritual awareness we can truly understand the combined forces of karma.

You may ask why people are not taught to understand the higher laws while in the Subtle World, but do many strive to learn while in the earthly schools?

The Thinker loved the Hermetic saying, "As above, so below."

305. Urusvati knows what We mean by "life." We say that life is service for evolution. One might find it simpler to say that life *is* evolution, but We emphasize the idea of service. Indeed, everything is in the process of evolution, but life's full expression can come only under conditions of voluntary service. It is the voluntary quality of service that indicates the rightness of the path.

In general, people dislike the concept of service. They dream about a time when there will be no need for it, and would be horrified to learn that all of life is unending service. They prefer to hear about Us, about Our labor and Our joy, and puzzled, they ask, "What kind of continual service is it when one can hear singing in the Brotherhood?"

People cannot understand that We use singing not as a pastime, but as a method for achieving harmony. It is hard for them to understand that art is a refined aid for evolution, and that We recommend the mastery of any art or craft as a rapid approach to service. A master will willingly agree to perpetual service in the perfection of his art, and feels no need to count the hours of labor.

Our life is a voluntary mastership and is not concerned with limits. Even on Earth it is possible to almost forget time, and service becomes joy. I affirm that one can prepare oneself for such service under all circumstances. One need not be a sage to accept life as something important and responsible. There are examples of even simple farmers who were ready to devote themselves to the idea of service. It was the loss of this concept of service that turned earthly life into slavery and insanity. But the time is approaching when people will be looking, even unwittingly, for the purpose of life. They will first refer to evolution in scientific terms, but the next step will be the acceptance of service as the right approach to life.

The Thinker taught that the concept of service can solve the riddles of life.

306. Urusvati knows that We do not advocate rituals. It is true that a united assemblage of people can produce powerful emanations, but this is possible only when there is true aspiration. But how many are striving? How often do we find them? In ancient times one could find perhaps three hundred heroes such as those at the battle of Marathon, but now everything is counted in the millions, and it is impossible to expect united action. Therefore we should transfer our attention to inner conditions.

People, through their own efforts, can become self-disciplined and moral, and produce healthy emanations. They should not burden themselves with rituals, and should realize that only inner striving will bring them to perfection. Let them learn to project thought to a distance. Let them visualize the Image they revere. For such inspiration rituals are superfluous. Everyone, in the purity of his own heart, can commune with the Teacher. Thus can Earth be filled with good aspirations. Such people will not be left in solitude, for the ultimate goal of Goodness will unify all seeking hearts.

There is no need to return to the old rituals, many of which have lost their meaning. The experience of higher exaltation comes instantaneously, and no words can describe its rapture. It is a feeling that is known only to the heart. Do not yield to rituals if the flame of your heart is burning brightly.

The Thinker knew that everyone has, as an inner gift, the ability to contact the Highest.

307. Urusvati knows what it means to see with the eyes of the heart. Every object is perceived by people in accordance with their inner state. People cannot accept the simple truth that *maya* originates in their own consciousness, and that it is necessary to escape from the snare of self-hypnosis.

Despite misleading outer impressions, man can glimpse sparks of reality. He can oppose the self-hypnosis of *maya* with the knowledge that dwells in his heart. People may wonder if this is not just another form of *maya*, with an equally deceptive appearance. But remember that in the Subtle World perception is considerably clarified, and that in the Fiery World reality is completely revealed. Even through the obstacles of the earthly world man can obtain some glimpses of truth.

It is true that *maya* remains impenetrable for the vast majority of people, for they do not even attempt to overcome "her." But there are a few seekers of truth who even in their earthly state can penetrate to the real essence of things. First, the seeker must learn to understand his own fleeting moods. He then will realize that the sun is the sun, neither cheerful nor gloomy, but that his personal, inner feelings can color even that great luminary.

He who wants to improve himself must know how to overcome his moods. If people were always aware of this task, they would avoid many errors. They would refrain from uttering unjust opinions and would realize that their inner feelings must also be just. Do not think that this is a superhuman task. On the contrary, it is a task of everyday life. For cooperation with Us, one must learn to see with the eyes of the heart.

The Thinker used to say, "Thank the Gods that I will never become blind, for as long as my heart beats it will also see."

308. Urusvati knows Our methods of healing through vibrations, which are similar in some ways to radio waves. These methods require cooperation, trust, and receptivity in the patient. Atmospheric conditions, which can at times interfere with Our currents, must also be taken into account. Many actions depend on attunement with the cosmic currents for their success. This must be well understood, or people will think that We at times withdraw Our help, and We may be accused of partiality.

Distrust disturbs the currents, and even if this disturbance is overcome by a special intensification of energy, the aftereffects of such a tension will be destructive. For a successful transmission of currents the recipient must be attuned to Us. It is not necessary for the recipient to send first; he must simply be receptive and not be surprised at the diversity of currents, which may feel pleasant or painful, depending on the condition of the various nerve centers.

It is necessary to know that the vibrations are directed to the nerve centers, and that one must be quiet so as not to impede the treatment. Remember that such vibrations can help all kinds of illnesses.

People are sufficiently informed about hypnotic suggestion, yet still cannot accept the idea that vibrations can travel over vast distances. It is a great tragedy that people welcome the most questionable concepts, yet often refuse to accept what is best for them.

The Thinker declared emphatically that healing can be received from space.

309. Urusvati knows how difficult is the art of the Good, which is how We describe the continuous, creative good will. One must learn how to discriminate between isolated, accidental good thoughts and actions, and conscious good will.

People themselves complicate this idea by fabricating numerous slogans which only confuse weak minds. They repeat, for example, "He is so kind, he would not hurt a fly." But We say, "He might not harm a fly, but indeed will kill the poisonous snake that threatens the life of his brother." To say this, one must first know which fly is harmless and which snake is deadly! Books can provide this information, but one must know how to look for it.

Much work is required before one can discern goodness. It is even more difficult to detect all the inner motives of the human mind. One should not judge only by outer deeds, but must examine motives. This art can be learned from the ancient sages. The circumstances of those days were quite different, but the scope of human thought was the same. Legends perhaps exaggerate the facts, but the essence of true achievement remains unchanged.

Thus, while studying the arts, let us not forget the art of the Good, which requires assumption of full responsibility and an understanding of the meaning of life. It is the most difficult of arts, but it speeds the way. An unskilled sculptor can ruin a block of marble, but an unskilled doer of good can break many hearts! Only by hard work can a sculptor become skilled.

Likewise, only profound contemplation can perfect the art of the Good.

The Thinker never tired of calling His disciples to perfecting the art of the Good. He said, "A field should be fertilized to produce good crops, and it is the same for the human soul."

310. Urusvati knows that the mundane and the Supermundane are in essence the same, because every earthly action is linked to all of existence. But when We speak about the foundations of life We call them supermundane. People should be taught by all possible means that the Supermundane is real, but man fears the Supermundane and tries to escape the grandeur of Infinity by burying his head here on Earth.

During a rainstorm most people will take cover in a shelter, even an insecure one, while a few will stand fast, facing the downpour in an open field. Similarly, while only a minority will understand the supermundane nature of life, the majority, full of doubts because of their fear, reject such an idea. Even the thought of life on far-off worlds seems impossible to them. In this, both atheists and religious believers are in agreement, and there are even scientists who still believe that Earth is the center of the Universe!

There are many beliefs by which people shield themselves from reality, and it is therefore necessary to goad humanity into participating in all aspects of life. Many ancient thinkers emphasized this, but unfortunately their advice came down in the form of maxims which today are read, but never applied. The thoughts of Confucius, Pythagoras, and Marcus Aurelius are recorded in the pages of history, yet the average man is loathe to accept their authority. People are ashamed to reveal the cause of their ignorance, therefore it is important to persist in reminding them about participating in the totality of life.

Many wish to be called Our co-workers, but for this they must learn to think in unison with Us. They may cooperate to different degrees, but there should be no room for distrust. First of all, the Teacher must find out how much the thinking of the disciple is purified and free of misconceptions. Only then can he be guided to the truth, and only then will mundane and Supermundane be understood as aspects of one whole.

The teacher should speak so that each word sounds like a familiar truth, but the results will be a new and deeper consciousness. We could use the word "higher" instead of "deeper," because, in truth, space knows neither height nor depth.

And where will our Supermundane be in a few hours? What new chemistry will affect us? It will not only touch us, but will also pierce the denseness of the entire planet. It will destroy certain metals and give life to new combinations. People cannot escape this laboratory; therefore it is wise and useful to participate in the work with all one's consciousness.

The Thinker said, "Participate in all of existence. It is meant for you and you are meant for it."

311. Urusvati knows well Our discourses that touch upon the life of the Brotherhood. Our thoughts, concerns, and labors are expressed in these messages for the betterment of life. There are some who feel that We give only ethical teachings; they do not realize that each Teaching is based upon observation and the experience of life.

We affirm that the conditions of life must be continuously improved, and thus We contribute with Our thoughts to the evolution of nations. But bear in mind that the difficult conditions at the end of *Kali*

Yuga require special measures, and understand how hard it is to resist the attacks of chaos. People underestimate this and simply want to gratify their personal desires. Very few try to comprehend the complexity of the counterattacks, which, unfortunately, people provoke by themselves.

Do not underestimate the power of human counterattacks; you can find fanatical declarations everywhere. Fragmentary messages and human outcries should not be ignored, for they all pollute space. Inexperienced people would want extreme measures for purification, but can you imagine these extreme measures applied daily? They would cease to be extraordinary, and the surrounding atmosphere would become strained to the point of explosion. Such methods cannot be applied without taking into consideration the final goal. Think, therefore, about the complexity of Our Labor and try to apply your forces in the same direction. Everyone can do something useful. Each consciousness can perceive the necessary path.

Thus spoke the Thinker, "Cooperation is predestined for all."

312. Urusvati understands the reasons for the disruption of thought. This occurs constantly but attracts little attention. It is usually believed that man himself interrupts the thread of his thought, but why then is the interrupted thought not replaced by another? Instead there is a complete cessation of the train of thought. Sometimes the interrupted thought does not return, leading one to conclude that an external influence has driven it away. This is precisely what happens.

The currents of space are of many kinds and influence human thinking much more than one imagines. Spatial messages could be assimilated in their original form, but because they often intrude forcefully into the consciousness as if in some unknown language, they cannot be understood. Such interruptions do not necessarily mean that a person's thoughts are poor or weak, for spatial currents can pierce even the most powerful thought. Man should understand this and not struggle against it. On the contrary, man can train himself to control the thread of his thought by being aware of the interrupting currents. If he is aware he can instantly make use of his ability to remember and deposit the uncompleted thought into the treasury of memory. Even if he is unable to withstand the power of spatial thought, he can nevertheless protect the current of his own thoughts. He can be like a pilgrim who temporarily uses a shelter during a rainstorm and later continues his journey.

One can even derive a benefit from such interruptions, because each of them carries a certain energy which one should recognize. The thoughts of space cannot always be transformed into conscious forms, but even in their formlessness they bring energy. Indeed, this energy may be coming from Our Towers! Remember that We send much and varied help.

The Thinker often said, "Who is the helping One? Who is present? I sense Thy touches."

313. Urusvati knows that so-called loss of memory is an illusion. Memory, as such, cannot be lost, but there are three factors that affect it. First, if one is absorbed with past events, current events cannot be perceived. Second, strong external influences can obstruct the natural access to memory. Third, damage to the brain can cause dysfunction of the memory. But in all these examples the memory as such, and the center of the Chalice, remain unimpaired.

In cases of amnesia a person can appear to lose all memory about himself, yet, if asked about what he can remember, his answer may be most unexpected. He might even recollect his past lives or vestiges of supermundane sensations. But physicians never ask about such things, and some of the most essential aspects of life are overlooked.

Even in childhood, the memory must be developed by overcoming these three undesirable conditions. The mind can be protected by labor, which guards against self-absorption. It should be understood that although We are surrounded by dangers and external shocks, they cannot affect the memory, and by being aware of this We are able to maintain clear thinking. Without the tension of challenges man grows lazy, but through vigilance his mind becomes disciplined, and he learns not to allow chaotic thoughts to obscure his memory.

People sometimes have flashes of remote recollections at the most unexpected moments. Their consciousness has preserved memories that cannot easily emerge from their treasury. A particular stimulus may be needed for the memories to surface, but they do exist!

The Thinker smiled when He said, "If man could unwind the skein of his recollections, he would see an endless thread."

314. Urusvati knows how often man's concept of the Subtle World changes. There were many periods when he was much closer to a correct understanding of the Subtle World. Entire eras saw an improvement of consciousness, but for no evident reason people would then fall into periods of ignorance.

An important book could be written about the fluctuations of human understanding. The psychic realm is not understood any more now than it was in antiquity, and this fact deserves special attention. It is logical to assume that man's evolution would result in a broadening of consciousness in all spheres; why then has such an important realm as the knowledge of the Subtle World remained so misunderstood? The reason is that man fears everything that lies beyond the boundaries of the material world. The consciousness strives to knowledge, but the earthbound mind will whisper that it is not necessary to know about the hereafter. Sometimes even well-informed people will begin to doubt, and thinking that the Subtle World does not exist, they undermine their previous accumulations.

When knowledge is for a time suppressed, mass disbelief will follow, but one should always remember that the consciousness will once again search for the Truth. One should not waste time in doubt, for the highest understanding was given and assimilated long ago. A courageous understanding of the future life is wise.

The Thinker used to say, "Courage is the ability to look ahead. The wise know that a cloud of dust is finite, and that nothing can obscure Infinity."

315. Urusvati knows that a sequence of events can be perceived in different ways. Imagine a room with a large gathering of people who are about to be poisoned. The question is, does the decisive moment occur when the poison is brought in, when it starts to take effect, or when people are beginning to die?

For most, only the third moment is significant. A few might have noticed the first signs of poisoning, but only the exceptional ones would have sensed the dangerous first instant, which is the most important. Thus, every event can be considered as a sequence of important moments. For some the moment may not have come, and for others it has already passed. And so it is, in all matters, great and small.

One should pay attention to the characteristics of each moment. Do not be deterred by the ignorant ones who ridicule and scoff, for they can perceive only the third type of moment and are only aware of the effects, while the creators of life know the first, causal moments.

One should also realize that events can be either accelerated or slowed. In essence they remain the same, but through some unpredicted circumstance a new significance emerges. All is in motion, and life cannot proceed without motion. In this grandeur of change and aspiration are contained the causes of key events.

The Thinker wanted His disciples to understand the true meaning of the sequence of events. He used to say, "Let us not be concerned about how we become corpses; it is better to comprehend the foundations of life."

316. Urusvati knows how some people try to cheat the Law of Karma. There are people who do this in ignorance of the law, but I am now talking about those who know about it and defy it.

Imagine a criminal who, having committed a crime, trembles in fear of punishment. But when the days pass and nothing happens he becomes bolder and decides that his crime was not so bad after all, and that perhaps it was justified by some higher law. Eventually the criminal grows impudent and scoffs at karma, calling it an invention of fools. At last, at a most unexpected moment the rebounding blow falls, and he blames karma for punishing him so unexpectedly at the prime of his life, when the punishment is particularly painful, forgetting that there are many factors involved in the timing of the karmic reaction.

Egotistically, man often believes that he himself

can decide the moment at which karmic law should act. One asks why karma is so delayed, another complains that it is too hasty, but no one considers the complexity of the circumstances of each event. Some see the cosmic laws as simplistic to the point of absurdity, while others think of them as so complex and ponderous that no action is possible. How can one collaborate in such extremes?

We have always stressed the golden mean, the middle way that includes a readiness to comprehend and accept the flow of energy that in human parlance can be called justice. Pure aspiration enables one to feel the power of this energy, but any impurity is like a threatening cloud.

The Thinker's concern was that the light of the sun not be obscured by human crimes.

317. Urusvati knows that each physical action is the result of a psychic action. This is not a new idea, yet people fail to recognize that thought precedes action, and when you speak to them about psychic action, they will think that you are joking.

One should understand that there are many subtle functions connected to each physical action, and that each action is produced not only through the will, but also through the influence of external energies. Thus the understanding of earthly manifestations can be infinitely expanded. When people accept the idea of such infinite collaboration, they will acquire a broader view of all of existence.

There should be an attempt to expand the boundaries of human concepts. Present schools are totally inadequate in fostering the expansion of consciousness. Today the average person would consider Our discourses to be insane or foolish! You know of people who scoff at Us because We attempt to teach humanity the purpose of life.

The evil forces zealously keep their vigil, ready to harm every beneficial undertaking. It is a mistake to think that these attempts of evil are casual; on the contrary, evil has its well organized followers. The inexperienced think that evil can simply be ignored, but We advise caution, and an increase in one's defenses.

The Thinker said, "I am here to fulfill an earthly task, but who is the Invisible One who has already created the prototype of my humble work?"

318. Urusvati knows that it is especially difficult for people to understand that psychic actions are instantaneous. They believe that earthly thinking requires time, not realizing that thought is instantaneous and that it generates lightning-like fiery decisions.

When a person says that he will think about something, he has already thought about it. The fiery decision already exists within him and when he says that he will think, he refers to the act of intellectual deliberation. It is instructive to observe the duel that takes place between mental and fiery decisions. The intellect can often distort a fiery decision, but the fiery seed itself remains intact. It secretes itself in the depths of the consciousness and reappears often. It is lamentable that man stubbornly refuses to accept the various states of consciousness that exist within him. This very awareness would help him to treat the process of thinking with caution.

Although We often tell people that thought is like lightning, they seldom understand what is meant by such a statement, believing it means that they must think quickly. We are not referring to the speed of reasoning however, but to the lightning-speed of psychic energy, which helps in contacts with Us. Psychic energy should not be accepted as a vague, occult idea: it is the very essence of existence. We try to impress upon human consciousness the importance of this natural essence of life; unfortunately, people do not like to look for natural causes, even of the greatest events.

The Thinker said, "How can there be anything unnatural in Nature?"

319. Urusvati knows how We labor for peace. Why then do We not rejoice at the many organizations dedicated to the promotion of peace? Simply because very few of them are unselfish in their work and the majority harbor hidden motives that are worse even than the drive toward war.

The matter of peace is a standard by which one must test oneself. To test oneself is to know how to draw upon new forces and achieve a new consciousness. It is a self-examination that must be performed within a context of absolute dedication to human evolution. Only then will peace be rightly understood; true peace will include the defense of the treasures of humanity.

Envy is a viper that grips the human heart and infects it with evil, and thoughts of peace then become impossible. Indeed, people can be envious in the most unexpected ways. Many surprises will await you when you learn to read the human mind. A man may have many treasures, yet will still envy his neighbor's meager success. Until the vices that obstruct peace are eradicated, true peace will not be possible.

Each benevolent thought about peace is helpful in space. The word *peace* should be repeated as a mantram, and it will strengthen all efforts to bring harmony. But woe unto those who promote pseudo-peace, which will lead only to corruption. Our Teaching is the Teaching of peace, of true peace.

The Thinker used to say, "I will stand guard to prevent the viper from crawling across the threshold."

320. Urusvati knows that each one of Us has contributed to the peace of the world in various ways. You remember Orpheus, who gave the people soothing melodies of peace, and how a certain Teacher tried to purify the Teachings so that people would know more and understand life better. Another spiritual Toiler preached that people should first of all make use of the most peaceful methods. And the Unifier of nations taught that peace can flourish only in harmony.

Those who work for goodness and peace suffer many hardships; where do such unbearable burdens come from? Every evolutionary step evokes the fury of chaos, and such fury is a response to every benevolent aspiration. But peacemakers can testify that their efforts for peace remain with them as their best memories. These efforts are not only recorded in the histories of nations, they are reflected also in the life of the people.

Is not the serenity that is derived from harmonious sounds within the grasp of all? But someone first had to discover ways of attaining peace through music. While many songs were sung in ancient times, it was considered necessary to point out their ability to evoke peace of mind. In this way a new harmony was introduced into the world.

In the same way, the command to use every possible resource for keeping the peace stands for all time to come. Although mankind seems to have forgotten Him who gave this command, it has nonetheless entered into human consciousness. One should always question whether all peaceful measures have been applied, but without causing the loss of human dignity. One should understand both the mundane and the supermundane measures; only through harmony and dignity can the beauty of peace be realized. Disregard of human dignity can only result in ugliness. He who knows nothing of beauty cannot think of peace, nor can the concept of unity be realized by the ignorant. Yet all people have reverence for the Unifiers. Thus We labor for peace.

The Thinker contributed greatly, daring to imagine a government of peace. What if people call such daring a dream? We know that dreams pave the road to Eternity!

321. Urusvati knows that in every significant aspiration there is an element that can be achieved. One of the most unrealizable dreams is that of world peace, yet humanity continues to pray for it. Difficult as it is to fulfill this dream, there is in it a fragment of truth that can be realized in earthly life.

Man has the gift of communication with his brethren. He learns that a life of enmity finally becomes unbearable, and that the family is ruined by discord. He should understand that this is also true about great nations, which become corrupt without constant, vigilant efforts toward improvement.

In these times it is not possible to expect peace, but we should understand that the coming era will be more suitable for an intelligent acceptance of peace. Therefore, everyone should speak about world peace even if only in the abstract. Let this word, which belongs to the future, be heard amidst today's clouds of hatred. Do not expect to hear such words at lifeless meetings. Let the best dreams be expressed by the young. Let them, in the armor of defense, lay the foundation of life. One should not interfere with the loftiest dreams.

There are many dreams that could be transformed into reality, even though they now seem unrealizable.

For example, people dream about education for all, yet there is much illiteracy throughout the world. And as long as slavery and barbarism remain in many areas, how can one dream about universal education? But We will say, not only can one dream, one must. Space must be filled with commands to begin campaigns for education.

One should not look upon illiteracy as an obstacle but as a reminder of the urgent need for education. How can we be proud that many schools already exist, when humanity has not yet outlived the shame of slavery, and education has not been sufficiently fostered?

The worldly-wise advise us to ignore the cruelties that surround us, but these "wise" ones are without life. You will be told many stories about the brilliant achievements of culture, yet the fact remains that slavery still exists. Moreover, it exists under a clever mask of sanctimonious hypocrisy; such a masquerade is particularly shameful. Yet instead of general indignation, one hears excuses for this shame.

The Thinker taught, "Beware of people who attempt to justify shameful deeds, for such people are enemies of humanity."

322. Urusvati knows that the concepts that We speak about must be fully understood. When We speak of slavery, We mean all forms of this infamy. It is not only the gross buying and selling of people, which, as We have often observed, was condemned by even the most fanatical conquerors, it is also the subtle humiliations inflicted on man that should be particularly noted.

Truly, slavery flourishes even more in enlightened capitals than in barbaric marketplaces. People have not freed themselves from the idea of slavery, and in order to satisfy modern standards of behavior they invent new pompous, hypocritical justifications. Behind these disguises is concealed a most hateful rapaciousness, and individuals are given less sympathy than dogs. Indeed, dogs are often treated better than humans.

Songs are sung in churches about human goodness, while just outside the begging hand is ignored, and no one shows interest or asks for the cause of the beggar's misery, or offers to ease his suffering.

Understanding another's misfortunes broadens the consciousness. Just one brief caring thought can create a salutary link, but, alas, even such brief thoughts are not often sent, and people ignore these karmic resolutions with cold indifference. They cannot imagine how much they separate themselves from Us and from the Subtle World, from which the best help could be received. Therefore, you must fully understand the foundations of life.

We have shown how the full extent of slavery is little recognized, and have cited examples from all aspects of life—in the standards of family life, the present state of education, and the general condition of humanity's welfare. These various aspects will provoke fierce argument because the concept of synthesis is not realized.

The Thinker pointed out that the nation's welfare begins in the heart of each person.

323. Urusvati knows that a person can be helped only within the limits of his consciousness. One can give a monkey a precious diamond, but he will just play with it and then discard it. Perhaps a passerby will then find the diamond and exchange it for a knife, which he will use to kill his brother. In the same way, one can accept advice only according to the limits of one's consciousness. Only intelligent aspiration will lead to the goal. People refuse to learn this truth, and think that they can make use of all precious things, but in practice We see that the most beneficial advice is unrecognized.

One should think of consciousness as a vessel that can contain all the human potential. When an ordinary cup is filled to the brim there is no room for more, but fortunately the vessel of consciousness can be stretched infinitely to accommodate the life-giving fluid. Thus, even the most wretched individual will not be deprived of wisdom if he can realize that the capacity of his consciousness is without limit.

People are not aware that their destiny depends upon the scope of their consciousness. They do not like to discuss the concept of consciousness, because this kind of discourse reminds them of their responsibilities. Such a reminder is always unpleasant, for behind it rise long-forgotten phantoms. But a courageous man does not fear ghosts and is able to benefit from the inspiring advice that has been recorded throughout the ages.

One may recollect that at the French court letters containing useful advice were written, but conditions were then difficult, and we should therefore respect the fact that even amid the extravagance of the court a voice about the useful life could be heard. Many calamities were thus averted. In this way one should examine the various eras.

The Thinker realized that the measure of man is determined by the breadth of his consciousness.

324. Urusvati knows how people reveal themselves in everyday life. Biographers make the mistake of thinking that the value of a person can be measured only by exceptional deeds, and because of this they miss the truth. Celebrities are often characterized by

the glory of their activities, their sparkling eyes and powerful, eloquent speech, but entirely different personalities are revealed by these people in their everyday life. They should be observed in their routine work and in the company of their near ones. Their true mentality, as manifested in thoughts and dreams, should be properly understood.

Above all, We value the achievement of harmony in everyday life. Most of human life passes in such routine, and people should be evaluated by how they stand this test of daily life—whether they can preserve harmony in their domestic environment, resist petty irritations, and rise above boredom.

Many unseen circumstances are hidden in daily life, and one must find in them the joy that elevates one into the Supermundane. May you all remember that you build your human dignity amid daily turbulence. This awareness will make your achievement permanent. We rejoice at the builders of harmony in life, and every day should become a stone in the foundation of this beautiful structure. If you love work, understand it as a substitute for time.

Can Our Life be imagined without total harmony in its daily routine? Not days, not years, but a succession of joyous works can provide the exaltation and strength to live without concern for time. We also have other joys, which the toiler can partake in. The intensity of Our labor brings Us closer to the music of the spheres; ordinary people usually do not notice when such a harmony occurs in their labor.

The Thinker taught that awareness of the resounding of space comes when least expected. "No human measure can determine when the harmony of the Supermundane becomes accessible."

325. Urusvati knows that dragons dwell at the

threshold. It is usually believed that they lurk at the bottom of fearsome abysses, or somewhere in the dark where people seldom enter, but in fact these dragons dwell at the threshold of the home, and one often meets them in the midst of daily life.

All that has been said about such dragons is quite correct. Their appearance is frightful, they are voracious, and they do not release their victims. They carefully watch those who enter and try to gain control of those who dwell in the house. They can change their appearance and rarely reveal their hideous essence.

The Dragon of the Threshold symbolizes the sentinel of human consciousness. These dragons are not mere abstract symbols, for they touch closely the daily life of every human being. Man's desires can never be satisfied, and his discontent is nourishment for the dragons. I certainly do not speak about man's thirst for knowledge, which is a worthy quest, but about his ordinary dissatisfactions. These are rooted in the base passions, where the accumulated discontent becomes food for the dragon, who wins the battle and rejoices in the feast.

In discussing the Supermundane We want you to recognize the obstacles that stand in your way. People can stumble, fall, or even be killed in crossing the most ordinary threshold. We have often spoken about the evil routines that man creates for himself. What then can one say about the threshold of loathsome habits? Indeed, it is dangerous to step over such a threshold!

Much wicked talk takes place at the threshold of evil, and dreadful curses originate there to the great delight of the dragons. We warn you to remove the dirt from your threshold. It nourishes the dragon, and he may grow so fat that you won't be able to squeeze past him through the door! One must realize that an evil environment is an obstacle to evolution. I can hear someone already exclaiming, "An old truism! We have known it for ages!" Friend, if you really knew this, your threshold would be cleaner.

Enough about the evil threshold. Let us assume that our friends have already realized the danger of feeding dragons. Now let us speak about the good threshold, which leads toward a good daily life. It may be an ordinary life, but if it is pure, the dragon will shrink, and turn into a small lizard. Thus, man is endowed with the power to bring about great transformations.

The Thinker said, "Is it not a miracle that people have the ability to transform evil into good?"

326. Urusvati knows that coarseness will be eradicated only by education. But one can be a learned scientist and still remain coarse. Clearly, formal education alone does not necessarily eradicate coarseness, but We should make clear what We mean by this word. A coarse nature cannot deal with subtle perceptions, and the science of the future will require genuine refinement, without which synthesis is impossible. A teacher must have reverence for all branches of science, but an awareness of synthesis is the product of long prior training.

If you ask the ordinary man what he considers coarse, he will probably suggest foul talk, blasphemy, and boorishness. But these are only some aspects of coarseness. The origins of coarseness are not recognized by most people. Only the one who deals with subtle energies can understand that coarseness is a violation of all that is subtle. People should understand that politeness is not a cure for rudeness. One can meet people who are polite, yet coarse, and they will certainly be the last to admit it.

Some may shrug their shoulders and ask whether

a book about good behavior is needed as part of the Teachings of Life. It is indeed, for you must acquire subtlety of understanding if you want to refine your consciousness. We are now speaking about concepts that are almost impossible to express in human words. Many basic principles are indeed inexpressible, and must be intuitively perceived. Such silent understanding and receptivity are bridges to future achievement. Not words, but an inner feeling will be remembered and will help lay the foundation of evolution. Thus, he who is refined in his feelings will never be coarse.

The Thinker said, "Know how to feel deeply, or people will think that you have a pig's hide."

327. Urusvati knows that there is a type of person who cannot distinguish between the tolling of church bells and the sounding of an alarm. What is wrong with them? Are their ears constructed differently? Indeed not, they simply misuse their free will, and when frightened by an alarm convince themselves that they are hearing the opposite, in spite of all evidence. Many people are guilty of this delusion, and it is impossible to convince them of their error when they have made up their minds to hear only what pleases them.

Such wilfulness delays progress. Ask several people to explain the meaning of a simple statement and you will receive the most contradictory and even malicious interpretations. The statement may be quite clear, but the free will can find a way to obscure its meaning and replace that meaning with its own notions!

The Thinker smiled and said, "People are always ready to answer before hearing an entire question!" What is more, their answer is colored by their impressions of the questioner—his figure, his attire, and sometimes even his handwriting. Handwriting does have significance, but certainly not in the case of those who judge without straight-knowledge. Superficial judgment is based on superficial signs, and is of little value.

Always remember the potential madness of free will. In this malady, one imagines that his will is unrestricted and begins to violate the fundamental laws. Such madness has been known since ancient times and can lead to great destruction. But the will is of value only when it is strictly in harmony with the laws of life. Most people do not understand this, for to them the will is equivalent to wilfulness, but a wise man knows that will and freedom are united in the Law of Be-ness. Unless we understand this harmony of will and freedom we shall distort facts and hear a joyous pealing of bells in the sound of a fire brigade!

The Thinker taught the understanding of the language of bells.

328. Urusvati knows that souls incarnate with good intention; such is the Great Law. Even the spirits in the lower strata, just before incarnating, receive a ray of enlightenment about goodness as the foundation of life. But just as the finest aroma cannot permeate space for long, kind intentions are dissipated by the influence of the varied conditions of life. A child is not evil, but can quickly succumb to inherited atavism. Also bad habits, formed from the smallest details of life, are the gates of evil. Thus the enlightenment so briefly experienced in the Subtle World is dispersed.

The process of merging into the dense physical body cuts off all impressions from the Subtle World. Nevertheless, many facts about life in the Subtle World can be obtained. The best way to collect these facts is from the individual testimonies of those who have received unexpected glimpses. This kind of evidence is usually honest, because these people did not expect anything and are amazed to have received any information at all. Thus, they testify to their impressions sincerely.

It is very informative to interview country people, who, being close to nature, observe many interesting things, but may not speak of them for fear of ridicule. It is clear that everyone comes into contact with extraordinary things, but the difference between people is in their attitude. Some pay attention to unusual perceptions, while others do not care to or are unable to open their hearts to things that are beyond the range of their intellect.

The Thinker taught people to concentrate intently upon extraordinary manifestations.

329. Urusvati knows that, in certain cases, passing into the Subtle World is accompanied by sensations either of extreme pain or extreme bliss. But these are extremes, not the average conditions that are experienced by the majority.

Let us take the case of someone who realizes the benefits of Good and who understands the power of thought. He will not lament leaving Earth, for he knows about his eventual return into physical existence. Such a person will fall asleep peacefully and will find himself conscious in the Subtle World. He will not suffer any pain, for his subtle body is not burdened by guilt—he committed no crimes, even in thought. Thus, he will not suffer from depression and will be able to relate to his new environment. He will drive away fear, because he understands that thoughts are his strongest shield.

It is especially valuable to know that even with an average degree of consciousness an individual can dispense with prolonged sleep in the Subtle World. In fact, he can begin to learn and work immediately. He can create his particular attire and hasten to join useful co-workers. He is ready to share in all the advantages of the Subtle World, and will even be ready to make contact with the higher spheres. Indeed, he can boldly approach the highest in full daring.

This person will think about the Subtle World as a joyous state of consciousness, and in such thought will create his future joy. He will affirm his previous experiences, for if he does not wish to do this, they will not enter his consciousness. People must remember this well, and understand the saying, "He who wants to receive, will receive."

The Thinker reminded people about this, for He knew that they deprive themselves of their own achievements.

330. Urusvati knows that the Subtle World can offer great help and mercy. Even where revenge and hatred seethe, the Master applies the maximum degree of help and persuasion. Unfortunately, the free will often resists and chooses to undergo terrible trials once again.

It is no contradiction when We say that every incarnating soul receives a ray of enlightenment, for no one is deprived of mercy. However, one must know how to make use of this blessing. You know that in earthly life the most useful advice is often rejected, and similarly in the Subtle World We often observe that illumination may be distorted.

Evil influences operate strongly in the Subtle World just as on Earth. Disembodied spirits bring with them from Earth the passions they have not yet outlived. However, such passions are not as dangerous as prejudice, because passion can lead to motion, whereas prejudice is stagnant and inevitably causes corruption. Do not conclude from this that We approve of passions. We only point out that in motion there can be a seed of success, whereas ignorance is quite hopeless. When We say "prejudice" we mean an opposition to true knowledge; this attitude is common not only on Earth, but also in the Subtle World. There are even those of a certain mentality who are convinced that knowledge is the cause of all human miseries.

I would like Our co-workers to imagine the various strata of the Subtle World, but there should be no false ideas about this. Many imagine the Subtle World to be a richly adorned paradise filled only with bliss. Yet, Earth groans under the pressures of murder, aggression, and falsehood, and the consequences of earthly delusion fill the Subtle World too.

We are not surprised when people do not accept benevolent advice; it simply means that the soil is not yet ready.

Please tell your friends that they should not assert in their earthly lives what they wish to be in the next incarnation. The fact is that the Subtle World provides possibilities so great that earthly limitations and measures can only diminish them. Life on Earth should be the expression of one's best accumulations. Often people begin to ponder upon their next incarnation, but it is wiser for them to postpone such thoughts until they find themselves in the Subtle World. They may then discover that it will not be necessary for them to return to Earth again, or that they will have to stay for a long time in the Subtle World to perform an entrusted task there. Such work brings one closer to the Brotherhood.

You remember the physician U., who stayed in the Subtle World for a long period of time in order to render great service to humanity, though his mission became clear to him only while in the Subtle World. Such an exemplary man is in stark contrast to those idlers who want to stay as long as permitted in the Subtle World, in order to delay facing the new tests awaiting them upon their return to Earth.

It should be understood that such defined times in the Subtle World exist for all, but some welcome them while others curse them. There are many who want to return to the earthly state before their time, while others try to avoid returning, at least for a short time, and will even invent some new task as an excuse to prolong their stay in the Subtle World. We could mention many different examples, but at the moment We refer only to those tasks that bring souls closer to the Brotherhood. When there is a relationship such as this, it is possible for one to develop while in the Subtle World, without incarnating.

The Thinker taught, "We can be useful in all states of being. Such readiness in itself is victory."

331. Urusvati is aware of foretold dates. People may be surprised to learn that events in China and in Spain were predicted ten years in advance of their happening. The evolution and involution of other nations were also indicated. At times these indications were given in symbols; for example, the coarsening of Germany was pointed out in visions relating to the Thirty Years' War.

The question may arise why some prophecies are received in definite forms, while others are perceived only in vague symbols. There are many reasons for this. Sometimes it may be a karmic situation, at other times it may be caused by a deliberate misinterpretation, the working of free will. Nations can be influenced in a benevolent way, but if free will is misused, it will only intensify the obscuring of consciousness.

And again it may be asked how it is that earthly events can be foreseen, and whether it is because they have already been manifested in the Subtle World. Such an idea has a sound basis. Actually, many events originate in the Infinite, but this does not mean that events on Earth are simply shadows of events that have already taken place in the Subtle World.

There are no words in the human language to express the correlation of events on the various planes. There are many currents in space that unite cosmic events.

A physician can predict the development of a disease by observing the very first symptoms, and various measures can be taken to avoid a fatal end. This applies also in the development of events, whose ultimate significance will depend on many influences. Our influence is always benevolent, but one should know how to recognize its consequences. If one is sufficiently observant, one will see that many events develop in unexpected ways. Shouldn't one conclude that behind them there is a Leading Hand?

The Thinker often tried to train His disciples to be open to unexpected developments, even those that are beyond human logic.

332. Urusvati knows that the law of the spiral is the basis of Cosmos. This is confirmed not only by physics, but also by evolution. The simple example of a screw will help one to understand the advance of evolution. The more threads there are on the screw, the better it serves its purpose. Similarly in evolution it is useful for the spiral to have many turns.

People usually are amazed that human consciousness appears to experience again and again the same achievements and the same failures. The question arises, why must one return if it is possible to move forward? But this "returning" is only illusory. Evolution never returns to previous points, but passes above them. People complain that they fall back into coarseness, but they do not realize that this state is not as before, for many new factors have entered their lives. It would be wrong to look upon life from one angle only. Life is a complete synthesis, and only in its multiformity does it reveal that the spiral has completed its turn.

It is very likely that we pass repeatedly by our former dwellings, but we make contact with them each time on a higher level, as in a tower with a spiral stairway on which we progress toward the Infinite. You must always remind yourself of the symbol of the spiral, otherwise many questions will remain unanswered.

It may seem that humanity has not shown any substantial progress during these millions of years. The point is that evolution proceeds, but the circle of its turning is enormous.

It is quite correct to say that people fall into coarseness and falsehood, but at the same time they acquire new knowledge in many fields. It is not easy to bring such extremes into harmony. In spite of this, let us love humanity.

The Thinker taught, "Love not the man, but mankind."

333. Urusvati knows what causes Us to choose an unusual system for giving Our discourses. The ignorant will say that there is no system at all, but simply countless aphorisms, some of which deal with current events, while others are unreasonably repetitious. Such is the opinion of the superficial reader, who cannot grasp the idea of the need for rhythm, which helps to broaden the consciousness. One cannot separate the discourses into formal subjects.

One could write a book about joy, but We prefer to give glimpses of joy, linking them with thoughts about grave dangers. Each discourse is given in a certain rhythm. You know that wearing many layers of the finest silk can keep one warmer than would a fur coat. Reiteration generates an accumulation of precipitations, providing an increased power of psychic energy, but these precipitations should be subject to a certain rhythm.

It would be unwise to put stress upon only one group of nerve centers. The foundations of life are manifold, and its refinement should have no limitations. Imagine the variety of impressions that strike your consciousness in the course of just one day! Varied are the precipitations and the rhythms, and the ordinary person becomes a co-creator of many events. Even if he does not notice these intense currents, they do exist. Therefore, we should approach the foundations of life in all their multiformity.

Joy cannot be just one joy. There are innumerable joys, and each of them touches upon a particular combination of nerve centers. People should think more about rhythm and multiformity.

The Thinker asserted that every good deed is rhythmical.

334. Urusvati knows that objects can be magnetized. You were able to observe that psychic energy can magnetize water, and that waters containing iron or lithium are very easily magnetized. One can also observe how water is gradually demagnetized in proportion to the decrease of psychic energy. This can be done with all objects, and it is not magic, but a scientific process. The important point is that the influence of the magnetizer himself be preserved.

The magnetism of objects can actually persist for centuries if the person who projected it does not withdraw his influence. Thus, the magnetic power lies not in the object itself, but in the individual. It must also be kept in mind that demagnetization can be effected by a special process.

There were cases when magnetized objects fell into the hands of evil people who were then able to use the beneficent energy for evil purposes. In such cases it becomes necessary to cut off the magnetic currents that permeate the objects. The energy should be maintained only where there is a benevolent purpose. This law is of paramount importance. Many previously revered sacred objects can be found for sale, but they are now used for selfish profit.

One should remember that minerals in particular are most easily permeated by psychic energy, because they are almost free of microorganisms, and their energy is less subject to change. This is not so with textiles and leather objects, in which microorganisms immediately assimilate the psychic energy and an undesirable, complex substance is formed. Therefore, We advise the destruction of such objects by fire.

It is a known fact that while a curse can remain active over centuries, the most powerful talisman becomes powerless in evil hands. Certain invocations can produce a great intensification of the power of objects if these objects remain long enough where the invocations were performed.

But now I want you to pay attention to another detail. It is not the object itself that is of importance, but the energy, which can be either renewed or cut off. If thieves think that they can steal living energy, they will find themselves before an empty pit. Thus, magic can be seen as a scientific act. He who has ears, let him hear.

We have often spoken about the influence of thought upon objects. Truly, it is easier to magnetize than to demagnetize, but the magnetizer himself can remove the magnetism when necessary through the concentration of his will. Such demagnetized objects acquire a neutral quality, that is, the living energy leaves them and they remain lifeless and subject to chaos, and can become the opposite of what they were.

Fundamentally, all legends are based on scientific truths. It was always believed that thought is the garment of an object. This idea refers to the accumulations of thought and the emanations of energy.

The Thinker strongly advised treasuring objects that were given with good thoughts and good wishes. He said, "We are not superstitious people but scientists, and We realize that he whose hand holds a gift close to his heart gives a part of his soul."

335. Urusvati knows that encounters with the servants of darkness are frequent, and that one should be aware of their versatility. There are manifestations that are clearly ugly, but there are others that are luminous, and only an expanded consciousness can determine the true essence of these entities.

The question may arise whether We ever encounter these enemies. Certainly, and We must not only constantly battle with them, but sometimes even converse with them. They miss no opportunity to approach Us during Our journeys, and attempt to sap Our energy for their own use. It is fair to say that the dark forces do not spare themselves. They courageously endure the pain caused by contact with Our energy, and are quite prepared to sacrifice themselves. It is lamentable that the so-called servants of Good are not nearly so devoted to their cause.

Indeed, it is not those who ferociously reject Truth who are dangerous, nor those who distort it, but the indifferent ones, the living corpses who remain unmoved by the word of Truth. We can only smile at the blasphemers and deniers, who do not suspect that by attracting attention to the truth they deny, they serve a certain purpose. Some force compels them to direct their energy into loudly denying the truth, while so many servants of Good whisper. Judge for yourself who is of more use, the one who whispers the Truth timidly and inaudibly, or the one who boldly and loudly attacks it.

Let us look to the past and we shall see that the brightest achievements were the result of ferocious opposition. If truth does not exist, to what purpose does this enemy exhaust itself? But if truth is alive, nothing can hurt it and slander will be its advertisement. We have often told Our adversaries that there is a law that turns their evil efforts into glorifications of truth.

In the same way, false prophets serve a purpose in attempting to give the multitudes their message. Therefore, let them continue to proclaim, in ignorance of the result. Let the empty shell of untruth fall away; the water of truth will continue to flow.

The Thinker, after meeting with a stranger, said, "He is not a good man, but he spoke much to Me about truth. Blessed be the Truth."

336. Urusvati knows how We grieve at every distortion of truth. We say that false prophets are less dangerous than "unfeeling, living corpses;" however, this comparison is relative, and you can be sure that We do not justify false prophets. Everyone knows that they work only for their own gain, and that their activity has nothing to do with the Teaching about the New Life. If one should ask those trumpeters of falsehood how much silver they have accumulated, they would remain silent, knowing that the Teaching is for each of them as a milk cow.

People may accuse Us of lack of logic, since on one day We say that the false prophets are not dangerous, yet We sternly condemn them on another; but relativity and antithesis are little understood. Indeed, worldly relationships are complicated, and an unwashed person will seem clean if compared with a chimney sweep. We shall not tire of reminding you that one of the signs of Armageddon is the enormous increase in the numbers of false preachers. They appear in all countries and offer whatever the crowds desire. We shall not belabor their distortions of life, but We can lament them.

The distortion of truth can be conscious or unconscious. Many people will assure you that their distortions are unconscious, but in reality they act consciously. The difference is in the degree of consciousness. One can often observe that the most incredible lies are uttered in the hope of a small personal advantage, or to assert the ego, or to make money. This pitiful gain is entirely out of proportion with the grandeur of the abused truth.

How amazingly perverse is the human mentality! People throw unmeasurable concepts upon the scales, and then will excuse themselves by professing that since they do not know the truth, they are not responsible for its distortion!

They should be told, "If you do not know what truth is, you can at least strive toward it. In such aspiration you will learn to love its first signs. The necessary thing is to learn how to love; this in itself will keep you from becoming traitors."

Once, when the Thinker saw a cloud of dust on the road, He exclaimed, "Who is approaching, a good messenger or a murderer? But I know, for my heart tells me that it is not a murderer who approaches."

337. Urusvati loves communion with Us. It cannot be ordered, it cannot be intellectually evoked, only the power of love can bring it into life.

Mark what I tell you. Often people come together for the purpose of united concentration of thought. Such an exercise is praiseworthy. Similarly, people gather together and send forth collective thoughts for the salvation of the world and the curing of illnesses. This too is praiseworthy. In these times there are many gatherings dedicated to the transmission of such benevolent thoughts. However, communion with Us is overlooked, even though it would help them in their good intentions.

We do not criticize those who attempt to unify and intensify their thinking, for in their own way they act worthily. But how much more intense would be their transmissions if each of them learned to love communion with Us! Everyone should dedicate at least a little time to mental unification with Us, but only love can be the bridge.

There is no need for stimulating artificial tension, or for counting, or for the repetition of hundreds of names. What is needed is simply a strong feeling. One must love the momentary contacts, and should feel the beautiful wings that they provide! We value each such bridge of love, which is built from love of labor. Contact with Us is established, therefore, on love and labor. However, any harmony can be disrupted and is difficult to restore.

The Thinker looked at the fragments of a priceless amphora and said, "Great is the power of man. He can break even the most precious vessel."

338. Urusvati knows that the human organism is

generously endowed with powerful substances. The chemical laboratory of a human being is truly amazing, and it can be safely said that nowhere except in the human organism are such powers stored. With good reason theories have existed since ancient times that any illness can be healed by the patient's own secretions. Let us also consider the fact that the chemistry of the human organism derives its subtlety from being under the direct influence of psychic energy, constantly renewed by its connection with the currents of space.

Powerful are human poisons, and salutary is psychic energy. Thus, when I speak about the necessity for psychic correlations, I advise you not only as a Teacher and humanitarian, but also as a physician. For example, I advise taking care of the spleen and keeping it clean. But at the same time I stress the need for preserving calmness and an atmosphere of solemnity. This may sound strange, for what can the spleen and a solemn mood have in common? In fact the spleen is the organ of harmony and must therefore be purified by a harmonious disposition. People assume that only the nervous system requires psychic influences, but such influences are also needed for various organs. The example of the spleen is indicative. I speak of this particular organ because it is rarely mentioned and needs special attention.

We are saddened when We see the violation of harmony. Imagine what would happen if a few members were suddenly to drop out of a group that is under Our influence. Great perturbations in the currents would take place, and the group would be exposed to many dangers. Likewise, if a patient swallows a medicine in a dosage prepared for many, dire consequences may befall him. And so one can cite many medical examples, for they remind us that psychic and chemical influences are interdependent.

The Thinker used to say, "I cannot bear the burdensome aura of a large crowd."

339. Urusvati knows that man's true nature is revealed at times of calamity—such is the way on Earth. We do not call this a law, because the conditions for each misfortune are different. It would seem that exaltation and happiness should have more effect than misery, but even the illusion of well-being renders people numb. How lamentable it is that most people can refine their feelings only through suffering!

Over many generations people have developed an awe for misfortune, and claim that it is the gods who send calamities. Man never forgets to pray for help, but he seldom remembers to give thanks for his happiness. It may seem hardly worthwhile to speak about such a thing, but it should be examined from the scientific point of view. The projected image of feelings of distress is an agitated one. We can observe their zigzags flickering on the screen, whereas rapture and exaltation produce perfect circles. It can be proved that disturbance not only produces poison, but also deadens the organs, whereupon the entire laboratory of the organism falls into disorder. This condition can be compared to the death of psychic energy.

Shock often causes loss of consciousness, but fainting must not be confused with stupor. Fainting is an unconscious numbness, but stupor does not necessarily exclude consciousness. External shocks rarely cause stupor, whose cause is far more subtle. While in a stupor, a person can often be cured of the first stages of a dangerous disease. Generally, it is incorrect to regard stupor as an illness; it should be seen an exceptional condition of body and mind.

It is a pity that the many aspects of such lethargic conditions are seldom studied. The important thing in such cases is not how to feed the patient, it is to observe the rhythm of the pulse and the activity of the brain. It would be wrong to awaken him, for he is absorbed in other worlds, and if it were possible to question him carefully, he would reveal many interesting things.

Folklore preserves stories about sleeping beauties and knights who remained in states of suspended animation. Folk wisdom observes this as a special condition that is followed by renewed energy and heroism. Truly, the time will come when medical science will be able to create these periods of absolute rest for the renewal of vital forces. Experiments for this took place in ancient times.

We experience similar conditions during distant flights. The important thing is that one must not overlook the first impression at the time of awakening. Under ordinary conditions it is difficult to be constantly vigilant, and the significant signs can be missed. Later, one may forget everything, and if pressed by clumsy questioning, will insist that he remembers nothing. We have mentioned this before, but such experiences are rare in Our Abode. Only at times when a general concentration is needed can We allow such methods; We do not want to miss any manifestation, and everyone's will is focused.

The time will come when people will be amazed how they needed suffering in order to grow, while missing many other possible ways to elevate their consciousness. Thus, one should realize how manifold are possibilities that We offer to people.

The Thinker said, "Could it be that man evolved from stone, since we see that a sharp blow is needed to ignite a spark in him?"

340. Urusvati knows that under normal conditions the human organism can successfully overcome diseases, but it is essential to understand what kind of organism we are talking about, and what conditions are best. The dangerous influence of genetic factors should be limited as much as possible. Governments should take measures to achieve this, and are only now beginning to pay some attention to this problem. Yet, people do not think enough about the natural environment. They are quite content with basic sanitary measures, and the essential foundations of life are overlooked.

It is not possible to promote health without a proper understanding of psychic life. People go to sanatoriums to improve their health, and ignore the fact that they will be closely associated with a random company of sick people. Such an environment can hardly have a positive effect. On the contrary, the association with those whose attention is focused upon illness can only intensify the fear of disease and aggravate their ailments.

It would be good to remember the remedy of ancient times when sick people would go into seclusion and remain close to nature. This was done not only in cases of contagious diseases, but when the organism was in need of renewal. Even now, there are those who prefer to live in mobile homes or in tents. Of course, a collection of many tents in one place only replicates urban conditions, but the fact that people dream of and look for seclusion reveals a healthy instinct for the preservation and restoration of health. We transmit thoughts of health, but of health correctly understood. It is especially important to think about health now. Many people are aware that the destruction of the nervous system has reached an extreme point. They understand that progress is impossible on this path of decay, but only a few know the significance of health in its full sense.

It is not psychology with its indifferent analysis that is needed, but enlightened striving toward the restoration of health. There are many cases of city dwellers who take jobs as farm laborers to escape the sickening environment of the big cities. This is a praiseworthy decision if one knows how to avoid crowds in the new environment.

Let us recollect various quests in which people sensed the need to change their unhealthy conditions. A longing for nature should be combined with psychic joy, otherwise the seeker will begin to weep at the first rainfall or other discomfort. The time will come when physicians understand that the human organism can fight diseases without outside help.

The Thinker said, "Even a dog cannot bear being disturbed during his illness. Is man inferior to a dog?"

341. Urusvati knows that harmony in life refines human feelings. Indeed, harmony is the only thing necessary; with it all will be subtler and loftier. Harmony is a great concept! Yet people seek it in external conditions and overlook it in the essence of things. For example, a primitive man may live in natural beauty, yet be far from harmony. The city dweller may be oppressed by the bustle of his surroundings, and be unable to think about a harmonious life. Even a refined philosopher can be crushed by the cares of supporting himself. Thus the fundamental law of harmony is forgotten.

People do not understand that the way to harmony is in the art of thinking. Deep contemplation is needed for the realization of harmony. Truly, only the art of thinking can refine one's feelings. But how does one acquire this art, which can sometimes be possessed by an illiterate person, yet elude the most learned? How can We teach man the art of thinking? Many will take this to be a clumsy aphorism. How can We explain to people that Our philosophy is based upon thinking about Infinity? With such ideals, earthly tribulations become bearable and manageable. Do not fear the lofty concept of harmony. It can be applied in all aspects of life, and every human being can develop a sense of it within himself. This state can be called by different names, yet it is the property of all. Everyone sooner or later will achieve harmony if the art of thinking is cultivated.

The Thinker stressed correct thinking. He wanted His disciples to feel themselves to be artists who could create new kinds of harmony.

342. Urusvati knows how persistent are the forces of chaos. They should be resisted consciously, because only through conscious opposition can one overcome them. Two currents can be distinguished—spatial chaos, and the chaos that affects the weak human will. Even good people can become victims of the attacks of chaos.

Certain events can only be explained by these attacks of chaos. You have heard about the girl who, even while the evil forces are attacking her, can heal with the power of her psychic energy. Even moderately good physicians oppose her and try to interfere with her *podvig*. There are many similar examples in various fields, and the remarkable thing is that individuals who are not even involved will also interfere.

It is astonishing that seemingly enlightened people are not ashamed to soil themselves by opposing benevolent work. Why do they become so savage and utter such shameful things? It often happens that they are obsessed, but it may also be a case of poisoning by chaos. Such circumstances should be studied scientifically. When their feelings are temporarily obscured, people can act in the most shameful manner without even realizing it. Later they may feel regret, but the deed has already been done, and karma determined.

One could object to the fact that people are held responsible unfairly for having succumbed to the attacks of chaos. However, by a vigilant free will they could have controlled themselves. How can one excuse people who carelessly blind themselves, then seek to justify their own carelessness? Thus, we should be able to distinguish between the conscious servants of darkness and those unaware victims of evil who also serve evil and can be even more harmful than darkness itself. The currents of chaos should be explained from a scientific point of view. Let as many people as possible learn about it, because this servitude to darkness takes place in both the dense and the subtle spheres.

The Thinker always warned about the attacks of chaos.

343. Urusvati knows that We carefully observe the life of animals. We keep dogs, goats, bulls, horses, and some smaller species of animals and birds. Our principal studies are of their psychic energy, although We also involve them in medical experiments. It goes without saying that We do not permit vivisection or torture. We do not train them by force, but by penetrating into their world of thinking. Only such an approach can bring trust and a correct response.

We must admit that observation of the thought and language of animals produces the most unexpected conclusions. Their language is expressed not so much in sounds as in gestures and glances, and remind us somewhat of language in the Subtle World.

People think that one should talk to animals, but such communication does not always lead to the best results. Animals understand thoughts, and do not need words in order to grasp with certainty the mood of their master. The horse and the dog know very well when their owner is cheerful or sad or disturbed. They also reflect the fears and anxieties of their owner and become fearful and anxious themselves. They understand such situations far better than people think they do. The important thing is to obtain their trust, which is not given easily.

Psychiatrists could benefit from observing animals; many puzzles would be solved. Since ancient times indications have been given regarding the importance of animals in human life. It was well-known that animals intensify the currents of psychic energy, but it was also known that they attract lower entities from the Subtle World. The psychic energy of animals can be beneficial, but it can also be dangerous, and one should act with caution. Animals should not be allowed too great an intimacy with people. Co-measurement is necessary in everything.

The Thinker frequently pointed out interesting facts about animal consciousness. His remarks were ridiculed on the grounds that animals have no intelligence and are therefore inferior beings, but the Thinker meant to show people that psychic energy works through all beings and throughout the universe.

344. Urusvati knows how heavy is the burden of the world. We can remind you of the suffering of Our Sister when embodied in Siena. It should be noted that the pains she endured were related to events in France and Spain. She experienced severe pains in the region of the solar plexus and by them was able to predict certain distant events. Often these events were felt more intensely than local ones. In the same way, one can trace specific links with previous lives.

These strong pains could not be stopped and there was often little time to alert physicians, who did not understand the true cause and tried to stop the pains by prescribing potent medicines. Even today, people do not understand subtle influences, and such lack of understanding hinders scientific progress.

During the lifetime of Our Sister of Siena the idea of telepathy was suppressed. Today much is said about telepathy, but its signs are still treated with skepticism. It is astonishing that even in progressive scientific societies there is doubt about it; this attitude only hinders research.

You have heard about the physician who was sent to investigate subtle manifestations, but could achieve nothing because prevailing conditions were not favorable for the success of his investigation. We want to encourage such research, but it is difficult to find some common ground for communication.

Urusvati can provide many convincing details to researchers, but it is essential that her testimony be listened to and correlated with that of Our Sisters and Brothers who have lived in the world. In such correlative studies one will be able to trace the evolution of knowledge about the subtle energies.

The Thinker Himself often experienced strange pains, which He attributed to the rays of the various planets.

345. Urusvati knows how many subtle feelings and influences fill one's life. Imbalance, that dreadful scourge, is the obstacle to appreciating and understanding life's precious gifts. After millions of years of evolution humanity is still ignorant about the art of achieving harmony.

What then do we see in this age, so proud of its discoveries? People reject completely all that is beyond the earthly realm and become victims of destructive imbalance. They forget their immediate responsibility toward Earth and begin to wander in a fog of abstraction, and if they meet those who have attained harmony, they despise them!

We should not attribute such hatred only to the forces of darkness. Many highly regarded citizens are the very ones who hate all that is harmonious, because they detest the idea of the unification of the mundane with the supermundane. Darkness has loyal co-workers among unbalanced people. If you see attacks upon useful undertakings, look attentively and you will see that the persecutors have not even the slightest degree of harmony within themselves. Study them and you will observe the inadequacies of their reasoning faculties and learn how to resist their trickery. You will learn when it is possible to remonstrate with them and when, because nothing can be accomplished in this life, a change of sheaths will be necessary. Yes, yes, yes, harmony itself is often understood as an abstraction!

Similarly misunderstood is Nirvana, in which the greatest intensification of one's faculties is sometimes interpreted as passive, unfeeling inaction. Equilibrium requires mutual tension, for both cups of the scale must bear equal loads. Therefore, both cups, the mundane and the supermundane, never stand empty. In his ignorance, man prefers to limit himself to one side or the other. That is why humanity is lame; but can one hop for long on one foot? Can one drag one's crutch into the Subtle World? I speak in jest, for sometimes a jest is better remembered!

The Thinker asked some narrow-minded intellectuals, "Why do you cripple yourselves by cutting off one of your legs? Verily, you will have great difficulty returning home."

346. Urusvati knows that if each person wrote down a description of something phenomenal that had taken place in his life, humanity could compile an extraordinary book in just one day. Everyone has had authentic glimpses into the supermundane and many could provide revealing accounts. Even those who deny it do not dare to claim that they can provide mundane explanations for everything that has happened in their lives.

The main obstacle to compiling such chronicles is the embarrassment each one feels in revealing his personal experiences. Urusvati remembers only too well how she was ridiculed as a child when she attempted to reveal her feelings. But that is an unavoidable experience for all.

I hope that some people will read My words to their immediate friends and will collect examples from the life around them. There is no need to be amazed about the little girl who suddenly began to speak twelve languages! And one can discover many other phenomena which could be explained scientifically.

When your friends begin to record their extraordinary experiences, please urge them to do it as simply as possible and avoid elaborate descriptions. They should not add their own interpretations but record the facts simply and accurately, with the utmost truthfulness. It is not necessary to place much significance in the fleeting lights that one sees, for they are small details of everyday life. Information should also be gathered from printed sources, although these cannot compare to one's own verifiable observations.

There are many books available that deal with psychic phenomena, and We will not waste Our time trying to convince the wilfully ignorant. At present, We only want to point out that psychic phenomena are increasing. One can also see that there is an unfortunate increase in fierce opposition. The forces of darkness are alarmed that the subtle energies are approaching the earthly plane. You must understand that the battle has reached its climax, and chaos is attempting to prevent evolutionary advance. But the New World approaches and nothing can stop the growth of consciousness.

The Thinker spoke about the inextinguishable fire of the heart. He understood the path of humanity.

347. Urusvati knows how distressing it is to have to withhold from people all that has been prepared for them. In fact, there are many new discoveries that cannot be revealed to people simply out of concern for their safety.

For example, powerful poisons have been discovered that are salutary when used in a certain way. But do people care about these salutary properties? Usually their first impulse is to experiment with the destructive qualities. Poisons often have medicinal powers, but to entrust them to irresponsible hands would be the greatest folly. The same can be said about all aspects of life. Discoveries are safe only when their use is goalfitting.

The question arises as to whether events caused by hatred can be goalfitting. You must realize that evil can be good, in a relative way. It is hard to imagine putting a limit on the number of miseries! Sometimes the only alternative is to choose the lesser evil, or, as the Romans said, "to take with a light hand."

When studying the history of psychic phenomena one can observe a rise and fall in the degree of their frequency. One might expect there to be a constant increase, but there are certain conditions that influence the manifestations. For instance, psychic phenomena increase during wartime, but they are of a less desirable type.

The same is true about most mass manifestations. Certainly a multitude intensifies psychic forces, but only rarely can the ecstasy of a crowd be of high quality. During quiet, constructive periods the manifestations can be very intense, because there is nothing to prevent the subtle energy from approaching the physical world. Moreover, people of a quiet and balanced nature create a more suitable atmosphere and intensify the phenomena. Thus, one may observe entire eras of evolution and involution.

People are not yet sufficiently trained to discriminate between these changes, because the science of psychic phenomena is not accepted by the majority. One must also bear in mind that We can help these phenomena in a variety of ways. Amidst the world's events Our energy is directed to those areas where there is a possibility of cosmic danger.

The Thinker pointed out the brilliance of the sun and added, "What dangers are hidden at times in this radiance!"

348. Urusvati knows the different ways in which people react to manifestations of the Subtle World. These manifestations often evoke shock and even terror. If people are constantly surrounded by inhabitants of the Subtle World, why is it that seeing them produces such extreme reactions? One should remember that although such subtle manifestations sometimes cause shocks, people can only react to what they actually see, and unaware that they are surrounded by inhabitants of the Subtle World, they show a pronounced fear of contact with these so-called ghosts. But such contacts are unavoidable, and We have ways of protecting people from truly unbearable experiences.

People fear the dead because they do not believe in eternal life. When this truth is broadly accepted, the world will be transformed. It is useless to speak of purification or sublimation before the continuity of life is understood. I affirm that at present people are far from an understanding of the structure of the three worlds. Nor will it help to simplify the scheme by division into two worlds; people will only become confused. Remember that in ancient times, too, very few accepted calmly the existence of invisible worlds. The majority feared these realms just as they do today.

The Thinker attempted to open this natural way of communication to His disciples, but only a few dared to face the truth.

349. Urusvati knows how emphatically We insist upon the need for harmony and unity. We often speak about unification, but now We wish to point out a special aspect of this concept—harmony. Only unification will bring right results. It is true that any kind of unification will intensify energy. Even unity in evil can be effective, but it can never be harmonious, for evil by its very nature is disharmonious. Also, unity in evil cannot last, and its results will be vague. But goodness is always harmonious, and it alone can produce meaningful results. Thus, by speaking of harmony We affirm goodness.

Each quality has many aspects, but they cannot all be revealed at once for they would not be understood. We first indicated unification in a general sense, and now it is time to point out the specific conditions that are required for the achievement of complete unity.

Are there perhaps certain invocations or physical exercises that can intensify this harmony? Certainly there are many such aids, but in the end they act like narcotics, producing only an imagined harmony. Such attainments are not beneficial and are not suitable for the Subtle World. Since the object of self-betterment is to become perfect for our future existence, We advise the use of the more natural methods of spiritual development. This is the new message.

People are either skeptical or they indulge in artificial methods and ignore all natural ways of broadening the consciousness. Yet such ways are the true treasures for ascent in the Subtle World, for those who dwell there have no artificial methods, and act only according to the fundamental laws of Nature.

We strongly advocate both labor and thought for self-perfectment. These will bring sublime accumulations that do not evaporate in the Subtle World, but, on the contrary, will lead to further knowledge. Thus We lay the foundation of harmony.

The Thinker pointed out, "Not the outward appearance but the power of thought will open the Sacred Gates."

350. Urusvati knows that all the advice We give is based on scientific truth. When We stress the benefits of an ethical life, Our chief concern is to preserve the fundamental laws of the Universe. When We say, "Purify your thoughts," We have harmony in mind.

Just imagine the power of a pure thought! You know that such a thought purifies the aura and emanates a radiant light. And what is more, purity of thought is the best defense against the dark entities that cling to every dark thought. I can already foresee the indignation of those pedantic scientists, in whose dictionaries dark entities do not exist! Well, We shall speak according to their consciousness, and tell them that every thought is in a way a magnet that attracts whatever is similar to it. Space is saturated with thoughts, and each of them attracts thoughts of similar quality. Whirlpools of thought exist in space, and grow amid the cosmic rotations.

Man has no right to produce chaos and cause harm to the manifested world. You must remember and understand that each good thought begets goodness, and each dark thought is a cradle of evil.

It may be asked how man can discriminate between his good and evil thoughts. Words can be deceptive, but at the deepest level of thought people do not deceive themselves. They understand quite well the difference between noble deeds and crime. The outward appearance of a deed is not its essence: this essence is clearly perceived in the heart of the author of the deed. Thus, man should not become a sower of destructive forces. Let everyone think about creating good. When people think scientifically they will understand the laws of ethics.

The Thinker warned, "Unless you acquire knowledge, you will remain immoral."

351. Urusvati knows the many reasons for the interruption of thought transmission. The main causes are the extraordinarily intense currents and the unexpected disturbances that must be immediately countered. But also undesirable entities may approach and try to obtain information that would cause harm if acquired prematurely, and that should not be revealed to them.

We can provide an example of information that was prematurely interrupted. Once, We sent a mental message about the sad condition of a certain Western country, but as soon as the first word, "space," was sent, unwanted listeners were discovered and the communication had to be interrupted. In order to fulfill Our intention We used a code word, which was sent at night. We continued with our communication the following night, not naming the country, because Urusvati could then understand the meaning of Our message.

I mention this episode to remind you about the caution that must be exercised in dealing with the filling of space. Even in earthly life people seek the opinions of experts in order to learn the meaning of events. It is the same when certain entities try to intercept Our communications in order to use the information for their own purposes.

Those of great experience accept the need to adhere to the laws of nature. Only the ignorant think that We need not submit to cosmic laws. It would be sad indeed if We were to unnecessarily intrude upon the karma of countries, peoples, or individuals.

What great harm results from a careless attitude to life! You know how unwisely some people extract fragments from Our books. This is very harmful, for one can never know how or by whom such incomplete quotations might be interpreted. We are concerned first of all about the accuracy of what is conveyed.

The Thinker was concerned about His disciples, wanting them to be responsible for every word they uttered.

352. Urusvati knows that one cannot perceive the exact moment of falling asleep, and that dreams or participation in the life of the Subtle World do not begin immediately. There seems to be an unexplainable transference into a new condition to which one must adjust. The same occurs in all contacts with the Subtle World, which are more numerous than one may think.

People may complain that contact with the Subtle

World is not frequent enough, but even during one's ordinary waking hours unusual sensations can be felt—perhaps a strange sense of being absent, or an awareness of some invisible presence. If people would learn to be attentive, they would see and feel many inexplicable phenomena. No special concentration is necessary for this, because subtle reactions come unexpectedly and cannot be anticipated. You know that the most wonderful phenomena have taken place amidst the most ordinary surroundings.

It is impossible to predict what kind of earthly circumstances will be most favorable for subtle manifestations. The only necessary condition for all is to be aware that every moment can bring a manifestation of the Supermundane. But while developing such an awareness one should not withdraw from earthly labors. We insist upon labor while on Earth.

The Thinker used to say, "Friend, are you ready for an unexpected communion with the luminous sphere?"

353. Urusvati knows that on the verge of awakening one must pass through a transitional state in which one belongs to two realms. Some people do not remember this state, but others retain impressions of subtle experiences.

When the ancients urged, "Know thyself," they were primarily concerned with the development of the power of observation. This process is no mystery. People should simply become more attentive to their own nature and to their surroundings, and should realize that they are responsible for the quality of their projections. It is strange that the interval between sleep and awakening remains unnoticed. People read about the particular qualities of drowsiness. The ancient initiates knew how acutely perceptive one becomes during this state, but this knowledge remained only with the initiates, who alone could remember their experiences. The average person, absorbed in his work, had no time for such observation.

But now We once again call people to develop attentiveness and to observe the idiosyncrasies of their nature even during labor. One should learn to combine one's ability to work with the power of subtle perception. Such a synthesis will transform life.

You should not assume that the initiates were withdrawn from daily life. From the biographies of the great, it is clear that they did not avoid the most diverse manifestations of life. And now too, labor should not keep one from self-examination. The new life requires collaboration with the two realms.

The Thinker used to say, "Friend, before retiring for sleep and before awakening for labor, utter a word of blessing. Verily it will open the gates of the two worlds."

354. Urusvati knows that very few have a right attitude about those who have passed into the Subtle World. Some grieve over the deceased, thus interfering with their ascent, and others criticize them, which is equally harmful. In some cases the deceased are completely forgotten, and this, too, is wrong. It is essential to have a proper, harmonious attitude.

Let us imagine a dear one who is in an adjoining room absorbed in some important work. Our first impulse is to safeguard his quietude and take all precautions against disturbing him. We provide the best conditions for the speedy fulfillment of his task. We are concerned about the work, and send our benevolent thoughts to him. We know that our dear one is near us, and although we would like to see him, we realize that we have no right to disturb him. We are patient, knowing that we shall be together at the right time.

In the same way, there is much to tell our friend who has passed into the Subtle World, but out of love for him we must control our desire and be cautious. We shall not allow a single word of evil, not wanting disharmonious currents to disturb his work. In short, we shall have a right attitude to the situation, and shall not grieve about the imaginary loss. How can we, knowing that our dear one lives and is near? Nor should we insist upon physical communication. If he is meant to, he will hasten to appear at the proper time.

One should be concerned about harmony, which is essential for both worlds. If an important task is being performed near us, we should not quarrel or make noise. Even in daily life people celebrate in the name of an absent one, and try, for example, to take care of the dear one's possessions. We act wisely if we behave toward the deceased as we would toward an absent friend.

You should have the same attitude toward Us. This attitude will broaden your consciousness and is beneficial for your inner life. It is lamentable that after millions of years We still must stress an intelligent attitude toward the life of the Subtle World. Let us be fair and admit that people do not understand the Subtle World; moreover, due to the predominance of technology, they are moving even farther from the true concepts. Literacy does not yet mean culture. Great calamities occur because of ignorance. We do not expect extraordinary refinement, but only that people manifest the best qualities of their spiritual nature.

The Thinker taught, "Let us send a smile of love to the deceased. Let us send encouragement to all pilgrims. May they rest peacefully at the crossroads. Pilgrim, tell us about the wondrous countries!"

355. Urusvati knows that, at times, people unexpectedly experience unusual psychic phenomena. They may receive radio transmissions, see through solid objects, or distinguish the presence of subterranean metals.

Let us elaborate upon this seeming suddenness of experience, for nothing occurs without a cause. Even when We speak about a "sudden illumination," it should be understood from a relative, earthly viewpoint. Although the illumination is sensed suddenly, it is the result of a lengthy process of the refinement of consciousness. Such refinement usually begins at an early age, or rather, is brought by the soul from the Subtle World.

People think that psychic powers are gifts from above, little realizing that these gifts are earned by the individual himself amidst all kinds of burdensome experiences. Usually, one does not recognize the presence of these seeds, which are ready to blossom at the first favorable opportunity. Furthermore, no one points out to the toiler the possibilities earned by him. A vessel filled to the brim is easily spilled. In the same way, accumulated psychic powers can be suddenly manifested at the least prompting.

People endure many humiliating situations and much self-doubt before they dare to speak about their powers. But the most difficult and incomprehensible potential for ordinary people to realize is their participation in cosmic events. The heart is strongly affected during such processes, but what earthly physician can understand the dangers of cosmic tension? As a rule, physicians do not even notice signs of cosmic suffering. They would rather accuse the patient of malingering than admit that cosmic disturbance could be the cause.

The Thinker long ago understood this kind of pain in the world.

356. Urusvati knows how painful it is to participate in cosmic processes. One may ask what causes such painful tension. The answer is simple—when even a particle of ectoplasm is affected a medium will suffer greatly, but ectoplasm constitutes only the subtle body. Cosmic experiences affect the fiery body, and cause far greater suffering.

One may further ask, if cosmic currents influence all living beings, why must only exceptional people undergo severe suffering? Again the answer is simple. These currents certainly influence the entire planet, but the degree of reaction to them varies, and when someone fills his Chalice and refines his consciousness, he places himself in the first rank of those affected. It is impossible then to avoid such suffering by altering his consciousness, for it has already attained a natural degree of development.

Who can stop the growth of consciousness when it has reached a certain degree of development? One should not interfere with the actions of a hero who has dedicated his life to *podvig*, for the destruction of darkness is the dream of every spiritual warrior. The battle is the same on both the mundane and the supermundane planes. By the use of vibration We may lessen the tension, but the cosmic battle requires a universal defense.

Defense and Nirvana are two mercilessly distorted concepts. People try to make them into something amorphous, vague, and passive, but such distortions are harmful for evolution.

People must consciously prepare themselves for a

state such as Nirvana, and this takes a long time. They must learn to love the state of mind that can be called all-containment. In the same way, people must learn to love the concept of defense, and think of it as the most intensified and vigilant condition. They must perfect themselves consciously, otherwise participation in the Cosmic Battle will become unbearable.

But how can man train himself for austere defense without contemplating cosmos? In practicing defense man displays the highest self-denial. He acts not for himself, but for the far-off realms. Everyone can understand that it is not easy to forget oneself for the sake of the far-off worlds. An expanded consciousness must go hand in hand with a solicitous attitude toward one's health. Human forces are frail compared to the currents of space.

One should develop clarity of consciousness. One should understand that in the protection of harmony lies Beauty. One must not allow doubts that will violate the order of harmony. Beautiful is the vigilance that knows and loves the treasures that it protects.

The Thinker knew the beauty of such vigilance. He said, "We learn, not for ourselves, not for Earth, not for the sun, but for the invisible Realms."

357. Urusvati knows how realistically a subtle entity can manifest itself. People think that such phenomena can take place only through the ectoplasm of a medium, but other processes of manifestation must be considered. These entities can also be perceived through the power of clairvoyance, which works not through ectoplasm, but through direct, fourth dimensional vision.

It is characteristic for certain entities to be attracted to particular places. In these cases, the energy that evokes the materialization has been accumulated in various locations, most often as precipitations on the walls of old buildings. Subtle entities strengthen their manifestations by use of certain layers of this matter. Such buildings could humorously be compared to old, worn-out garments infested with microorganisms that make them "come to life," as it were.

People frequently complain that they have no visions. These visions do indeed occur, but people do not pay attention to them. For example, the sight, in broad daylight, of human images, which then immediately disappear. Unfortunately, the human mind would rather fabricate all sorts of artificial explanations than find the true cause for such manifestations.

The time has come when it is necessary to bring the Subtle World closer to Earth, but it is impossible to do so without the cooperation of humanity. Even those who are ready to accept the existence of the Subtle World expect some tremendous shock that will immediately transform their entire life. Our help is in proportion to human cooperation.

People must accept the existence of the Subtle World and free themselves from superstition and bigotry. These two vipers deprive people of the possibility of communing consciously with the Subtle World. Do not think that We exaggerate the dangers of superstition and bigotry. The lives of most people are based upon these prejudices, which deprive them of freedom of thought and so fill them with ignorant convictions that they deliberately close their eyes and ears to the most obvious manifestations. If one wants to see, one must have an open mind. Negation closes the keenest eye. On the other hand, one must beware of false, imagined visions. Thus, there remains only one way—the golden middle way, which We have already stressed. He who follows the middle way knows an all-embracingness that excludes or changes nothing. This is not an easy way, for it requires a refinement of consciousness.

The Thinker taught not to fear the middle way.

358. Urusvati knows how varied are the rhythms of Our communications. At times they flow slowly and distinctly, but at other times so rapidly that it is almost impossible to hear them. They may be shockingly loud, or may become almost inaudible, like the softest whisper. Sometimes they strain the centers, but usually they are beneficent. Do not suppose that these variations are the result of Our unbalanced minds! You should seek the cause in the spatial currents. The example of Our communication is of use to anyone who studies the energy of thought.

People are impatient in everything. To explain each phenomenon they hasten to create their own rules, and through such arbitrary, willful interference, they interrupt the most valuable manifestations. This is why it is so important that you be reminded about the variety of Our communications. One should bear in mind that if Our force can be affected by cosmic currents, it is even more difficult for the efforts of beginners.

When We speak about purification of thinking We have in mind primarily liberation from preconceived notions. Imagine someone experimenting with the receiving of direct communications who then tries to introduce his own thoughts. Such a student will only mix up the messages. There have been many such cases.

When receiving communications from a great distance one should be particularly careful not to allow interruptions. Through carelessness in receiving, many words can be lost. Much experience is necessary for one to be able to perceive the various changes of rhythm.

When We speak about Our Inner Life We primarily want to impress upon you the diversity of conditions that surround you and Us. It is an annoying fact that people fail to understand that we are all surrounded by the same currents of energy. Only when you realize this will you come close to Us. This closeness will evoke reverence, or in other words, acceptance of the Teacher. Alas, it is seldom that the Teacher is accepted. At times people may feel sparks of devotion, but such flickering will only irritate the atmosphere. We do not speak about Our authority, but about the principle on which harmonious communion can be built.

The Thinker insisted upon respect for the Teacher. He said, "In the dark of the night one should look for the Guiding Hand. The Voice of the Guide is a joy. But this devotion should continue not only in the darkness, but also in the sunlight."

359. Urusvati knows that clarity of subtle vision is developed in the course of many incarnations. This quality is correctly called clairvoyance. Glimmers of clairvoyance are not unusual, but steady vision is acquired only with great effort. Urusvati has testified correctly that even in her childhood she possessed clairvoyance with full, unwavering images.

It is interesting to observe how slowly people acquire this ability. Often the perceived images tremble, the features become distorted, parts disappear, or the images may become stretched out of proportion or change their expression. Even the most kindly face can acquire a look of malice. Due to these distortions people imagine that they have been approached by an evil spirit, but the cause lies in their own inability to develop subtle vision.

Certainly, amid fuss and commotion it is not easy to concentrate one's attention upon the image, especially when the contours of its aura tremble. It is a mistake to attribute these fluctuations of the aura to the imagination, for they are often caused by the wavering aura of the observer himself. You must remember that the majority of auras are not steady, and this can affect even physical sight.

In ancient days students were required to develop subtle sight. For this purpose, the student was asked to observe an object, then suddenly was asked to close his eyes and describe it. This is not an easy discipline. In these tests, although the student thinks that he has memorized everything, he has in reality absorbed only the general outlines, and the object's distinctive features have eluded him. But it is precisely in the distinctive features of an object that one can find its essence and style.

The ancients paid much attention to the study of the psychic nature of man, and such studies took place not only in the temples, but also in special schools, which, when later established in Greece, were called Academies. Many subjects were studied in them, including the legends, which were the main source of information about life in remote antiquity. Even now, scientists who study folklore can find there traces of profound wisdom.

We should investigate the heroic achievements of the ancients; we will find in them similarities with the achievements of modern science. As a matter of fact, the ancients not only dreamed about future scientific achievements, they were aware of many of them. If scientists were to look at the treasures of folklore from a scientific point of view, they would find many confirmations of the knowledge of ancient people.

The Thinker once saw a shepherd who was followed by his large flock of sheep. The Thinker smilingly asked, "By what magic do you compel the animals to follow you so obediently?" The shepherd answered, "I live with them and love them, and they feel that they are safe if they follow me."

360. Urusvati knows how often people attempt to attribute subtle phenomena to gross physical causes. For instance, noises in the ear that are experienced by many are physical manifestations that provoke varying interpretations. Doctors often attribute them to abnormal blood pressure, but this is simply another external symptom. The true cause of such pressures is the touch of subtle influences. Actually, there are three kinds of noise—one is a peculiarly dull, continuous noise, another is like a reflection of the pulse, and the third you have described as like the sound of cicadas. This third type, a curious, very rapid pulsation, is especially characteristic, and is the sign of a particularly subtle energy.

These noises cannot be explained by a decreased function of the heart, or by irritability, especially since they occur unexpectedly and independently, with no connection to any previous physical experiences. They may be due to the pressure of cosmic currents, but it is more likely that they are the touches of the Subtle World. Thus, we come back again to the subject of contact with the Subtle World. People should look more within themselves, and should fulfill the ancient maxim "Man, know thyself."

Therefore it is not only physicians who are equipped with the necessary knowledge about such matters; ordinary people can also give wise advice if sufficiently experienced and introspective. Long ago it was known that, even amid the most ordinary daily routine, it was possible to be in touch with reflections of the subtlest energies. Indeed, from the very depths of man's nature explosions erupt, as if a seal were opened by some special touch.

There is a curious state of mind called *idée fixe*. I am not referring to possession, which may have similar symptoms, but to obsessive, constantly repeated assertions, which can have a special significance. Medical science considers the *idée fixe* to be dangerous, but this is a baseless judgment. If we accept this opinion, we must then consider many splendid scientific minds insane! It is time to revise the notion about the insanity of genius, otherwise we will have to conclude that fools and dolts have sound and healthy minds!

We have repeatedly condemned the dark obsessions that lead to evil and crime. It should be understood that it is the influence of subtle energy alone that results in the healthiest state of mind. The benevolent influence of subtle energy is the great blessing that inspires man to ascend the ladder of evolution.

Only by observing human actions can one discriminate and sense the subtle differences between good and bad people. You will see that the one who labors for evolution is filled with ideas. But who would call these ideas fixed? It would be right to call them leading ideas. Pay heed then to all the manifestations of nature.

The Thinker said, "Whether I serve Nature, or Nature serves me, does not matter. The important thing is that all my knowledge and experience are offered in the service of the Common Good."

361. Urusvati knows that with each generation there are changes in world outlook, customs, and even language. It is not easy to recognize the New Era when in the midst of it, but from a distance every observant eye can see how agitated is the substance of life.

There was an ancient practice of sending observers to certain places, to stay for a period of time and then return. With the coming of the new generation, the same observers were sent again to these places. We use the same method, so that Our Messengers may witness the formation of a new generation. Only in this way can We acquire a fresh and correct impression regarding the evolution of a particular nation.

Many will doubt the very possibility of such evolution, for they themselves are stagnant. But evolution is a law of Nature. The difficulty is that people see only from their own point of view and are therefore unable to progress. They imagine that everything ends with their demise, and cannot understand that life has its own continually changing, vivid waves.

Such immobile people will find themselves in a most lamentable position when they enter the Subtle World. They will regret that during their earthly existence they did not mingle with different generations or find points of contact with a variety of mentalities. The ancients wisely experimented with various generations. And you too will learn how to feel at home among the most diverse mentalities. Remember that We, also, had to undergo such experiences.

The Thinker compared such tests with the tempering of a blade. He knew that only by the alternate application of heat and cold could indestructible strength be forged.

362. Urusvati knows that intention equals action. More accurately, We can say that intention is more significant than action. Action discharges energy, whereas intention accumulates the energy that will be manifested as action. Therefore, when I advise being careful about intentions, I have in mind the maximum benefit.

People frequently leave their earthly existence with many intentions still unrealized. The ignorant think that these intentions will remain so, not understanding that life does not cease and the opportunity remains for intentions to be fulfilled elsewhere or at another time.

Blessed are those who have a store of good intentions, for they will be beautifully realized. Truly, every intention will bear fruit, every promise will be kept, and every goodness glorified.

People complain that their merits are unappreciated, ignorant of the fact that life continues after the death of the body. He who believes that everything ends with his departure from Earth is a poor man, for he has robbed himself of the treasures of fulfillment and will enter the Subtle World unprepared. Where then will he be while his consciousness is so obscured? Alas, he will be confined to a place in the dark regions of the lower spheres that he could easily have avoided, where he will be subjected to negative influences that will impede his progress even more.

Various religions deal with the idea of the continuity of life, but these hints are not sufficiently convincing or people would try to prepare themselves for better progress. Some people try to buy a better future with monetary donations, but gold has no value in the Subtle World. Good deeds combined with a good consciousness will bring joy on Earth and in the Supermundane Realm. If the instrument is tuned, it will resound in harmony with the higher spheres.

Sometimes people hope that there will appear a Guide who will save them from any abyss. These selfish people do not understand that the Guide suffers when descending into the lower spheres. Others think that there is enough time in Infinity, and that while on Earth they can enjoy themselves without limit! Alas, once beyond the earthly boundaries, they will learn to evaluate their losses.

You are quite right in your feelings. There can be no merriment while Earth cries out from the burden of calamities. While hunger exists there can be no gluttony. And what kind of dances can be performed against a background of violence? Truly, I say that merriment is indecent in these days of calamity.

You are also right in assuming that the waves of distant transmissions are quite varied. Some may be caught by certain intended receivers, but others may reach the most undesirable listeners, and in this respect caution is always needed.

The Thinker knew about this when He said, "May my thoughts reach those who will appreciate them."

363. Urusvati knows that labor engenders one of the most sublime joys. One would expect this truth to be accepted by all, but alas, labor is usually considered a burden and people dream only about holidays. However, We shall share with you Our concept of labor. We work always amidst the most tiring conditions and also have holidays, but Our holidays are periods of communion with the Highest Spheres.

There are some who would consider that such communion is labor also, and they would be right, for the exploration of the higher spheres requires much energy. Absolute concentration is required and the apparatuses must be controlled with skill. Recently, Urusvati experienced a powerful shock when one of the levers broke in My hand. Such unpredicted complications often occur, but there is a great difference between the breaking of a lever during routine work and a complication in the apparatuses used for communication. Yet, despite inevitable complications, the labor of striving toward the higher spheres is a true festival.

Amid earthly chores you too can create festive labor. Self-examination however is needed in order to decide which particular work one might consider a festival, and to learn what kind of work increases one's strength.

Rest is best achieved through change of work. Yes, yes, yes, it will be a long time before people understand this paradox! Nor is it easy for them to recognize that even the process of thinking is labor, for who can understand that man creates something real when thinking?

People are reluctant to accept the idea that a routine task should be followed by a period of concentrated thinking. How then can they imagine the kind of thought that kindles the fires of space and builds structures in the Subtle World? Even those who write about the significance of thought do not apply to themselves the rule about the inevitable and irreparable results of thinking. Man is a strange being, quite ready to accept the idea of the influence of someone else's thoughts, but oblivious to the results of his own thinking. Thus man neglects his own possibilities. I believe that the time has come for people to cease lecturing and to apply themselves to strict self-betterment.

Why is it that psychic research societies so often stagnate? The members themselves obstruct their own progress. It is an unwholesome situation when the researchers themselves are unable, first of all, to test the purity of their own intentions.

The Thinker was greatly concerned about the purity of the intentions of His disciples, and used to ask, "Precious substances are available even for the usual ablutions, but what substance can be used for purifying our intentions?"

364. Urusvati knows that world events usually affect those who participated in their inception in past ages. Events in any country affect those who are currently involved in them. But they also affect those who, in past lives, helped to build the country. They, too, reverberate to the violent calamities that befall the nation they created.

You can imagine the anxiety of Sister O., who was connected with two countries and now is witness to their suffering. Likewise, He who directed a nation toward righteousness during its revolution is now saddened to see it rush toward destruction. Indeed, how can one remain indifferent when the best intentions are thwarted?

You also are filled with anxiety because you were once involved in work connected with the suffering nations. One can already witness the humiliating fate of one particular nation that could have been in a favorable position. Gradually the events are taking shape in the West, with its feverish campaign against ideas of community. But the false communitarians are even worse than those dreamers who think of themselves as founders of the New Era.

Anxiety surrounds the nearby spheres, and special care should be taken for the preservation of harmony. These are unprecedented times, and the human consciousness is unable to perceive them properly.

The Thinker warned His fellow citizens, "Do not overestimate your knowledge, for events may take place that will reveal its inadequacy."

365. Urusvati knows that it is extremely difficult for materialized entities of the Subtle World to reproduce the sound of the voice. This is understandable, for an entity is more accustomed to transmission by thought, and reproducing the voice is difficult. Of course, in cases of special harmony this difficulty can be overcome, though such a degree of harmony is rare. People do not know how to approach subtle guests in order to determine their needs.

It is possible to observe a complete materialization or a transfer of objects; rarely however can one witness a manifestation of the earthly voice, for it is far more difficult. True, mental communication is possible, but unfortunately people do not yet know how to use it. So much would be achieved if people could sense the subtle conditions.

This ability should also be developed in relations between people. What a pity that so many good achievements are obstructed simply because of a lack of care and understanding. Indeed, great care for one another is needed, particularly amid the more oppressive currents.

You have experienced the onrush of anguish. Such anxiety should be analyzed, and can be traced to the repercussions of world calamities. You should record them as the explosions of Armageddon, whose astonishing waves shake the whole world.

The Thinker could recognize such days by a particular beat of His heart.

366. Urusvati knows that outer appearances do not serve as an indication of the inner life. To obtain a clear idea of the inner life, one must have a knowledge of a man's aspirations and intentions. Learning that someone was a philosopher, physician, king, or warrior will not show you the inner man; it is far more important to learn the underlying motives that prompted the actions of these individuals.

And so We now give you the outlines of Our Inner Life, pointing out the principles that lie in the foundations of the Brotherhood. Alas, people have too often pictured Us as celestial beings, but nothing good can be derived from such an idea, for it appears to isolate Us from Earth. Indeed, when We discuss the Supermundane Realm We certainly do not imply isolation from Earth. After all, all of life is supermundane, for it is permeated with the subtle energies.

The time will come when people will be compelled to turn to a more subtle mode of thinking. Evolution is created by man himself and nothing can impede it. Even the present state of evolution will in the long run serve a good purpose as a unique *tactica adversa*, for in his attachment to technology man will drive himself into such a dead end that no way will be open to him but to turn to the joy of the Subtle World.

It has been prophesied that if man escapes the catastrophe he will turn toward the refinement of life, and the time will arrive for the coming together of the two worlds. Even now the time has come! For example, the densification of the subtle body is no longer considered as supernatural, and there are those people who, while in the physical body, know how to consciously release their subtle body. From both sides the parts of the bridge are coming together. Lightning can unite these two parts, and We wait with great vigilance for the time when the bridge will be joined. Then Our work will change course, and We shall proceed to the far-off worlds.

Therefore, the first task of humanity is the building of the bridge of the Temple. The second task of learning communion with the far-off worlds will be easier. What some people now perceive vaguely will become a normal condition of planetary life. Do you not think that for such tasks it is worthwhile to preserve Earth? But as yet only a small minority thinks in this way.

The Thinker foresaw how few there would be who care to save the planet.

367. Urusvati knows how physical and psychic phenomena are intimately linked. For example, because of extreme physical exertion a person may see sparks of light that are similar to psychic phenomena. Therefore We advise calm and concentration of the mind in order to prevent sudden physical shocks. Thought should be directed to Us, but in a state of mental equilibrium. We even advise a partial realization of the Infinite, for nothing contributes so much to one's balance as the sense of Infinity. There are many different methods of acquiring calm, but awareness of the Infinite is the most effective.

Uttering the name of the Guru also creates a strong bond, but this, too, must be done with serenity, for any excessive exertion will invariably produce a disturbed atmosphere. Realize, however, that calmness is not inertia; on the contrary, just as in the state of Nirvana, it is full of inner vibration. Many will not understand this and will see only contradiction. They will argue, "How can calmness be filled with vibrations, and how can a calm invocation of the Guru's name be so effective? How can a calm prayer be more effective than a cry of despair?"

It is hard to express certain ideas in words. It is hard to explain the difference between the power of calmness and the oppressive force of aggression. Only those who have trod many earthly paths will understand the value of calmness, particularly during the days of Armageddon. Calm reigns in Our Abode, where even the slightest imbalance can cause a great calamity. Calmness should be cultivated everywhere in the world.

Urusvati quite correctly stresses the building of character in the young. Indeed, it is more important than a strictly intellectual education, for only the building of good character can lay the foundations of calmness and productive labor in life.

The Thinker warned His disciples, saying, "Preserve calmness, or you will fall into the inferno of hell."

368. Urusvati knows that the world-outlook changes with each generation. But few individuals grasp this, for an entire generation is rarely studied. Amid life's confusion people are not accustomed to paying sufficient attention to the thinking of youth, and believe that by using the old textbooks, they will strengthen traditional concepts. But these books are obsolete, and young thought finds its own way.

Twenty years is the measure of a generation. This division should be kept in mind, otherwise you will perpetuate the same old injustices.

For example, imagine the hostility that arises in a certain country where the population has been living in hatred for a quarter of a century and has transmitted its hostility to the next generation. Is this just? Even when the original enemies no longer exist, and the young generation has begun to think in a new way, there are those who will wish to impose upon the young minds earlier antiquated concepts. One should always remember the span of the generations so that injustice will not be done.

The essential meaning of a society should not be judged by the outward conditions and customs of life which can remain unchanged from one generation to the next, but by its inner growth and striving. You should understand that I am not talking abstractly. I am observing a certain nation in which people are creating a new world-outlook, yet there is a strong opposition that attempts to force the nation to revert to the ancient concepts of past generations. Casual, short-sighted observers tell the most contradictory stories. It would be appropriate to ask these observers from which generation they have drawn their judgments.

One must insist upon clear discernment, or misjudgments will be committed and the new generation accused of crimes of the former generation for which they are not responsible. It is difficult to form a correct judgment, which is why one must learn to understand the causes and effects of life in general.

The Thinker often questioned His listeners, "Of whom are you really speaking, a son, a father, or a grandfather?"

369. Urusvati knows that there are certain individuals who can foresee the direction of evolution. Such co-workers of Ours can be found in different countries and ages. We use them as channels through which We transmit the varying degrees of aspiration that correspond to the needs of evolution. But it should be understood that such striving individuals are rare, and will feel out of place in any generation. It would be correct to think of them not as dwellers of Earth, but rather as guests, filled with memories of better worlds. Indeed, earthly life is not easy for them. They are filled with the spirit of service to humanity, but this concept is little understood on Earth. These toilers cannot find a common language with coarser earthly people. It is to be lamented that time so distorts their ideas, although eventually their words find some degree of recognition. All that I have said here is also true about Our own work, but through the centuries We have become sufficiently aware of the turning of the Wheel of Life. We understand that in motion much is consumed; even huge meteors are burned away, yet some of them succeed in carrying their diamonds to Earth. Only a calm understanding of earthly processes can reveal the whole range of accumulated knowledge. We call such observations a clarification of consciousness.

The Thinker fully understood that His Teaching would be subjected to many distortions. He used to say, "Only in the clouds will the signs of Our intentions be fully recorded."

370. Urusvati knows that self-betterment must begin with the eradication of small, but harmful, habits. We particularly stress the importance of daily habits. People believe they must overcome the main obstacles at once, only to find that such drastic measures are beyond their capacity. One may also often observe instances when people imagine that they have rid themselves of their major sins, yet remain burdened with little ugly habits. A tree bent by the weight of ugly fruit, developed over ages, is a sad sight indeed.

Bear in mind that it is not easy to rid oneself of petty habits. Among them there are always some of which one is not even aware, and which only a keen-eyed observer can discern. Yet, the uncovering of such hidden habits often leads to complete transformation. Remember the ancient saying, "If you seize the lesser devil by the tail, he will lead you to his superior."

The wisdom of folklore should always be remembered; it will lead to a practical application of the Teaching, rather than a superficial reading. Many people read all the books, but remain without knowledge. Sometimes such unreceptive readers even regress, and prove to be worse off than if they had been illiterate. People should try to understand exactly what has been assimilated from their reading, and what can be useful in its application to their lives. Let them ask themselves what negative habits they have successfully overcome, and write down those paragraphs from the books that have influenced their minds in a beneficial way. How can one expect harmony amidst the uproar of disharmony if the smallest habits remain untouched and unchanged? Thus, do not forget to warn friends against the dangers of petty habits.

The Thinker was careful about His habits, and knew how to relinquish any of them. His motto was, "Do not carry unneeded stones in your pockets."

371. Urusvati knows that in preparation for Infinity the earthly path is filled with both danger and joy. However, there are three kinds of doubters. The first asks, "And where is the promised joy? So much is said about joy, but now we hear only about endless dangers! After all, it is only because of the promised joy that we pay attention to instructions."

We shall say to him, "Ignoramus! Is not the overcoming of chaos a joy? Is not the bringing of light into darkness a joy? Is not the understanding of service a joy? If your concept of joy is the joy of the bazaar, our paths are not compatible."

Another angrily complains, "You remain in complete safety, yet all you offer us is continual danger." We shall answer, "Ignoramus, what makes you think that We are safe? Everything is relative. Our dangers may be invisible to you, but there is no such thing as life without danger. You must realize that one of the greatest joys comes from the awareness and understanding of danger. Through vigilance and awareness man becomes victorious, and this victory is joy!"

The third doubts the concept of Infinity. To him We shall say, "Ignoramus, your heart has become harder than stone if you have lost the joy of Infinity.

Man should realize that he is called to saturate Infinite Space with thought. The realization of the infinite power of thought is in itself the highest joy. Imagine what a beautiful garden of thought has been given to you, and rejoice at this knowledge." In this way one can nullify all doubters.

Bear in mind that certain terms should be understood relatively. For example, one may speak of "spiritual drought," but few understand the meaning of this condition. Yet it does come about, due to an intense but unbalanced concentration, when the consciousness is greatly elevated while the centers are unable to adjust themselves. Thus, temporarily, man cannot express his consciousness. Such turns of the spiral of consciousness are unavoidable.

The Thinker once said, "Today I felt as though I knew nothing. This is a good sign, for it means that tomorrow I shall probably learn something beautiful."

372. Urusvati knows how great are the dangers that We must overcome. You know about the terrible consequences of the explosion that was experienced by Our Brother V. Space absorbs many shocks! Nevertheless many terrible events take place as the result of disregarding Our Indications. Some people will argue and take issue with the beneficial advice, while others outwardly pretend to follow it, yet inwardly rebel. Pay particular attention to this second type. If people could only understand how worthless are their false, superficial smiles! The most useful advice loses its significance if it is inwardly rejected; then nothing is left but the husk.

Also remember that a large number of useful instructions are distorted. Let us take, for example, the question of food. We are decidedly against a meat diet. The normal progress of evolution has been retarded in part because of the eating of meat. Yet there are instances, such as a shortage of food, when dried or smoked meat may be eaten as an emergency measure. We are decidedly against the drinking of wine. As an intoxicant it is inadmissible, but it can be used in the treatment of certain illnesses. We are decidedly against all narcotics, but there may be cases of such unbearable suffering that a physician has no choice but to use them. There are those who may object to this, and ask if it is not possible to use suggestion against pain. Of course, it can and should be used, but it is not easy to find a person with sufficient power of suggestion.

Our instructions are quite clear, yet there will be people who try to confuse others and cause harm. These troublemakers will assure everyone that We allow the use of wine, narcotics, and meat, and they will demand absolute abstinence. Yet, should they be hungry or ill, they will be the first to accuse the Teacher of allowing them no exceptions.

Besides hypocrisy, one can also expect to see great cunning. People will deceive themselves in order to justify their own weaknesses. Yet they will not stop to think about the dangers they create for themselves. On the surface they appear to be Our co-workers, yet where is the reverence that should be at the foundation of all collaboration?

The Thinker used to say, "Do not believe all assurances of love! The great foundation of the world needs not assurances, but actions."

373. Urusvati knows that culture is the common heritage of all humanity. Despite differences in customs, creeds, and languages, every act of culture is the possession of all mankind. The unification of the world through culture is the first step toward the transformation of all life.

The objection may be raised that each nation has its own culture. You can answer that culture should not be confused with customs. The objectors will also insist that there are great differences in the written languages of the various countries. But in speaking of culture We have in mind not the alphabets or the style of expression but the intended meaning and ideas. Compare the finest creations of the various nations and you will see that the basic ideas are common to all. Thus, We can affirm that even in diversity there is a unifying international aspiration.

It is a joyous fact that the essence of human nature strives toward perfection. Man ignores this ever-present impulse, and will even rebel against this prompting of his higher nature, yet deep within the recesses of his Chalice the seed of culture radiates! Sooner or later this seed will sprout; this is why everyone carries within himself a sense of his humanity.

One then may wonder if the many who are filled with fury and hatred also bear within themselves a seed of culture. Yes, but it is deeply buried under their accumulation of crimes. They will find an Instructor in the Subtle World who will point out that such a debased state is inadmissible. Verily, people must understand that each day can be radiant with humaneness.

The Thinker was concerned that His disciples should understand that universal humaneness radiates even in the far-off worlds, and that everyone is a citizen of all the worlds.

374. Urusvati knows that every thinking person searches for the Primal Cause. Some seekers use subtle approaches, others coarse ones, yet all seek. The common mistake is in attempting to investigate the Highest Cause without first studying the more accessible ones. In doing so people ignore the need for common sense discrimination in daily events. He who has sufficient wisdom to perceive the causes of the simplest daily occurrences earns the right to dive deeper and to soar higher. Perceiving the causes of daily events refines the thinking process. It is instructive to observe how sometimes an entire chain of events can be broken simply by an exclamation or glance, yet those who are present do not notice and afterwards will completely forget the original cause.

In Our mental Messages We sometimes use just one word. Such a hint is filled with meaning, yet not all who receive such hints pay attention to them. One must acquire experience in concentration in order to become vigilant, especially since the cause and effect are often separated by a lengthy period of time.

Similarly, people pay little attention to the "cementing of space," and question why thoughts should be sent forth again and again that are essentially the same as those that have been sent before. Little do they understand that Our repetitions are intended to fill space. It is not enough to make decisions; a suitable atmosphere must also be created for Our thoughts, and such weaving demands lengthy efforts. People also should understand that their intentions must be enveloped in a protective shield, and much can be facilitated by constant calm and affirmative thought, directed with intention.

The Thinker used to say, "Intentions are like a sword without its sheath. Anything can damage the blade, and only if it is sheathed will it retain its sharpness."

375. Urusvati knows how unwise are those who abuse their dwelling place. It is difficult for people to realize that irritability is especially undesirable during meals and before retiring to bed, and they find it incomprehensible that dark thoughts and curses can cling tenaciously to their dwelling place. The most beautiful dwelling can become a den of dark entities when people refuse to acknowledge the energy of thought.

Just as there are objects permeated with the most benevolent vibrations, there are also cursed objects. People forget that their emanations have the ability to attract antithetical entities. People do not know that any place can be changed into a good and beneficial one. And how can one curse a place that has become unpleasant precisely because of human foolishness? People should remember that their irritability and blasphemy will return to them as a burden. It brings to mind a terrible picture of a man who has unwittingly put his head in a noose and only realizes it when his own neck is being broken.

Further, people do not think that by their blasphemy they impede Our work. We have to expend much energy purifying those places that they have polluted. How can one permit such lack of discipline? Most obscenity is uttered because of ignorance. And some people might say that they feel imprisoned because of not being allowed to speak freely. But they should understand that many crimes and miseries are caused by casual, thoughtless words. Some places are so permeated with blood and curses that it is better to leave these poisonous locations and start a new life elsewhere. Let time itself clear away the dark emanations.

The Thinker warned that thoughts and words should express intentions which later will not have to be denied.

376. Urusvati knows that it is impermissible to build with one hand, and destroy with the other. But one can often observe precisely that, when one half of a man's personality is dedicated to constructive work while the other half commits blasphemy and destroys his previous achievements, and even his values. We advise applying oneself completely to the constructive work or not attempting it at all.

This instruction also applies to the cognizing of the Subtle World. On the one hand man seems to wish to bring the Subtle World closer, and on the other he tries to thrust it aside. People are instructed to believe in the phenomena described in the Bible and other sacred books, and at the same time are forbidden to touch upon these domains. One can cite countless examples of scientific investigations of the Subtle World that were forbidden and many beautiful achievements that were abruptly stopped. It is terrible to think that some people are compelled to believe blindly, and that learning is forbidden to them!

One can imagine the many negative forces impeding much that is ready to manifest. The boundary between the earthly world and the Subtle World has an ugly twist that can be traced to such imperfection. The battle at the boundary of the two worlds is great, therefore We advise you either to approach with full devotion or not to make contact with the Subtle World at all.

There is much blasphemy. People hypocritically repeat the words of the Teaching and at the same time think without shame about inadmissible actions. Those of whom I speak should take note. The instructions that are sent can only be applied to life in full measure. Whom then will the hypocrites deceive?

The Thinker used to say, "It is not possible to deceive the Invisible Forces."

377. Urusvati knows about the nature of battle in the Subtle World, where all things are created by the

mind alone, and destroyed by the mind alone. One can imagine the clashes that take place when fury contends with the courage of justice. The battle takes place in the various spheres and its quality corresponds to the quality of those spheres. It is particularly frenzied in the sphere closest to Earth, where reign passions not yet outlived. All earthly errors survive here, for those who bear them have not been liberated from their passions.

Among the inhabitants of these spheres may be found many political leaders who while on Earth believed power to be the crown of earthly achievement, and are still unaware that their unrestrained desires are a burden to the earthly atmosphere. In fact, these souls without harmony are ever ready to storm not only Earth, but Heaven also. They know no peace and derive their destructive power from their fury. There is nothing puzzling in the resultant battles, and many of these madmen perish while others continue to survive. Even the most difficult karma requires existence, if the Law of Karma is to be fulfilled.

Those with a tendency to destroy harmony increase the burden of their karma. One should ask what happens to those who do not survive, who are "killed" by the explosions of thought. They fall into a deep sleep, an unconscious state that holds back their progress. In this way many descriptions of heavenly battles are not far from reality.

Unfortunately, people often make crude earthly comparisons that only serve to increase their misconceptions about the Subtle World. Examine human history, and you will see how the striving for Truth is impeded by human imaginings. The crude descriptions of the Subtle World do not correspond to its true condition. For example, the fury of the subtle entities is quite different from earthly rage.

The Thinker believed that earthly thought cannot attain the degree of refinement it reaches in the higher worlds.

378. Urusvati knows that the Law of Karma postulates the continuity of existence, or rebirth. Many would prefer the idea of complete annihilation to that of the spiral of karmic reactions. There is an ancient proverb, "Karma is an executioner who guards his victim." In other words, karma will not allow criminals to be destroyed and thus escape their punishment.

Indeed, sometimes terrible and obvious evildoers continue to exist, although, humanly speaking, it would seem only just for them to have been destroyed. But is it possible to apply human measures where the Law of Absolute Justice operates? Sometimes the evildoers are punished by prolonged illness or, though in good physical health, become subject to the terrors of psychic unrest.

One should not think that crime may be excused because of mental imbalance. We should search more deeply and look for causes rooted in the past. Such a study will clarify the concept of karma. The wise do not fear this law. Generally, humanity can be divided into two groups, those who fear the consequences of karma and those who accept them calmly. Avoid those who fear, for they almost certainly sense the approach of karmic retribution. They may not yet know anything about its effects, but in the depths of the Chalice the long-forgotten viper is rising to the surface.

Mark well the way in which people differ according to their attitude toward the doctrine of reincarnation. Some are able to accept the full justice of this Law, but to others it seems monstrous. Perhaps those who are fearful have vague memories of their previous deeds, and have good reason for their present fears. Thus one can note the division of humanity.

The Thinker taught His disciples not to fear the Law of Karma. He said, "The hunter enters the forest with much hope. How else can he set out? Without hope his hunt will not be successful."

379. Urusvati knows that so-called sacred pains do not differ outwardly from ordinary physical pains. Physicians will find the most routine explanations for them. You recall that two of the greatest sages of India were stricken and died, one from cancer of the throat and the other from diabetes. What can such ailments have in common with sacred pains? Both cases indicate that a selfless outpouring of psychic energy can result in unexpected afflictions.

You also know about the sacred pains of Upâsikâ, whose doctors would never have accepted the true explanation for them—that they were the result of excessive self-sacrifice. There are those who will object to such an expending of psychic energy, but are such objections proper? One could just as well question the value of the self-sacrificing lives of Our Sisters in Spain and Italy, who both stand as lofty examples of workers for the Common Good. They struggled against injustice and ignorance, endured terrible abuse, and demonstrated patience beyond understanding. Both suffered from sacred pains. No one could diagnose their various ailments, which broke out unexpectedly and ended just as suddenly. No one could trace the cause of their pains, least of all those for whose sake the energy had been expended. But their sublime self-sacrifice led to the glory of ascension.

One Hellenic sage, observing his very good health, was quite saddened, and remarked, "I would rather give my energy where it could be of use!" There are many examples to show that great service to humanity is not necessarily associated with good health. It is also well-known that some ill people live longer than supposedly healthy ones. Remember that giving one's energy is the highest generosity and mercy.

The Thinker said, "It is wonderful that everyone has within himself invisible resources."

380. Urusvati knows that those who do not ponder upon the goal of existence during their earthly lives prepare a dark future for themselves after death. Urusvati saw a woman who, though good and kind from an earthly point of view, never thought about the meaning of life. When she crossed into the Subtle World she was utterly helpless, and did not even know how to accept the help of her Guide. Urusvati performed a good deed by visiting this disembodied soul and showing her that help and guidance were very near.

Most people cannot understand that even having such a fine quality as kindness while in an earthly state is not sufficient, for it is also necessary to think about the future path while still on Earth. Even if such thinking is elementary, it nevertheless will develop the imagination. Without some idea about the next world the disembodied soul is confused by its new and incomprehensible surroundings. If, while still on Earth, man cultivates thoughts about the joyous experiences that await him in the next world, he develops his imagination and prepares himself for entry into the corresponding spheres.

It is within human capability to greatly facilitate entry into the Subtle World. Indeed, great is the joy when one can enter these new conditions as if into a welcoming home, to find there all those for whom one has yearned, and to sigh with relief that one more earthly journey has been fulfilled. But such a state of mind can only be the result of conscious imagination. Therefore, please understand why We direct you to everything that develops the imagination. We know how gradually this precious quality must be attained. We would not be able to help mankind without making use of imagination, which goes hand in hand with foresight!

The Thinker taught the development of the imagination, without which the third eye could not be opened.

381. Urusvati knows that tolerance is a fundamental necessity for evolution. Every sign of tolerance must be valued. We, Ourselves, could not help people without the highest degree of tolerance. All one's inner fire of enthusiasm must be used for the Common Good, for dull indifference is most deadly. Truly, fierce opposition is often more justified than unfeeling indifference.

We often smile at our heated opponents, for in each of them there is a particle of affirmation. But on the ice of indifference no flowers can grow. This explains why, in the Testament, the Lord chose the cold and the hot ones, and spat the lukewarm ones out of His mouth. Some will not agree with this. The fact is however that He does help those whom He rejects. How is it possible to convince the lukewarm one that he is potentially full of fire, and that his apparent tepidness can be ignited into a great flame? Opposition turns into affirmation; this is the pattern of existence. But those who in the Testament are called lukewarm do not easily ignite.

Unfortunately, there are too many of these lukewarm ones, producers of cosmic waste who obstruct evolutionary development by their inertia. They fail to benefit at all from their stay in the Subtle World, and We are unable to help them, for they produce no fiery emanations that could serve as a conductor for Our influence. So many benevolent arrows are blunted by the thick skin of indifference. It is easier to strike a spark in a negator than to break through a shield of indifference. Fire can be ignited only where there is inner friction.

One should learn to distinguish each small particle of energy and pay careful attention to it. People furiously shout, "He is not one of us, crucify him!" Fools! He is indeed not one of you, he is of fire! Only the ignorant extinguish the light and then remain in darkness, complaining about their cruel fate.

The Thinker taught that even the smallest particle of energy should be guarded. "Be thrifty builders!"

382. Urusvati saw the many different apparatuses in Our laboratory, each of which operates with the assistance of psychic energy. The time will come when people will recognize that the functioning of machines is dependent upon the psychic energy of the person operating them. This should not be regarded as magic or something extraordinary. People should know that they transmit some of their psychic energy to every object they touch. Uncontrolled energy has very little effect, but when it is realized and organized it will manifest itself more strongly.

At times people notice a particularly intense manifestation of psychic energy. They may call such a state inspiration, or attribute it to particularly high spirits, or sufficient rest, or renewed strength. However, they simply sense the intensity of their own energy. They could achieve better results if they would realize that the source of such energy always abides within themselves. No special invocations are needed; one need only remember the treasure that lies dormant within everyone.

Another factor should be kept in mind, that psychic energy is developed especially during conscious communion with Hierarchy. This communication should be practiced throughout one's entire life, and will then become firmly established. The Image of the Teacher will become ever-present, and the flow of the new, vital currents will be manifested in all endeavors. This will become the foundation of the feeling that people call optimism. Such straight-knowledge helps even machines to do their best work! All Our apparatuses are designed to respond to psychic energy. Not everyone is able to make use of Our methods, but every thinking person can progress on the same path. The difference between Us and others is that, due to lengthy experience, We know how to focus Our psychic energy.

The Thinker said, "I know that my power is multiplied when I appeal to Heaven. May Heaven provide me with a particle of its power."

383. Urusvati knows that a true aspirant is ever ready to defend Truth. It is wrong to think that Truth needs no defense. That might be so in a cosmic sense, but from an earthly point of view Truth must be affirmed so that it not be distorted.

Despite everything, sparks of Truth penetrate the human consciousness. Today the average person would not sneer at some ideas that were rejected half a century ago, but this acceptance has come at such sacrifice, and with so little progress! The sad fact is that the losses sometimes exceed the achievements. How then should the aspirant defend Truth? If he is slandered, thrown into prison, or killed, who will hear his last words? Therefore, a special wisdom must be applied in proclaiming and defending the Truth. Complete co-measurement must be applied.

We most definitely do not want to lose useful people. We frequently advise caution and the avoidance of unnecessary dangers. The experienced and devoted aspirant understands how best to apply the accumulated energy. Imagine a scientist who, while absorbed in an especially important experiment, abruptly leaves his work to rush and give aid to victims of an accident in the street. Some people will criticize the abandonment of important work that could have been of benefit to humanity, but a refined consciousness can perceive the boundaries of heroic action. We know how imperceptible this boundary can be. So many factors are placed on the scales that balance is achieved with difficulty.

The Thinker said, "The burden is so great that We do not know what things must be jettisoned during the journey."

384. Urusvati knows how potentially harmful it is to apply earthly measures to supermundane circumstances. I am referring to those people who read about the Foundations of Life, yet approach the Truth in an earthly way. They have a sense of proportion when dealing with minor events, but when confronted by major tests they cannot find a proper approach, and rely on their limited, earthly judgment. However, it is precisely in extraordinary circumstances that one should apply a supermundane level of understanding.

People do not know how to invoke the Forces of Light when threatened with danger. On the contrary, they cast their doubts, regrets, and even accusations into space, even though they are fully aware that such faintheartedness does not help them. They know that accusations are not invocations, and that only the latter can increase their strength.

The ancient people acted far more sensibly. In times of danger they turned instantly to Heaven, and in silence and without thoughts opened their hearts in receptivity to the Higher Forces. They understood that earthly words are useless in such circumstances and could not express their need, and they allowed the Higher Force to flow unimpeded into their consciousness. They were certain that in time of need benevolent help would come. They knew that space is fully inhabited, and that the Good Ones are always ready to provide help.

One can observe how the approach of various subtle entities, even though not altogether negative, can shock the whole organism. If the influence of human beings upon one another is strong, the influence of the invisible worlds is far more intense, especially when the subtle entities direct their attention to a particular individual as a chosen victim. The disharmony caused by invisible entities is not uncommon and can cause physical indisposition. Urusvati knows what We speak about.

The Thinker could sense the presence of invisible beings. He addressed these unexpected guests calmly, asking them not to burden Him, but to help according to their abilities.

385. Urusvati knows how much We insist upon unification. People often think that this rule has only ethical significance, and do not understand that unification increases energy and provides strength. You can imagine how much easier it is for Us to send help to those who are harmoniously unified. Indeed, much energy is saved, for the united energy is focused upon one idea, and such concentration results in an intensification of power.

People should learn to understand that each ethical instruction is also scientific advice. I stress this fact because I see that so many who study the Teaching do not apply it in their daily life.

In addition to the fact that unification evokes an intensification of Our help, it acts as a "pump," pouring forth spatial energy. People do not realize that when they are united their energy is increased many times. Only through scientific methods may skeptics be convinced. Let your scientists show you how united forces are multiplied, and when this progression is calculated, humans will realize once again what has been entrusted to them in their earthly life. Why should you not learn that cooperation is the best magic? Even those who do not know Us should ask themselves if there is not somewhere a precious Source of energy that could be utilized in life. Every such acceptance serves as an approach to Us.

The Thinker understood that human energy becomes inexhaustible when one trains one's thought upon the Highest Source.

386. Urusvati knows about salutary rhythm or the so-called "natural" yoga. In the Middle Way of Buddha's Teaching, in Plato's writings on ethics, and in the schools of the Eye of Horus in Egypt, we can find instruction about the yoga that is linked with earthly life. Especially at the present time one should pay particular attention to the natural development of psychic energy, which should be studied and also applied in life. It is true that psychic energy acts independently, but now I am speaking of its conscious application.

You should assure people that each one of them possesses this treasure and can utilize it in thought, amidst daily life. But for this one must first of all understand the process of thinking, which continues unceasingly whether one is asleep or awake. However, there are two currents of thought, one in the brain, and another that registers in the depths of the consciousness. Usually, people are not aware of the deep consciousness, and do not realize that the most precious knowledge is not received through the brain.

People should learn about the process of ceaseless thinking, which works like a pulse and generates a beneficial rhythm. This description is instructive. It indicates that good thinking is also healthy thinking, and produces a benevolent inner fire.

Urusvati knows that the healing flame can easily be brought into the darkness of the astral world. The subtle body is like a chalice filled with phosphorus. It can be an inexhaustible source of light and beneficial rhythm.

We love to pass through the dark spheres to scatter the sparks of Light. Every man, no matter in what condition, can be a source of Light.

The Thinker said, "Goodness is Light."

387. Urusvati knows how diverse are the sensations experienced during and after flights into the Subtle World. Usually these sensations guide one to the Highest, yet at times they can be unpleasant and even painful.

Confirmed skeptics will insist that all such sensations are illusory, nothing more than disturbing dreams resulting from bad digestion! But those who have experienced the Subtle Realm certainly know of their reality.

Why then do these sensations differ so greatly during contacts with the Subtle World? They should not be attributed to fluctuating moods, but are caused by the chemistry of the various spheres. Physicians should study and compare the statements of those who have experienced these flights and they will see that the sensations in the physical body correspond to the impressions derived from the various strata of the Subtle World. There may be confusing or even contradictory sensations, such as symptoms similar to those caused by poisoning. Evidence thus gathered indicates that the subtle body is not altogether free of physical characteristics.

The chemistry of different strata is varied, and as one approaches inhabited locations, their emanations can be felt more strongly. Even places that are not entirely negative can emit disordered emanations that cause pain to the physical body upon the return of the astral body. Thus, experiments with astral flights produce many different physical reactions. The time will come when such flights will be scientifically supervised, but every path of research is full of thorns.

The Thinker often sensed the separation of His astral body, and at such times He directed it mentally toward those spheres where He could learn something new.

388. Urusvati knows that there is a ceaseless struggle between the various strata of matter. The statement, "Light overcomes darkness," has become a truism. Undoubtedly light does overcome darkness, though the complete dispersion of chaos and darkness is a very slow process. There are many gradations between light and darkness. This should be understood where both physical and all mental processes are concerned.

One may rightly ask why certain cogent ideas are so slowly assimilated by the human consciousness. For instance, it is astonishing that, despite much proof, the concept of reincarnation is such a difficult doctrine for most people. After all, one should understand that the realization and acceptance of this law by all people would signal an end to chaos, and transform the entire earthly life. Compare those who have accepted this doctrine with those who oppose it, and you will understand who is of Light and who is of Darkness!

The alternation of the waves of acceptance and opposition is amazing, but the real battle takes place in the supermundane realm, and Great Forces participate in it. It is difficult to discern the boundary between unconditional acceptance and complete negation. At times opposers are closer to the truth than those who mechanically affirm the letter of the law without understanding its meaning.

It is interesting that some people have experienced the Subtle World, yet will not admit it. This is particularly true of "bookworms" who read all kind of books, but whose consciousness cannot assimilate anything. What a great load of ignorance impedes the cognition of every Law! One can often see the fury of certain people who detest any manifestation of the Invisible even when it can do them no harm. This is simply a reflection of the battle between various strata of matter.

The Thinker knew that the feet of humanity are firmly mired in chaos.

389. Urusvati knows that the law of attraction and repulsion operates in all the worlds. This law is a vital one, especially in the realm of thought, for there the mediating energy is most active. It is instructive to observe how this law operates in the Subtle World, where its manifestation is more evident than in the material world.

People assume that in the Subtle World one can always remain in the sphere that accords with one's spiritual affinity, but this possibility is conditional. In truth, everyone is attracted to a certain sphere, but this does not prevent the sending of thoughts into other spheres. These mental bridges can serve as media for new contacts as long as repulsion is not operating. And if the directed thought is clear and kind even this obstacle can be surmounted.

In the Subtle World negative feelings such as malice, revenge, and general harmfulness will exhaust themselves because they are useless. The spirit ultimately awakens to the fact that no gates are opened by such keys. Likewise on Earth, people who are ardently absorbed in their work have no time to dwell on petty offenses or injustices. Work demands their complete attention. In the higher spheres evil thoughts do not exist, for evil is of chaos, and in harmonious spheres there are no conditions for discord. Thus an attraction is created, and the Magnet is brought into operation.

Even in the physical world clear thoughts will grow and lead to the heights. Such thoughts should not be shattered by petty misfortunes. After all, most grievances are born of mistrust, and when people eventually learn to trust the Higher Forces, they regret the energy spent on complaints. The best thought can be generated anywhere in the world.

The Great Thinker Himself taught people to find refuge where there is no despair.

390. Urusvati knows that most people enter the Subtle World with their consciousnesses burdened by earthly habits. During her flights into the Subtle World Urusvati frequently observed how even some good people build their astral existence according to their earthly patterns. It is amazing that the new conditions do not inspire them in their new task, and among these astral inhabitants there are some instructive examples. For instance, people who were unduly absorbed in their physical ailments continue with similar concerns in the Subtle World. They are accustomed to their many medicines and cannot imagine that this aspect of their earthly life is no longer necessary for their now disembodied state. Making use of atmospheric chemistry, they invent new medicines; unfortunately these astral experiments are forgotten in their new incarnations!

It is astonishing that medical authorities do not explore the chemistry of the atmosphere. They prescribe seaside or mountain air, but do not investigate the unusual chemical characteristics that permeate the lower earthly strata. I do not refer to poisonous fumes, which are evident and can be easily traced, but to the higher chemical compounds, which can be studied by means of astrochemistry and astrology. The power of astrochemical emanations must be verified. We study this realm, and know that the subtle spheres contain unique possibilities. People on Earth can also participate in these studies, and if these observations are begun now, new treatments will emerge. All that is necessary is an open mind, but earthly habits are the primary enemies of all new investigations.

The Thinker advised His disciples to ask themselves now and again, "Have I deprived myself of something?"

391. Urusvati knows that the Teaching of Life is free of contradiction, yet the superficial reader is always ready to see contradictions in it. For example, although We speak of the battles of Armageddon in the Subtle World, We also speak of the peaceful conditions that exist there. There is no contradiction in this, for even on Earth, at the time of the most frightful wars, there are countries that remain neutral and at peace. So it is in the Subtle World. Remember—as on Earth, so in Heaven.

However, the reverse is not true. Earthly events are limited to this small planet, whereas the realms of the Subtle World are incomparably more vast, and all measures are applied in terms of the Infinite. People are not yet able to understand that the Subtle World includes things that are not compatible with earthly concepts.

The spheres can be defined schematically as separate, but when studied in detail they are seen to be interconnected. Although on Earth everything appears distinct and classified, in reality all existence is subtly linked in the most diverse ways. This is even more so in the Subtle World.

I speak a great deal about this vast Subtle World, not only because one should know as much as possible about it, but also because of its closeness to earthly life. There are many who will say that not enough has been revealed yet about the Subtle World, but the same could be said about earthly life, which is filled with wonders far surpassing anything in the imagination. Why not extend these wonders into Infinity? Then we shall grasp the possibilities of the Subtle World.

It is only because of inattentiveness in their earthly life that people fail to imagine Our existence. Even those who affirm that they know Us will have doubts after their first disappointment, and will lose faith in Us and in the Subtle World.

What then will happen if We tell you that the Subtle World is also filled with all kinds of difficulties? Those who have been interested will scatter, forgetting that their running away will not free them from having to enter the Subtle World. But is it not far better to provide oneself with the information that is needed for the future journey?

The passing into the Subtle World is like the fleeting moment of a dream; the one who has been resting in sleep will, upon awakening, find himself in completely new surroundings, and his thoughts may become so confused that, not yet adapted to the Subtle World, he will not think to call for the Guide's help. Does not the same thing happen in earthly life? No one speaks about Guides while in the earthly state, and in the Subtle World this close bond often goes unused.

In the Subtle World even dear ones cannot help if they are rejected, for rejection nullifies any offered help, and forced help can break the hand! But the one who enters the Subtle World already aware of it is greatly blessed. Energy will not have to be spent in adapting, and can express itself in soaring upward. Long ago it was said that the higher spheres should be conquered and that they belong to those whose consciousness can embrace them.

The Thinker instructed the departing ones, "Gather all your strength, in order to direct yourself toward the Highest."

392. Urusvati knows that for the foreseeing of events there must be a harmonious combination of many conditions. Human thought is necessary, astrological signs are important, and the cooperation of Higher Forces is essential. How else can one foresee an event that will occur in future decades? If we are able to put together all the relevant circumstances, it must be clear that the image of the event has already been impressed in the sacred records of the Subtle World.

Many wonder how human thought can be of importance in such foreseeing; examination indeed shows that human thought is also involved in predicted events. However, thought alone cannot inscribe the image in the Subtle World. When the currents meet from both above and below, an unusual and characteristic imprint of the future results. Regarding this, we should mention the interesting fact that the events are depicted in very brief images, as if telegraphed. Only keen eyes and ears can grasp these images of the future.

It is particularly important to understand how human thought can cooperate with the Highest Spheres. One should not forget the old saying that a man's nature is created by his thought. We preserve many tablets on which it can be seen how people have created their own evolution. Urusvati frequently saw how the future history of various nations was recorded. We do not advocate the artificial unification of countries, but look into their future, where We can see the consequences of past mistakes. When people begin to project the idea of peace in their thought, it is possible that an entirely different formula will be recorded on these Subtle Tablets.

For the Thinker, daily thought was associated with the process of fertile contemplation.

393. Urusvati knows the contrasts and complexities of the principles of life, which even in the simplest cases can easily be misinterpreted. For example, We indicate that attention should be paid to all details of life's events, but at the same time warn against self-indulgent absorption with illusion.

Some people will argue that it is impossible to draw a clear line between reality and illusion, and it is true that only through straight-knowledge or the highest intuition can one discriminate between them. By refining one's perception reality may be seen in its true proportions, but a correct point of view must be obtained. For example, people may rejoice at the beginning and sorrow at the end of an undertaking, but looked at from another perspective it might elicit a quite different reaction, and they would rejoice at the end while bearing good will toward a beginning that is fraught with dangers.

Most people forge their convictions and beliefs in ignorance of a future life. Such limitation binds the free will and creates a narrow view of Cosmos. The modern mentality has not changed much and repeats the errors of the ancients. In most cases only the terminology has changed, and the understanding of essential meaning is no deeper. Our work is considerably complicated by the gross conventions invented by the human mind.

Long ago the Thinker was concerned that one's mind and head should not be constricted, even by a crown. He used to say, "A crown is no good if it does not fit."

394. Urusvati knows both grief and joy, and who does not? Yet, the Golden Mean brings them into balance; for this reason the Sage taught the Middle Way. But people fail to recognize where the higher joy is and where the depth of sorrow. Frequently, although the arrow of sorrow has already passed, they will persist in their fear and suffering, and likewise, although joy may already be passing, they try to prolong it and remain under its spell.

We certainly do not advocate lack of feeling, in which suppressing grief also erases joy. We will never advocate indifference, for that would be death. On the contrary, in everything We emphasize life, but warn against phantoms. Thus, We advise full awareness of the painful sting of grief and the fresh breath of the highest joy. On Earth as well as in the Subtle World one must be able to accept joy and overcome sorrow.

It is said about a Warrior that he is unchanged in joy and in sorrow, in victory and in defeat. It is not about indifference that We speak, but about a degree of intensity that, by its velocity of motion, prevents perception of extremes. I often speak about a bad experience and at the same time refer to joy. In the speed of his movement the pilgrim passes quickly over both mountain and abyss. He is so absorbed in his mission that his striving carries him over all obstacles upon the wings of success. Likewise, We are in such tension that Our striving carries Us through, with new measures of time and events.

The Thinker, while absorbed in His earthly labors, prayed, "Let grief not be a stumbling block, nor joy a blinding ray."

395. Urusvati has stated correctly that her ailments increase during world calamities and the illnesses of her near ones. Space groans and the heart aches.

So-called sacred pains are caused only by an excessive outflow of psychic energy. But how can we disapprove of the generosity of one who serves the Common Good with all his will and being? One cannot place a limit on self-sacrifice when rendering help to humanity.

The outflow of psychic energy can be of two kinds, intentional or spontaneous. The first is easily understood, for it is thought that sends out the waves. However, the second kind is not always understood: it is the result of the uniting of the power of directed psychic energy with the main magnetic current. The Teacher urges the disciples to turn to Him, and because of this a connection with a powerful current of energy takes place. The Teacher expends a great deal of energy. You can imagine what effort is needed to exert an influence upon many countries, and to unify so many diverse free wills.

More than once I have told you about wonderful, dynamic people who gave all their strength in selfless service. They suffered much, but their lightning-like discharges of energy were healing for all of space. They could not know where the salutary results would occur, and only later, when in the Subtle World, were they able to witness their victory.

We all know how the heart aches for humanity, and We draw strength only for the sake of the future. It is often difficult to stand firm on the path to the victorious future.

The Thinker emphasized that every path is trodden for the sake of the future.

396. Urusvati correctly observes that space sometimes falls silent and seems to be utterly without sound. One might mistakenly think that his hearing has been lost, but the true reason is that these are the instances when We have sent a special barrier to protect the sensitive ear from the howling and groaning that fills space. Why should the heart be burdened with such unbearable sounds of suffering when the accumulation of energy is needed? We know how difficult it is to bear the groans of space.

It can be claimed that such groans do not exist. The inhabitants of the lower strata of the Subtle World are so attached to the familiar conditions there that they cannot perceive the higher manifestations. Let them remain in their imagined well-being. On Earth, too, some dance amid fratricidal wars, and their insensitivity extends into strata of the Subtle World, making self-perfectment impossible.

We know how necessary it is to protect the sensitive ear from the excessive pressure of the roaring in space. Special caution is needed when the courageous heart is ready for limitless *podvig*. Such striving hearts must be safeguarded.

Space resounds continuously. From the keynote of Nature and the music of the spheres, to the groans and roaring of space, a trained ear can perceive all sounds. We call them trumpet calls and can define the quality of the spatial tensions accordingly. It should be noted that in ancient times people knew how to pay attention to the signs of space. They did not understand the precise meaning of the signs, but they certainly understood that the music of the spheres resounded only when the currents were propitious, and that the groaning signified malevolent currents. Thus one may at times hear the trumpet call without knowing its cause.

We constantly listen to the resounding of space, and experience and patience have taught Us to distinguish the many gradations of sound. We have some apparatuses that enable Us to register even the weakest atmospheric rhythms, but the essential knowledge comes through clairaudience.

The Thinker asked, "Why has Heaven become silent? Is it possible that a thunderous arrow is approaching?"

397. Urusvati knows that in addition to the epidemics that are known, there are many others that are not recognized. For example, there is a type of drowsiness that suddenly afflicts groups of people. Certainly, this is neither lethargy nor sleeping sickness, but is the result of a decreased psychic energy. It is important to note that this condition may simultaneously afflict the most diverse types of people.

Indeed, such an intensified manifestation cannot

be explained by or simply be attributed to the sensations of individuals. Perhaps it could be ascribed to a general intensification of atmospheric pressures, but even this explanation is incomplete. It might also be explained as a need for energy for some supermundane purpose. It is impossible to observe the scale of these epidemics because people are not accustomed to discussing their sensations. They will even be ashamed of their drowsiness and will try to overcome it, not realizing that it may be related to their participation in some important action.

Likewise, little attention is paid to the irritation of the mucous membranes. These epidemics occur frequently, particularly at the time of world calamities. People do not consider these inflammations as anything serious, they have no explanation for them, and often attribute them to a simple cold. We would advise you to pay serious attention to all sensations, but at the same time not to become self-indulgent or succumb to hypochondria! The impact of sensations should be realized in the depth of one's consciousness.

The Thinker used to say, "O, Thou Unknown One, accept my strength if it can be of service to others."

398. Urusvati knows that in addition to verbal intercourse and instruction there are mental communications of equally deep meaning. Such transmissions of thought require at least as much concentration as is needed for verbal exchange with Us.

Much has been said about contemplation and concentration in the transmission of verbal messages. But now We speak about an act of mental transmission that is like a lightning bolt, so intense that it is beyond describing in words, when only the most penetrating straight-knowledge is acting. Such straight-knowledge derives its power from the accumulation of consciousness. No time is needed for such communications. They are at the threshold of ecstasy, and an active love is expressed in them. One can understand that words are inappropriate when the essence of thought is aflame. But one must be trained to master these lightning flashes of thought.

Not the cold reasoning of the intellect, nor forced pretense, but a purified, unutterable thought will deliver the call of devotion. I have already said that one should not beg for personal help. Unuttered communication will transmit it. How beautiful is the proximity manifested in the lightning-thought, when silence is more eloquent than words.

The Thinker said, "O Guru, Thou Invisible One, when I tell Thee my best words, I know that my thoughts of love for Thee have not yet been expressed."

399. Urusvati knows that metals can accelerate the transmission of thought at a distance. This phenomenon was known even in the remote past, and from this knowledge grew an entire science dealing with alloys. Different images could be cast with a proper fusion of metals. Even today such objects can be found, but the characteristics of the alloys cannot be analyzed without damage to the images themselves.

One other condition prevents the correct study of this knowledge left to us from antiquity. Originally the images were placed upon insulated metal plates, but since the plates were never permanently fastened to the images, the secret of combining metals was safeguarded. We have already spoken about this insulating plate upon which the hands were placed.

Later, the original scientific objectives were obscured, the images became the property of the temples, and people began to worship them, having forgotten their original purpose. In ancient times the creation of alloys was studied thoroughly. People desiring to communicate with each other had duplicate images, and they knew that favorable conditions had to be maintained.

I speak about these ancient achievements in order to put to shame many of our contemporaries, who are proud of their numerous discoveries but often cannot maintain the simplest conditions necessary for their experiments. Furthermore, people do not wish to learn patience. They should think about what great patience was needed by the ancients for the investigation of alloys. As the centuries passed some metals were forgotten and later rediscovered. It is instructive to note how many things were forgotten by humanity! Among these was radium, which in ancient times had another name; it was called "heart of the firmament."

The Thinker treasured an image that was sent to Him from India. He said, "People may think that this is made from an ordinary metal, but no! I feel the heart in it. It radiates warmth and is able to heal."

400. Urusvati knows how uninterested and forgetful people are about past eras. Not realizing that today's culture is linked to the past, they demean it and thus limit their knowledge of the present. The recent past is vaguely remembered, and the ancient periods have been completely forgotten. Thus do people restrict the scope of their life awareness.

It is remarkable that, while in the Subtle World, people receive information about the earliest eras, but only a few are able to preserve any memory of this knowledge during subsequent incarnations. If they later find relics from these ancient periods, they generally do not recognize them. But tangible proof, such as physical contact with objects of those eras, is not really necessary. The essential thing is to preserve deeply within one's consciousness the assurance of their existence.

It is a fact that there exists a definite continuity between eras. Thus, the ancient cultures of Egypt and the Mayas were linked with Atlantis, which in turn was linked with Lemuria. The true impressions of this must be brought from the Subtle World and remembered, just as the lives in the far-off worlds should be remembered. While some memories persist in the form of fairy tales, they do not convince people. Such obliviousness to the past and the future limits man's consciousness and makes him a slave to the present.

We are always saddened when We see that even science, which should serve to broaden the consciousness, limits it instead.

The Thinker used to show an ancient stone and say, "Let this witness remind us about the bygone life."

401. Urusvati knows that four things must be experienced for the transformation of earthly life: the perception of the past, the perception of the far-off worlds, the perception of the Subtle World, and the perception of Hierarchy. But can man grasp these four foundations? Every thinking person will agree that these fundamentals are not difficult to understand. They are inherent in the foundation of one's concept of life, and as soon as they are absorbed, the most ordinary life will be transformed into a beautiful reality. But in order to acquire these realizations one must cultivate one's will, for only a free will can make real those concepts that are dead for many.

The ordinary man will say, "What have I to do with a hierarchy that I do not see? Why do I need a subtle world that cannot be applied to my own life? Of what profit or use to me are far-off worlds? Let the past die with all its coffins and bones." He does not understand that the past does not lie only in its bones. He does not understand that the far-off worlds are the equilibrium of Cosmos. He cannot recognize the Subtle World because he does not hear the Voice of Silence. What is Hierarchy to him who imagines himself the King of the Universe?

Do not think that I speak unjustly. Unfortunately, such dull consciousnesses are in the majority. They seek nothing and do not admit to the existence of anything beyond the confines of their home. Their consciousness is inactive and seems dead, but without the effervescence of consciousness the will cannot be aflame. Consciousness does not whisper to them that the transfiguration of life is within their grasp. We feel the burden of this dead weight on the planet.

The Thinker said, "He who rejects thought need not go on living."

402. Urusvati knows that idealism and materialism are illusory concepts. There may be those who will say that the four foundations I have named are idealistic and do not conform to a materialistic outlook. But these learned deniers have not troubled themselves to examine each concept from a truly materialistic point of view.

How can they say that the scientific study of the past, the life of far-off worlds, or of still-undiscovered energies, is not materialistic? And as far as Hierarchy is concerned, each denier has his own "hierarchy" and reveres it even more than We would recommend for the true Hierarchy! If we examine each concept from the materialistic point of view we will come to the conclusion that everything that exists is matter. But what about idealistic convictions? They, too, cannot be outside matter, although they touch upon its highest strata. Thus we see that both materialism and idealism are poorly defined concepts.

Man strives to cognize the Great Reality and for this he possesses the ability to reason. He has come to the correct conclusion that thought is energy, and this shows that valid research will bring tangible results. Man follows an intensively scientific path, and providing that the science is pure and unprejudiced, there are no notions, however lofty, that are not compatible with scientific methods.

Humanity proceeds by the way of scientific theory, but progress is too slow, and ignorance impedes any acceleration. It is time for outworn concepts to fall away, otherwise self-important innovators will prove in the end to be the most obstructive.

The Thinker warned His disciples not to become victims of limited, backward definitions.

403. Urusvati knows that the majority of people, instead of choosing responsible cooperation, prefer to remain in a state of passive learning. They prefer to be listeners and readers, and when the hour comes for them to demonstrate the power of Spirit they disperse.

One must remember the acts of betrayal in history when the traitors displayed an extraordinary ability to disappear. Traitors can always be found among the most learned followers, but this is not surprising, since without knowledge they would have nothing to betray. It is instructive to study the fate of these traitors. Sometimes they ended in dark despair, but more often their lives deteriorated into dreary stagnation.

Do you remember the fate of the betrayers of Upâsikâ? It was seen that they lost their "gifts" and in frustration hastened into the darkness. Some of them tried to reform, but the burden of karma weighed heavily, dimming their wits.

Certain dates are given to humanity as a reminder of those betrayals that affected the karma of entire nations, but even such striking examples hardly touch man's consciousness. Just as a small stone produces a small splash, an unfeeling heart cannot be effective against darkness. But occasionally, on a Day of Remembrance, even such a heart will know how dark is the traitor.

The Thinker pointed out that the Gods do not forgive betrayal.

404. Urusvati knows how highly We value thought about art. Art refines one's taste, but it also helps one to understand thought-images. It is necessary to accustom oneself to every kind of perception. We may read much about various phenomena, but it is not easy to transform what is read into actual perception.

For example, one may have read much about thought-images, but when actually passing into the Subtle World one becomes confused by the profusion of images in space. Only experienced observers who truly understand art and who can make use of the loftiest images in their thinking can interpret this phantasmagoria. Nature is certainly the best source for such imagery, but one must know how to observe it. In this, the works of the great masters will be helpful. Like magnets they attract the eyes and feelings, and through them people can learn how to approach nature.

Space can be filled with beautiful images that will help to prepare the way to harmony. Yet people commit a grave crime by filling space with ugliness. It will take a long time and much suffering for humanity to realize how criminal it is to create ugliness and evil. Understand this in all its aspects. The manifestation of beauty will heal and will lead one safely over every abyss.

The Thinker repeatedly asked, "When shall we at last rise from the dead?"

405. Urusvati knows that in evoking new energies great caution must be exercised. The summoned energies whirl in space, and one cannot know the extent of their dissemination, or whether there may be an oversaturation of space. A forced evocation of such energies may provoke dangerous cataclysms. There are known examples of catastrophes that have been caused by the unbridled greed of humanity. It is impossible to foretell when the overloading of space may occur, but one can see the increasing dangers.

Interplanetary currents can be exceedingly burdensome, but the danger is not in them, for spatial currents are inherently balanced. It is the lightminded use of man's free will that can release the devouring monsters that disturb equilibrium. People may not know that they can disturb the equilibrium of the planet, but it is in their power to call forth devouring energies of such strength that spatial voids will increase.

People are straining the energies, ignoring the fact that every beginning has its end. A cannon's fire can cause rain, but this is just a primitive example. Radio waves thicken the atmosphere, yet the number of radios increases without limit. Factory owners do not care what diseases they cause, and one can observe many resultant cases of irritation of the mucous membranes and malignant tumors. People do not regard their own wilfulness as a likely cause, nor do they realize that new victims will appear who will pay with their lives.

We can say with certainty that all Our warnings will be met with ridicule. There are two kinds of ignorant people: some are ignorant because of their lack of learning, and others precisely because of their learning. The latter are the more dangerous for they allow no contradiction. One cannot talk with them about the Supermundane, but they should know that one drop may overfill the vessel.

The Thinker took care that His disciples should speak to people about past cataclysms.

406. Urusvati knows that *pralaya* is a systematic and unavoidable phenomenon. Night follows even the brightest day, and labor and vigilance are followed by sleep. Collected treasures are hidden in their secret repositories only to reappear, transformed. These changes can be observed not only in great cosmic phenomena, but also in everyday life.

Let us cite the example of cultural change. The appearance of new culture seems to depend upon the destruction of former achievements. But after careful study one can verify that the repeated efforts of human labor have not been in vain, and in time begin to reappear in a transformed way.

We can provide many examples from life, when the apparent destruction of something actually assisted in its regeneration. Take for example the knowledge about Our Tower. Humanity seems to acknowledge it at one moment, and in the next almost forgets about Our very existence. These waves are not accidental, and each wave of evolution has its *pralaya*. Only such changes produce the spiral of knowledge.

The same process occurs with periods of creative activity, but the wise know that every labor must have its period of rest. We do not intend to encourage or provide justification for idlers, but are speaking about enlightened workers. They will recognize in their hearts the ebb tide that heralds the flood of creativity.

The Thinker taught people to understand the ebb and flow of the tide of creativity. He used to say, "The sea of humanity has its succession of energies. Let us thus receive the gifts of the Muses."

407. Urusvati knows the sensation of rapture and awe that is sometimes called ancient, or primal awe. This feeling can be caused by many experiences, ranging from the music of the spheres to a thundering storm, which would strike not fear but awe in the hearts of the ancients, who sensed their powerlessness in the face of the elements.

We can all remember waking at times in the grip of unexplainable terror. This feeling can be caused by world events or by impressions from the lower spheres, but it is often the result of the influence of the elements.

People do not clearly distinguish between the sensation of fear and that of awe. Moments of darkness can provoke a sensation of awe that is very close to a feeling of anguish. This is sometimes called world-anguish, for there is something cosmic at the foundation of such straight-knowledge. Every refined thinker experiences these weighty sensations, for without them existence is not complete.

Some may ask if We also experience such sensations. Indeed We do, they are familiar to Us and We experience them very strongly. There are those who would like to think of Us as free of such feelings, but without them the music of the spheres would not resound. The refining of such feelings will affect one's entire way of life.

Everyone who wishes to come near to Us must be ready to rejoice and also to suffer. Life is full of sunrises and sunsets.

The Thinker constantly pointed out that people do not know where is the end and where the beginning.

408. Urusvati knows why after even the most vivid dream not all its details can be remembered. Even the strongest subtle experiences cannot be accommodated by earthly reality. This is not because the memory cannot retain extraordinary impressions, but because the nature of Earth and that of the Subtle World are completely different.

It is not surprising that man is so limited by his earthly body, for it could not possibly withstand the tension that often predominates in the Subtle World. Because of the fineness of structure of the inhabitants of the Subtle World, they enter easily into the atmosphere of the subtle energies, and the same force that can destroy an earthly body strengthens them. This should be remembered, for one can hardly imagine how different is the nature of these two worlds.

Failed experiments in materialization have also shown that earthly criteria are not applicable in the Subtle World. During such experiments there is always the possibility of disruptive discord among those present. Also, one should consider and test the atmospheric currents, and record what has occurred in that same location prior to an experiment.

The incense used to harmonize the atmosphere is only a palliative and cannot destroy many chemisms. Yet, for every experiment the best conditions must be prepared. Sometimes an experiment is successful even though the conditions are not perfect, but much additional energy must then be expended, with adverse effects on one's health.

The Thinker taught that not one drop of the divine energy should be wasted.

409. Urusvati knows how often people ask for the

impossible. If they could look into the remote past they would understand why certain conditions are not possible for them, but only in the rarest cases are people able to lift the veil of the past.

A broadened consciousness can provide the signs that will enable people to sense what is possible and what is not. By listening to the voice of one's consciousness, one can discern these limits, but it is not easy to find the key to the portals of consciousness. People obscure their consciousness with their passions; instead of a wise warning, they hear the voice of their own selfishness, and cannot see where active help lies and where their own delusions are. It is still more difficult for people to find their way in this labyrinth when they do not understand which of their passions predominates.

Often a fervent desire fails to achieve its goal, whereas a barely pronounced word proves effective. Here again is evidence of the Subtle World. The power of earthly wailing may have its effect, but thought that is in accord with the Subtle World is far more powerful. People think so little about the Subtle World that they may be unaware of this accord. It is hopeless to expect that Our messages will be received completely if the heart is not open. Many times We have advised keeping the gates of the consciousness open, but, unfortunately, bars and bolts prevent the admittance of help.

The Thinker begged His disciples, "Do not close your souls."

410. Urusvati knows that people are rarely able to communicate mentally when appealing to the higher spheres. Through all ages help has been offered in various verbal formulas, but many of these have lost their original meaning in the course of time and are repeated by people with little understanding.

One may ask in what language and in what terms it is best to appeal to the higher spheres. We will answer that this is possible in any language, but it is best to use your native tongue, which most easily expresses the thought. Let your expressions and your way of thinking be your own; why use the memorized words of another when you can freely express your own feelings? When people speak to each other they rarely use the words of others, and in addressing the Highest should speak in their own individual way. People should understand that the highest consciousnesses need not be addressed with conventional formulas or memorized verses when a direct appeal from the heart is more personal. In everything a heartfelt expression should be used without embarrassment, for the simplest words are always the most potent.

We take care to speak simply, and when it becomes impossible to convey the more complicated feelings in words, a silent, mental message will be of help.

The Thinker used to say, "When I cannot express my feeling in words, I just offer thanks, for I am sure that help has been given."

411. Urusvati knows that impatience is an undesirable trait that is frequently confused with other qualities. For instance, it can be compared to aspiration, but is quite different in its essence. Constant aspiration is harmonious and generates beautiful rhythms, while impatience is discordant and acts fitfully, disturbing the rhythm. Impatience demonstrates ignorance of the basic law that the essence of Being is in a state of constant motion. Only patient, alert, ardent observation can reveal the power of energy.

Therefore find the balance between action and

patience; without this equilibrium you will find no rhythm and no true cooperation. An unbalanced person will say, "I can wait no longer!" and in these words reveals his impotence. The lack of power is lack of will, because will is developed through human power. If we examine all these traits, we shall come to the conclusion that they are subject to human power.

One will exclaim, "I am impatient by nature." Let him rather say that his habits have brought him a loss of will. Then let us take the other extreme, those who understand patience as inaction, and in this error engender new sufferings. Truly, the most assiduous patience can be combined with intense activity.

If people cannot discern the constant motion of the Substance of Being, they can still perform good work within the limits of their abilities. The ancients used to say, "Let us work while we wait." Skills are the best discipline for patience and are within reach for all humanity.

Let our labors serve as a reminder about active patience. Patience gives accuracy to our work, and in the high quality of labor we shall understand the meaning of harmony.

The Thinker said, "I would like to have in all labor the resounding of the chords of space. The Great Music is the labor of our Patrons, the Muses."

412. Urusvati knows that the decay of consciousness is worse than any war, pestilence, or earthquake. It steals up unnoticed and commits acts that will horrify future historians. It causes people to lose their self-respect, to become malicious, and to ignore their own necessary contribution to future generations. The decay of consciousness causes writers to produce repugnant images, and nonentities to sit in judgment.

Remember what is written in the *Vishnu Puranas*,

in whose ancient prophecies one can recognize the present time. It may seem that the monstrous time described is exaggerated, but observe what is now taking place and you will agree that the ancient predictions were even an understatement. Yet people, manifesting real confusion, have no interest in ancient warnings.

It is especially horrible that the majority does not want to understand present events. They dance, trade, and think that the present time represents the peak of achievement. Compare what is happening now with the events during other periods of decline, and you will find that they have symptoms in common. People once dreamed of conquest and considered themselves the lawful masters of the world, but how suddenly these Towers of Babel collapsed! Many symbols have been left to humanity, but they have remained decaying relics.

The Thinker foresaw these calamities. He said, "Do not count the days until that time when you are asked to account for all your hypocrisies. You had better wash yourself clean today!"

413. Urusvati knows that spatial currents, beneficial in their essence, can become destructive when they contact the foul atmosphere of Earth. Often the most beneficial chemical compounds can be made into virulent poisons by the addition of a single ingredient. The same takes place when spatial currents are affected by the brown gases of Earth. The planet itself is not to blame for these harmful fumes. It is the king of the planet, man, who produces the poisons.

Some scientists will agree, although with reservations, that human emanations transform the atmosphere. No emanations are as powerful as those of man, who is capable both of healing and poisoning everything around him. It is not so much the infectious sickness of people that poison the atmosphere, but their irritation, anger, and malice. Let us examine how few good emanations appear at the earth's crust at one time compared with the multitude of malicious thoughts.

I am not speaking in abstract terms, but giving medical advice. Humanity suffers from irritations of the mucous membranes and malignant tumors, which occur with such frequency they are taking on the dimensions of epidemics. Many causes have been proposed, but the fact that such epidemics are the result of spatial influences is ignored.

Healing and cleansing measures are needed for Earth. The infected layers must be purified, and only man can do it. If inhabitants of Earth consider the state of their psychic energy and are careful not to worsen it, the process of improvement will begin. The most dangerous epidemics can be stopped by invisible forces, and one can begin such defense in one's daily life.

The Thinker warned, "Do not admit malice, the source of all disease."

414. Urusvati knows that poisonous currents act not only upon those who create them by their acts of malice, but also upon others who are innocent of such acts. Refined organisms may be the first to suffer, and the responsibility is heavy for those who contribute to the poisoning of the currents.

One can study the extent to which the poison created by humanity has spread. Man can be likened to a foolish archer who shoots his arrows aimlessly in a thickly populated city without caring where they strike. It was this way in remote antiquity, and it is so now, to an even greater extent. Science must explain to humanity that such a production of poisons is clearly inadmissible. Compare man's many technical achievements with his neglect of psychic energy and you will be ashamed that this most important domain has been forgotten and even condemned.

Many of today's psychological notions are inapplicable to life, and in the present state of the planet man cannot waste time with such theories. We must agree that everything that does not lead to the transformation of life should be regarded as useless, and in this there must be no difference of opinion. One can move forward or backward, but to go back among forgotten fossils would be unendurable.

There should be no difference of opinion between you and the Guiding Forces. It is possible to think in different languages, or wear different clothes, but there must be no deviation from the Foundations. Think about Our Towers. It would be unwise not to collaborate in the purification of psychic energy.

The Thinker was horrified when He noticed that people overburden themselves with negation. He said, "It is better to load oneself with a great rock than to deny Be-ness."

415. Urusvati knows that every teacher may find himself in a position similar to Ours. As long as he simply instructs in the fundamentals of life he will be listened to and agreed with, but as soon as he appeals to people to actually apply his precepts, the listeners disperse. Such is the fate of much of Our advice.

People agree that the advice is good and meant for the best, but they do not want to apply it to their own lives. If something is acknowledged as good and worthy, why then is it not applied? Attention should be paid to such inconsistency. Many instances can be cited in which the most useful and easily accomplished action was rejected. Afterwards, some regretted having rejected the good advice, but life had already begun its new turn.

The Teacher will say that it is useless to regret the past, and He will be right, for regrets are fetters. But one should examine why the advice was not applied, and among the reasons we will find fear and selfishness. These vipers can turn the most attentive listener into an unbridled opponent! In his negation he will develop a peculiar bravado, and will cheat in order to justify himself and his deviations. The Teacher knows these human traits, and He will not regret the spilled seeds, for the earth may produce an unexpected yield. We have observed over and over how different listening is from actual application. We look into the future, and in this aspiration We find steadfastness and courage.

The Thinker wished that all friends could meditate upon the future.

416. Urusvati knows that waves of energy can be disturbed not only by crude material means, but also by subtle gaseous substances. A complete investigation of the disruption of sound and other waves can, and should, be conducted. Earth is enveloped by a cloud of gas, and during the last quarter century this sinister cover has condensed remarkably.

It is astonishing that many experiments succeed in spite of this obstacle. I have in mind primarily the transmission of thought to a distance. True, the energy of thought is penetrative and not bound by distance, but even it is subject to disturbance by gases. People do not know what harm is inflicted upon evolution by their creation of destructive gases, and no one can estimate how far these gases spread and what compounds they form.

Nor have we even mentioned the deadly products created for deliberate destruction. Everyone knows their effect upon the atmosphere and the soil; such poisons are the disgrace of humanity. Furthermore, besides these, many new gases are produced which contribute to this sinister cover of Earth.

We could make available to chemists the opportunity to invent a neutralizing gas, but using it would be very difficult. Even if it were possible to protect a limited region, the degree of containment and neutralization of the destructive gas could not be determined. Humanity creates new dangers and pays for them with new diseases. Humanity bears the responsibility for its own health on Earth, but it is unforgivable when the subtle spheres are harmed.

The Thinker long ago observed how poisonous the smoke from furnaces and bonfires could be. When He saw lighted torches, He remarked, "Whose destiny is it to inhale such poison?"

417. Urusvati knows that the planetary current at every moment has a unique significance, but this simple truth is not understood. People strenuously resist the fact that all existence is in a state of continuous motion. Even the beauty of such a current in limitless space fails to stimulate the imagination of humanity.

Yet, how can we understand evolution if our consciousness has not accepted the principle of motion? People know about the movement of the planets, but do not apply this law to themselves, and while Earth rotates, humanity clings to the idea of immobility. Thus every word about the beauty of motion is undermined by the inertia of human consciousness. In such a state of discord with Be-ness how can one expect speedy development?

In daily life one can often see a primitive personality in otherwise learned people. Because of this We have suffered from human opposition in all Our experiments. It is particularly striking that so many people who regard themselves as modern are actually hopelessly archaic. I affirm that until the cosmic current is recognized there can be no true progress.

People sometimes attempt to advance by leaps, prompted by fear or prejudice or by their passions, but it is impossible to advance by leaps. A steady, systematic motion is needed in everything, and only through the Golden Mean can one progress.

Likewise, remember that We welcome collaboration based upon free will, for destiny is based precisely on free will. How can We convince people of this truth? A manifest awareness of the Subtle World will be the threshold to progress.

The Thinker said, "Our good fortune is that our progress cannot stop."

418. Urusvati knows how difficult it is to recognize a person who has achieved the breadth of psychic energy required for a true perception of reality. No outward traits will reveal the one who is capable of such broad perception. No learning or knowledge is required, no particular physical characteristics, but simply an understanding heart that is open to the mysteries of consciousness.

But this lotus does not open easily, and errors are possible. People are too easily influenced by superficial impressions. They tend to forget their first, direct impression, and are too readily influenced by the second, which in its superficiality is more conventional. Also, judgments are too often formed under the influence of the words of others, and it thus becomes impossible to return to one's first, immediate impression. People forget how many obstacles they themselves create.

Every co-worker needs to know all the possibilities. Of course, there exist many co-workers, but they are scattered all over the world, speak many languages, and belong to different traditions. These superficial barriers must be overcome if one wants to approach people and be able to recognize their true value.

Thus, in Our labors much energy is devoted to understanding the human heart. It is not sufficient to judge by first impressions only. One must look into the consciousness of others under a variety of conditions.

The Thinker advised His disciples to examine the consciousness of others by day and by night.

419. Urusvati knows the many kinds of forgetting. It is good for a person to be able to forget those harmful old rags, malice and revenge, that stand in the way of progress, but this ability is rare. More often man ignores the useful instructions, because they disturb his habits and make him ill at ease.

How can We remind people of their responsibility and duty? I say, by repetition, and though people cannot stand it, they need such constant reminders. It is difficult to remind without repetition. But We have been trained well in this, and are able to repeat while always adding something new. Sometimes a single hint can add newness to a whole sentence. We must learn to continually propel the spiral of fostering useful principles.

The lazy will ask if it is worth taking such pains over things that will be forgotten anyway, but they do not know about the saturation of space, which can be so filled with thought that people are influenced without spoken words. Personal labor thus becomes spatial, and fatigue is impossible.

Teachers must convince their students of the great joy in working for the saturation of space. It does not matter if the listeners show signs of forgetfulness, for they are also a part of living space, in which every useful thought unfolds as a beautiful flower.

The Thinker said, "Let us be gardeners and help the flowers of eternity grow."

420. Urusvati knows that each dropping of the sheath, when in harmony with karmic law, must be met with joy. One should set off on such a new journey full of hope or at least imbued with curiosity—it is good to love to travel and to develop within oneself a sense of mobility. This feeling will be most useful in the Subtle World, for even there one can sink into an immobility of spirit.

We know that striving must not be abandoned by the dwellers of the Subtle World, for it is needed for the sake of perfectment. How then should one strive toward the brighter strata? One could undertake the far from easy task of approaching the earthly strata for the purpose of doing good. But people on Earth cannot imagine how painful it is to approach their sphere. They think that these approaches are rare, because they do not notice the profusion of evidence that surrounds them. For instance, people readily believe that each sound or color can produce certain sensations. This is true, but many of the sounds and colors of the Subtle World have an even more powerful effect, although the earthly senses cannot normally perceive them. Therefore mankind must train itself to observe these subtle sensations, which training will prove useful in the Subtle World.

We must not forget that each dweller of the Subtle World must help his earthly brothers. Such charity is the best guarantee of mobility of spirit. Let us think of helping our brothers and sisters under all conditions. We must not think that we are separated forever from any strata. Wherever there is calamity, we can render help, and no one should think that there is anything beneath his dignity.

We serve humanity, We love humanity. Many workers remain in the earthly spheres so that they can continue working amidst all calamities.

The Thinker often repeated, "Unseen Friends, how can we express our gratitude to you?"

421. Urusvati knows about the so-called devourers of air, and also the similar devourers of psychic energy and of spatial currents. They all suffer from states of imbalance for which there are many causes—atmospheric, atavistic, or karmic, and people can be excessively influenced by these causes because of their personal habits.

People long ago found ways to restore their equilibrium. One of the ancient methods was *pranayama*, by which, through rhythmic breathing exercises, one could find an equilibrium that protected against an excessive intake of energy. Nothing can be more destructive than consuming an excess of energy.

People are usually not aware when they devour energy in excess. In some ways such people resemble vampires. It is not easy to cure them, for they do not recognize their illness, which can also be contagious. It begins so imperceptibly that neither the victim himself nor those close to him notice that he is becoming a devourer. He may feel some pain, but he can also feel the flow of psychic energy that allows him to influence those around him. One cannot say that this state is always harmful, but the boundary line between the proper power and excessive tension is a fine one.

The Thinker carefully studied the balance of all the

forces of man. He used to say, "Let the Golden Mean indicate the right measure of needed strength."

422. Urusvati knows about the problems involved in the transfusion of blood. The physical properties of the blood are already being taken into account, but these are primitive considerations, and two additional aspects should be mentioned. It will soon be learned that the psychic quality of blood is of particular importance, and the time will come when its karmic condition will also be taken into account. Only by attention to all three aspects will the right results be obtained.

The ethnic characteristics of blood become less evident as the nations are mixed. But a reading of the aura will reveal other, psychic differences. Karmic harmony between the donor and the recipient is necessary, therefore the transfusion of blood of close relatives may not be the best. People will need to discern the karmic connections, and in this task astrology and clairvoyance will be useful aids.

It can be said that these methods take too long when an immediate transfusion is needed. But, aside from emergency cases, there are those in which a day or two makes no decisive difference. Even in the case of an operation that cannot be delayed there is time for analysis, and it is most important to be cautious when determining the quality of blood.

Mixing supplies of whole blood is proof of ignorance. From both the physical and the psychic point of view one should consider what incompatible elements have been indiscriminately combined to produce a false cure instead of a real one. People fail to understand what they are preparing for future generations. On the one hand they seem to care about the purity of future generations, but on the other thoughtlessly transfuse mixed blood.

We are sorry to see how indiscriminately people handle the most powerful substances. Psychologists must broaden their knowledge, for it is they who can give the needed advice to humanity. They must teach people to think more subtly, so that they are able to discern the limits that must not be crossed.

The Thinker often said, "Blood is the precious bond between lives."

423. Urusvati knows the many future medical developments that are foreseen. Psychic energy will be understood, and patients will be examined to determine the quality of their psychic energy. Treatments will be enhanced by the application of the appropriate energy. It will be possible to surround a patient with a special kind of pure air that will augment his energy, and even the energy transmitted by a loving family member may be utilized.

It will be possible to study the sources of many ailments that are latent in some people. Even now, special attention is paid to such carriers of disease, but their number is far greater than may be apparent. Carriers of specific latent diseases could be studied for research that would be conducted without harm. Many useful new measures will be applied when people pay sufficient attention to the energies within themselves.

We can recall examples from ancient times that indicate an understanding of this inner energy. For example, it was customary when giving a gift to place one's hand upon the gift and even to hold it close for a while. Thus the magnetism of the donor was transferred to the object. Sometimes the gift was wrapped in hair or dipped into magnetized water. If even in ancient times people had an idea of Primary Energy, surely by today we should be able to apply it scientifically!

The Thinker advised that to convince a listener one should place one's hand upon his shoulder.

424. Urusvati knows that self-control is needed for all experiments with psychic energy. It is important to maintain composure, for both foolish lightmindedness and untimely agitation will both lead to inaccurate results.

Ask one who is sitting upon water or walking on coals and he will say that no agitating thought troubles him. All such phenomena require balance. The ability to control one's feelings is the result of long training. It can be achieved in the midst of everyday life, when one experiences many occasions for the disturbance of equilibrium.

The slightest doubt will also decrease one's nervous stamina. Those who doubt cannot sit upon water or walk through fire. It is instructive to observe how the smallest doubt can destroy. This may be so fleeting that one does not notice it, yet it succeeds in disturbing the circulation of the blood. One cannot hope to arrest one's pulse when the attention is divided, but it is not easy to free oneself from divided thought. Frequently thoughts carry along their "mirror images" which weaken the action of the basic thought. These unwelcome companions are the result of insufficient mental clarity.

We frequently perform exercises for clarity of thought, for thinking requires practice. Even the loftiest thinker will not deny that he too must exercise this capacity, just as a musician must practice constantly for clarity of sound. Let fools insist that they need no such exercises. Composure, too, is acquired through the exercise of thought.

The Thinker taught, "Exercise your thought, or it will not flow freely."

425. Urusvati knows the importance of education. It is the nourishment of everything lofty and refined. People can understand that a careful upbringing provides many opportunities for a proper education, but education alone will not complete one's upbringing. Every child comes into earthly life with an already formed character. It is possible to ennoble and elevate this essential character, but its basic nature cannot be changed. Educators must recognize this truth. They first must discern the unchangeable essence of a child, and educate accordingly.

We would not be distorting the truth if We said that the human essence is formed in the Subtle World. All family and earthly influences are but external and supplementary, since the seed of one's nature has already been acquired during the subtle sojourn. Fortunately, a mother can sense this essence, sometimes even before birth, and begin to work zealously and sensitively to prepare the child for its earthly life.

But how seldom we meet with such a consciously careful upbringing! Even the best teachers sometimes find themselves in such difficult conditions that they have no possibility of paying attention to the individual qualities of their pupils. In some families the question of upbringing is not considered, and the children are left to themselves with no caressing hand and no parental voice to tell them about the marvelous world.

We insist that teachers be provided with better conditions of life, so that they may devote themselves fully to the most refined methods of upbringing. But such circumstances do not yet exist, although even now the complexity of life and of scientific discoveries demands careful thinking in setting children on their path.

Our Sisters labor greatly by helping in the education

of children. The little ones can tell many tales about being visited by beautiful women and even playmates. There are many such phenomena, but adults do not like to listen to children's stories. These visits are necessary, and sometimes, by one such contact, a child can be reminded of the task that was accepted in the Subtle World. Many children's tears are dried by these luminous visits. Great is the labor of these Sisters, the Carriers of Light. Supermundane work requires self-sacrifice, for it is performed under the most varied and often extremely unpleasant conditions. To raise children properly one must learn to impart joy, and thus transform daily routine into a festival.

The Thinker appealed to mothers to give their children the best images of the marvelous world.

426. Urusvati knows that most people cannot perceive the beauty of the Subtle World. Even in the earthly world people have difficulty grasping the manifestation of beauty, and then only sense it in a crude way. Amidst the subtler harmonies they will feel themselves to be as if in a fog. How many are able to rejoice at the wondrous beauties of light, and will not the music of the spheres seem monotonous to the ear torn by earthly cacophonies? People will better appreciate the harmony of the higher spheres if, to a certain degree at least, they can accept the best earthly harmonies.

Since ancient times people have believed that the Subtle World is gloomy, misty, and cold. But such a notion can be applied only to the lower strata—or perhaps those who have crossed over were both blind and deaf! This is why We insist so much upon the refining of human nature. Only after having conquered chaos while in the earthly sheath can one be sensitive to the beauty of the Subtle World.

People may listen to the most exalted words yet not apply them in life. When We speak about upbringing, education in the perception of beauty is the most important aspect. Man must belong to Beauty! He can perceive it in every sunbeam. He can accept it in the harmony of sounds. Poverty is no obstacle, for Cosmos is open equally to the poor and the rich. Let earthly teachers learn to train people in the perception of Beauty.

The Thinker said, "He who does not know the ways of Beauty will not dare to turn to the Divine Heights."

427. Urusvati knows about the filling of space with thought-waves. You can imagine how strained is the space around Us, with waves of the most varied intensity and content intercepting one another. But often these waves are alike in intensity and can interpermeate. It is impossible to tell which hours are the more silent, for the waves invade from both hemispheres.

In Our normal work We must set aside time for the reception of communications from a distance. But this is not easy, since an organism that is tensed and refined cannot help resounding to calls from everywhere. Remember that, in addition to any direct appeals to Us, space thunders with world events. And now this cacophony has reached such a degree that it can endanger the human organism. Thought-waves, like arrows, pierce the mucous membranes; the throat, the ears, the eyes, and all other mucous tissues can be affected. There are times when thought-waves are even strengthened by the mutual opposition. One cannot always see the explosions of black projectiles. Unearthly Forces are active in them, but earthly thoughts treble their effect.

We must postpone many experiments when the world is in such a state of tension. We must quiet the moans, alleviate the pain, and provide counsel. Only the divisibility of spirit enables Us to respond simultaneously to so many varied and urgent events. People do not realize the degree of saturation of the atmosphere. They think that We should be able to do everything, yet they themselves continue in their opposition. These aspects of Our life are little understood.

People talk about ceremonial rays. It would be better if they thought about rays of urgent assistance. In the midst of conflagration, a special collaboration is needed. We have already spoken of the time that is worse than war, and now such a time can be seen. Observers may think that its limits have been reached, but there is limitlessness in everything.

The Thinker paused at a precipice and observed, "It seems that the abyss is bottomless."

428. Urusvati knows that the writer who collects historical information about Our Brotherhood is performing a crucial task. Let him not hurry to complete it, for much data comes unexpectedly.

Let him also gather those poetic fictions about Our Towers, of which there is an abundance. This legendary material must be recorded, and collected in separate chapters. People will be interested to learn how these notions were interpreted by different cultures. The songs of different nations will also remind us about the Unknown Place toward which pilgrims of every kind are striving.

Every principle that has nourished the many centuries must be scientifically investigated. In addition to the printed sources oral traditions must be collected. The investigation of how these notions have been interpreted in the minds of different peoples will prove particularly instructive.

Often people preferred to see the Great Teachers

in the attire of their own country, which lent a special character to the Image.

And so We ask scholars to describe the Brotherhood, each one in his own way. There will be some very negative descriptions, but remember that in some negation there is contained a degree of affirmation. You have already seen how Truth, when persecuted, flourishes beautifully and cannot be destroyed by empty, abusive words. Every Truth is affirmed by people in their great achievements. Thus We call upon the researchers.

The Thinker also called for the investigation of legends.

429. Urusvati knows that human radiations can be seen by the naked eye. We can cite many cases in which people emitted radiation when in a transport of exaltation. True, the onlookers paid no attention to this manifestation or tried to explain it as a reflected outside source of light.

Often the hand that is writing about a lofty subject radiates a light that can be seen against a white sheet of paper. The radiation then accumulates in the manuscript and imparts to it a special significance. These luminous emanations of light remain for many centuries.

People can sometimes notice an unusual light in the eyes of one who is in a state of so-called inspiration. The eyes shine not from any outside source but from an inner fire. When people notice such natural manifestations, it is not a poetic invention! One must be trained for this perceptive ability, for then the power of observation will develop and many phenomena will be more frequently seen.

The teacher should continue to remind the pupil about the vast numbers of natural phenomena that have remained unknown due to ignorance. In Our observations We are particularly saddened by the fact that people often pass by the special, precious proofs of the subtle nature of man without even noticing them.

The Thinker taught that everyone is given the gift of being able to perceive the subtle nature.

430. Urusvati knows that it is possible to see not only the human aura, but also the ectoplasm, which is an essential part of our subtle nature. It is well known that subtle beings make use of the medium's ectoplasm, and weave from it their visible garments, but I wish now to remind you that everyone possesses this immutable phenomenon. Subtle beings circle about all of us and use pieces of it, with the result that the atmosphere around man is filled with shreds of this substance. Many people often notice misty spots that float past in space and assume varied forms. Physicians explain these manifestations as resulting from the imperfection of human vision, but they actually demonstrate the efficiency of our eyesight!

You may also ask how to counter unwelcome visitors—only through the valor of the spirit, not permitting them to contact your essence. Urusvati knows how these unwelcome guests have recoiled; it was not even necessary to drive them away, for they could not penetrate the protective net. Such natural protection is always the best, but for this, training of the spirit is required. Depression is the most gloomy magnet, and irritation also entices these ugly guests.

One might ask if an outflow of ectoplasm affects the health. Indeed it can, depending particularly upon the nature of the thieving, voracious inhabitants of the lower strata who do not care about the harm they commit. But thoughtful beings can also approach, and they hasten to replenish the stolen ectoplasm.

Remember that ectoplasm is exuded not only at special seances, but constantly, and only a strong and courageous consciousness prevents an excessive outflow. But what a dense atmosphere is formed by these shreds, and people have to breathe this refuse! Yet, there are also wonderful secretions, known as the food of the gods. We will speak about these later.

The Thinker taught that the surrounding space is filled with subtle substance.

431. Urusvati knows that there can be a beneficial exchange of one's earthly ectoplasm for the higher energies. The Beings of the Higher Spheres can use these particles of ectoplasm, and in return They send active inspiration and strengthen the vital substance. In this way We can make sure that during communion of a natural, high degree, when saturation with a high substance occurs, no harm is done. However, for such communion one must be able to strive toward the Highest. All unhealthy contrivances will only lead to a loss of strength and evoke the ugliest companions.

Man himself is fully aware when he does something unworthy. He must learn from the smallest daily examples and develop within himself a persistent striving toward the Highest.

Likewise, anyone who knows about the Great Service will remember that any unworthy action will cause pain to someone. Old governesses used to say to children who had done something wrong, "Your angel will weep," and this warning reached to the very depths of the children's hearts. Truly, each unkind action causes someone to suffer. What Higher Communion can there be when natural laws are violated? People may think that everything is admissible, even robbery and murder! But who are They who will approach the place of crime?

The Thinker called upon people to try to find invisible Helpers.

432. Urusvati knows that the help of the Higher Beings is usually accomplished by spiritual means, but the help can also be material. Tradition often relates the appearance of departed dear ones who came to give useful advice, but stated that they were allowed to help only once. Similar indications can be found among different peoples throughout the ages, and such testimony is quite true.

Only in extraordinary cases are We permitted to intrude upon karma and act by earthly means. Let friends remember that even in the higher spheres there exist limitations governed by the Law of Karma. The inhabitants of Earth cannot imagine how difficult it is to approach them with material help. Usually spiritual help precedes, but it is thought to be a mere coincidence and is rarely accepted.

We are greatly saddened when Our advice has been rejected or its application delayed. However, even Our material help is not always accepted. The usual excuse is that Our methods are too unfamiliar. But people cannot see that the conditions of Our help may be quite beyond their earthly understanding and judgment, and their unwillingness to accept it is due to a lack of imagination. They cling fast to the only way they see out of a difficulty, and unfamiliar suggestions are unacceptable to them. That is why it is so helpful to listen to the traditions of different peoples. Only by comparing the most varied opinions can one imagine the diversity of existing conditions. One should learn to listen to the slightest appeals. The heart will tell when they are true.

It is a great joy for Us when We see the power of observation that has been developed naturally. The

Science of Life demands first of all an understanding of the fundamental laws.

The Thinker used to say, "I cannot express in words how far we proceed in accordance with the Great Laws, but the heart knows the inexpressible essence."

433. Urusvati knows that even the Great Ones have manifested different qualities in each incarnation. Observing a whole series of incarnations, one can see clearly the necklace of accumulations. In this regard it is particularly instructive to note the great variations, succeeding one after the other. It should not be thought that qualities are accumulated by any earthly way or that each incarnation is a continuation of the preceding one—the law of evolution is far more vast in its outlines. From the supermundane heights it is easier to see just how the spirit must perfect itself. There is no contradiction in the fact that the spirit develops in accordance with supermundane processes.

It is not only in the sequence of incarnations that various accumulations occur. One can observe changes of desires and aspirations even within one human life. This may also happen by involution, when one falls into savagery and dullness, but let us not speak now about such gloomy manifestations. On the contrary, let us stress how much good one can accumulate during one earthly life—one can learn without limit! The impulse of a growing consciousness will disclose how varied are the ways of seeking.

And in this quest We help. We direct people's attention to new books. We inspire useful turning-points in discussion. We send thoughts about new discoveries. We send warnings about harmful errors. It is joyous to render this help unnoticed. We value those fighters who bravely repel the assaults of darkness. People should recall how they were instructed in the Subtle

World, how the Luminous Beings approached them, and how the growth of their consciousness permitted these Instructors to come close. The same thing takes place in the earthly life.

The Thinker sometimes confided to His disciples that He felt two lives within Himself, one of light and the other of darkness, but that the one of light was the guide to the higher worlds. He said, "The life of light is always vigilant—call it, and it will answer."

434. Urusvati is aware of the common misconception that the forces of evil manifest more powerfully upon the earthly plane than the forces of good, and that evil images appear more clearly than the misty forms of the beings of light. However, this is true only from the earthly point of view, and although earthly observations are not without merit, the strength of subtle entities does not lie in their degree of visibility, but in the power of their energy.

It is true that the entities of the lower strata are fed by earthly emanations, and are drawn toward the earthly sphere in an attempt to devour human ectoplasm and continue to commit evil. However, their actions are not in accord with the laws of the Universe. They need not be taught evil, they learned it while in the earthly state and continue to practice it intuitively, because goodness for them is meaningless. There is no need to assume that some special hierophant of evil is necessary for an evil action to occur. On Earth, the most insignificant, gloomy person can commit sufficient evil, and near him are the subtle entities that know all the delights of evil-doing.

But let us turn to the Luminous Powers. We have already described how careful They are in the use of Primary Energy, and how They observe the laws of the Universe. They know that a lawless waste of energy affects the entire universe, and They labor to preserve the equilibrium. Can this Great Labor be compared to the petty attacks of evil? Who could say that a planet can exist without Light? Who will dare to compare the dull glow of evil beings to the radiance of the higher spheres? Let us not forget that people need these reminders.

The Thinker sometimes exclaimed, "Citizens, you use your eyes and ears strangely. You turn only to see evil deeds, and strain to hear only evil."

435. Urusvati knows that, as the increasingly poisonous atmosphere attacks the tissues, inflammation of the mucous membranes has become the scourge of humanity. It is impossible to imagine how multiform are the symptoms of this sickness of our times. People attempt to relate these symptoms to previously-known types of disease; they do not understand the unique characteristics of this epidemic. Often the symptoms seem to be harmless, and physicians cannot determine the cause or the course of the illness. It is therefore important for physicians to study the human organism by all available scientific methods.

No one can say when an inflamed tissue will become further damaged, with all the attendant consequences. On the other hand, the inflammation may abate, and this must be watched with equal care. Nourishment is needed for the organism to regain its vitality, and a simple, non-acidic diet should be recommended.

The symptoms of such illnesses can be quite varied. Some organs will experience pain directly, but since the inflammation of the membranes affects the entire nervous system, pain can also be experienced in other areas of the body. This is why a thorough examination of the whole organism is necessary. Generally speaking, mucous membranes are involved in the most varied functions of the organism, and they are the first to react to the saturation of the surrounding atmosphere. In this way, even if no harmful process is taking place, it is necessary to be very attentive and careful.

Remember that this epidemic was foreseen long ago. When We spoke about Armageddon, We had in mind not only war, but all the devastating consequences of humanity's confusion. But one should not fall into despair, for a depressed state opens the door to all that is poisonous. It is wise to know that Armageddon is accompanied by epidemics. We cannot limit our awareness to known forms of illnesses, but must be ready to face the most complicated and unusual symptoms. Physicians must be able to recognize these new diseases, which are now appearing everywhere.

The Thinker said, "Can anyone be so filled with self-importance that he thinks he has studied all the manifestations of Nature?"

436. Urusvati knows that methods of treatment by vibration are quite different for each individual. Because the variety of vibrations is so great it is not possible to prescribe them without experimentation, and for this three aids may be used. One is the healer's clairvoyance, another, the pendulum of life, and the third, indications given by the patient while under hypnosis. Only by one of these means can one discover the required vibrations. The treatment itself can take place by means of an electric apparatus, but the laying on of hands may also be used.

I use a special apparatus, which Urusvati has seen, that requires certain conditions not available to ordinary physicians. This does not mean that treatment by vibration is not possible for them, although under all conditions a particularly sharp perception and flexibility of mind are required. The physician may decide to use one kind of current, then decide quickly that he must alternate it with another. He must also know whether a cooling current or a hot one should be applied. There should be no mistake in this, or undesirable results may follow.

Keep in mind that during the epidemic of which We speak there may be an accelerated development of symptoms, and one should be able to recognize them. Strong vibrations should not be used by insufficiently experienced people. Each new method should be tested on mild illnesses rather than dangerous ones, and one should verify which of the three aids is necessary, for their application and the reactions to them will vary with the individual.

Urusvati has sensed Our vibrations many times. She knows how varied they are, and that the time for their application is also variable. The vibrations can be pleasant, but may at times be difficult. And when there is full trust, their intensity can be increased.

The Thinker said, "Trust is the most reliable weapon. But where is the limit of trust? Man knows that trust is limitless."

437. Urusvati knows that some of Our predictions in scientific and social fields have already been realized. Our thought reaches the minds of many scientists. Though they may not realize why they have started research in a certain direction, We must not upset them by saying their thought was inspired, since they do not believe in the transmitted continuity of ideas. We must not thrust this concept on those who believe that they are the only source of their ideas! Therefore, should you notice that someone has obviously made use of your ideas, do not object. Let everything useful grow in all fields.

But it is regrettable when scattered ideas provide

only fragments of an intended whole. Yet even in such cases We shall say, "Let every seed grow that is of benefit to humanity. Let all friends become accustomed to the sowing of ideas without rivalry, and without infringing upon one another's rights. One should rejoice at every harvest."

We know well enough that ideas do not belong to Us, and that We are only the transmitters of these gifts from space. It is not possible to identify who has originated each thought; even on earthly paths such investigations are impossible. What then can one say about the Higher Worlds, about the inexhaustible Source of Thought!

We will also learn to rejoice when we recognize that we are links in the chain of collaboration. There will be no dejection where the unbreakable bond with the Highest is recognized. It is mankind that can maintain this bond and thus receive the Shower of Good.

Let friends rejoice with Us when somewhere a branch of knowledge has already blossomed. Even if the gardener is not close in spirit to us, let us seek the best that is in him. Let us not reject anything in which there may be a seed of evolution.

The very same thing was said by the Thinker, "If the greatest negator says only one word of truth, we will listen even to him."

438. Urusvati knows that each of Our Indications helps to open the gate. However, there is no Indication that does not require labor for its fulfillment. There are many stories about Our unheard-of splendor, but little has been said about Our Labor. When one considers the most intensive human labor and extends it to infinity, the quality of all supermundane labor can then be understood.

Humanity should be advised to multiply the intensity of labor. Especially during these days of Armageddon is this advice needed. Everyone can continue his labor, but must intensify it. Only such care about the effort and quality of labor can help to diminish the confusion of humanity. The one who can find within himself the strength to labor, even amidst confusion, creates equilibrium in his environment. This is especially needed when entire nations fall into madness.

One must not allow people to mock peaceful labor during times of war. We labor not for today, and not for Earth, but for the most severe Battle. But do not think that these words have been understood by everyone. We can see how perversely the most precise Indications are interpreted.

When you are asked what should be done, answer, "Work as never before. Let everyone do his best, even if his work is the most simple, everyday task."

You may be asked if it would not be better to concentrate mentally. But this beautiful state can be destroyed by spatial currents and whirlwinds. Besides, ordinary people do not know how to think, and waver like reeds in the wind. But during such winds one must hold fast to something secure. In labor will people's consciousnesses find this support. The teacher must accustom his pupils to work and must praise the best quality of labor. This perfectment will lead to an expansion of thought.

The Thinker liked to point out the women carrying water. He would say, "They do not know whose thirst they will quench."

439. Urusvati knows how often it is necessary to explain even Our clearest Indications. For example, it has been asked whether a pupil has the right to absorb the energy of the Teacher. Some will find in this a contradiction with the Indication concerning discussion with the Teacher. But it is clear that a conversation has nothing to do with absorption of energy. It includes no pleas, but simply broadens the consciousness, and every expansion is an increase of energy. Such discussion does not consume the energy of the Teacher; on the contrary, it helps to strengthen the aura, which is beneficial for the pupil. Yet some cannot understand that a true pupil will not burden the Teacher with requests. The disciple knows well enough that all that is possible will be done. He understands the state of tension in which the Teacher tirelessly sends out His energy.

Some people express communion only by asking for help. Perhaps traditional prayers have accustomed people to demand earthly blessings from Deity. This error is common in all teachings—people stop striving toward illumination and restrict their communion with the Highest to requests for an increase in earthly benefits. Thus, it is necessary to explain that the Teaching of Life cannot contain contradictions. Let those who fail to understand ask, and they will learn that the Teaching knows life in all its aspects. Let them remember that a devoted pupil communes with the Teacher in one unified current of energy.

The Thinker indicated how much people can multiply their strength by immersing themselves in this one current of energy.

440. Urusvati knows how people attempt to excuse themselves, claiming that because of their earthly duties they can find no time for higher communion. But let us compare their most important earthly duties with the sparks of even the least enlightenment. Let us examine them from a distance of several decades, and we will find that while the earthly affairs have faded, the enlightenment has remained clear and even grown more vivid into a beautiful affirmation. Such a comparison between earthly affairs and illumination can reveal the true values.

Let us not delude ourselves into thinking that people will easily understand such values, although everyone preserves in his heart the beauty of higher communion. And how much stronger this grows when one has friends to whom one's highest feelings can be confided! This sharing becomes a kind of amplifier, and with united striving the surrounding atmosphere will be purified. Thus will people understand which deeds are the best. Let them also find the balance between earthly labor and glimmers of illumination.

There is no contradiction between intense labor and the striving for illumination. Everyone who has experienced moments of illumination realizes that they are timeless and are achieved not by reasoning, but by the feeling that blooms in the powerful dignity of labor. The simple truth that labor is prayer is not always clear to people, and a good deed is accomplished when one repeats this truth.

The teacher should have several skills in order to inspire his students beyond intellectual exercises to a higher quality of craftsmanship.

The Thinker insisted that His pupils choose a craft and learn to find perfectment in it.

441. Urusvati knows how necessary it is to correct all misconceptions. We have mentioned *pranayama*, and at the same time have pointed out natural ways of ascent. Is there a contradiction in this? No, because We do not reject *pranayama*, and even point out its usefulness, for in certain cases *pranayama* may be a kind of remedy for the organism.

However, We always advise simple *pranayama*. Breathing is an important process, but, as in everything, a natural *pranayama* is the best and is in accord with contemporary conditions. People should not devote only a certain time of the day to the purification of breath, but should practice it frequently during the day. For instance, it is healing to inhale fresh prana several times before making an important statement. Public speakers often use this method, but they rarely do it consciously, and it is precisely the conscious inhalation of prana that will transform their breathing. Thus, the objector should understand that We approve of *pranayama* of a certain quality, but the ancient painful practices must be revised.

Certain views of the caste system must likewise be reformed. In ancient times its restrictions were wisely applied, but evolution has since taken many turns. It is now wise to reevaluate the conditions of life, and we must not allow prejudiced thinking to be an obstacle.

The Thinker taught that there should be no condition of slavery on Earth, for the nature of mankind is divine.

442. Urusvati knows that every event is a link in a long chain of causes and effects. From the earthly point of view one may perceive an event as important, but in fact all occurrences are subject to the same law, and who can say where the birth of great events takes place?

A broadened consciousness enables one to look back and identify the sources of events. It is important to acquire this ability so as to understand the progression of events, not by reason, but by straight-knowledge. One should not ponder at length over the origin of every daily occurrence, but the path of life must be understood. Only in this understanding of causes will a natural foresight develop.

We must learn to anticipate events that are links

of an already-forged chain. I am not speaking of clairvoyance, which is as yet attainable for only a few, but of a natural foresight based upon an understanding of causes, both recent and remote. However, it must not be thought that this ability is easily attained. The broadened consciousness shines brightly, and its light allows one to look back as well as forward. The path already trodden is familiar because of its many signs, whereas the future way shows only unfamiliar outlines. How then can the wayfarer distinguish them?

We have often spoken about straight-knowledge; let communion with Us help this natural development. In this growth it should be understood that some common, everyday occurrences are far more significant than so-called world events.

The Thinker pointed out that everyone at some time is a propeller of remarkable events, but such moments are rarely recognized.

443. Urusvati knows not only cosmic joy, but also cosmic sorrow and cosmic anxiety. Cosmos is alive, and the manifestations of its life are reflected in earthly feelings. One may be troubled by earthly turmoil or have personal sorrows, but cosmic feelings are inevitably added to these. They may have nothing to do with personal life, they may not foretell earthquakes or other calamities on the planet, but they affect the sensitive heart.

As a rule, people do not understand that their Primary Energy is limitless. Supermundane experiences cannot be expressed in earthly words, yet, because they possess all the qualities of the human microcosm, one may say about Cosmos that it rejoices and grieves. It is correct to think of cosmic thought as sentient, and the sensitive human heart will vibrate in consonance with the great ebb and flow of cosmic energy.

Undoubtedly this energy is One, but its manifestations vary greatly, and the human mind attempts to assign a specific name to each of its variations. One can imagine how many false perceptions arise from such arbitrary classifications of the One Energy. It is true that particular qualities of this energy seem to manifest by chance, but this perception is relative, for in Cosmos nothing happens by chance.

One can sometimes feel the breath of Cosmos. From ancient times people have sought the rhythm of breathing, and in this search they try to approach the Great Breath.

The teacher must explain that there can be experiences of three kinds—personal, planetary, and cosmic.

The Thinker saw unity and trinity in everything.

444. Urusvati knows that the stronger the perception of the all-pervading Primal Energy, the more powerful it becomes. For this reason it has been called the living, or divine, energy. People utilize this Primal Energy best when they accept it as immutable law, feel its power, and love it.

A sensitive physician will prescribe a patient's favorite foods; the same is done when a preferred substance is indicated for the success of an experiment. Even the simplest man has an inner sense of what is especially close to him, and remarkable experiments could be performed comparing the different substances that are especially suitable for each organism. It can be shown that man himself senses what is best for him. But everything superficial must be eliminated, or drunkards will insist that only alcohol is good for them!

In order to discern a person's inclinations it is sometimes necessary to use hypnosis, under which he will name not only the foods that are useful, but also the minerals, metals, and plants that are most needed for him. Thus a striking, unique individuality will be revealed. Quite different things may be named, which at first glance seem to be mutually exclusive, yet highly refined chemical experiments may reveal that combining them will prove to be useful.

In all things the fundamentals of individuality must be recognized, especially at present. People try to equalize and generalize everything, but nature reveals individuality in every phenomenon. When one understands the generosity of this principle, the evolutionary process in nature, in which the value of individuality can be seen in everything, comes easily to mind.

Even those who rebel against the usual human categories must accept the law of individuality. There is no phenomenon on Earth in which a vivid individuality is not revealed. For example, We have spoken before about ectoplasm, which is inherent in everyone, but every manifestation of ectoplasm is individual. The same principles may be said to apply in the liberating of the subtle body. The usual forcible methods only create obstacles, for such prescriptions do not consider the individuality. Thus do We value each person's unique approach to things.

The Thinker used to say, "Every man has his own inimitable way."

445. Urusvati knows about the limitlessness of all mental processes, of which the free will is one. By means of the free will people can oppose even cosmic forces. Be not surprised if I tell you that even cosmic laws can be shaken by the efforts of free will, which is why there are so many karmic misfortunes. Instead of following the cosmic way, people provoke great upheavals, and by the insistency of their free will affect the harmony of Cosmos. It not only affects Cosmos, but reverberates increasingly, gaining strength throughout the spheres.

The sages of antiquity tried to appeal to the conscience of people by relating tales about epic heroes who could converse with the far-off worlds, but the legends remained mere fairy-tales. Even in this century, the Age of Energy, people pay no attention to the energy of thought. One can rejoice that transference of thought is being studied in some universities, but unfortunately this research has been limited to a few mechanical methods that will never enlighten humanity regarding the importance of thought as the subtlest energy.

The realization of the energy of thought must help to discipline the free will. It must be understood that dire planetary events are caused by the impetuosity of unbridled free will. Earth is now experiencing Armageddon, and in this calamity the free will is of great importance. Supermundane forces could not precipitate such a calamity without the long-term participation of humanity.

I beg you to pay attention to this epidemic of psychic madness. We cannot attribute what is taking place to any particular group of individuals, and must recognize that the people of all nations contribute to the world's upheavals. One should not think that events are born and die of themselves. Perhaps the seeds that were sown two thousand years ago are now sprouting. So carefully does space guard the phenomenon of thought.

The Thinker pointed out that people can recognize their present condition of being when looking back into their ancient repositories.

446. Urusvati knows that the free will also acts in the Subtle World. In the Higher Spheres it is harmonized with the highest psychic energy, resulting in true collaboration, but in the middle and lower spheres struggle is often sensed. Some entities there do not wish to recognize the goalfitness of the Law of Existence. It is especially deplorable to observe how they attempt to avoid incarnation. These entities know that because of their karmic load they cannot advance any further in the Subtle World, yet prefer even their state of confusion to the necessity of undertaking a new earthly path. We call their condition a state of confusion, but it could also be called a state of torment. No one mistreats them, but they feel the impossibility of further progress in the lower strata. Such resistance by the free will indicates that, because their consciousness did not broaden during their earthly life, there was no inclination toward an understanding of Cosmos, and there certainly was no love for Hierarchy. This condition must be thoroughly understood.

Many people talk a great deal about love and devotion, but do not manifest them in life. They often speak about the Teacher, yet make no effort to forge a strong bond. We do not mean that people should depend completely upon the Teacher. On the contrary, We advise independent activity, but within the heart there must gleam the lamp of love. Only then will the responding flame be kindled. Explain it as you will, even as an electric current, but the current of true love is a strong bond, and true confidence grows only from love.

The Thinker believed firmly that love is a divine gift.

447. Urusvati knows that calmness is required for higher communion. The stirring of water may be necessary for some experiments, but should you wish to study the depths of a well, you must have a calm surface and clear water.

People are often confused as to whether calmness is possible when the world is in such commotion. But We have in mind a calmness of consciousness which, if attained, becomes inviolable. Then, although one may express indignation through the outer centers, or in words, the consciousness will remain serene. Such a state is not easily attained, and will not come from mechanical methods. One can extinguish outer flames by means of rhythm, but the steadfast consciousness is born of the link with the Highest.

Every spark of consciousness must be safeguarded, for violent whirlwinds rage around it. Tempters will come that cannot even be imagined by the human mind. They cannot tolerate the serene consciousness, for every broadened consciousness is for them an obstacle on their gloomy way. But we should not regret that the broadened consciousness is a target for dark beings; we should rather rejoice that these beings of gloom will stumble against the clear consciousness.

One who has experienced the serenity of a broadened consciousness can imagine cosmic storms, but knows that they cannot upset the equilibrium of the Universe. These words should be a reminder of Our calmness, which is based upon long experience, and in which collaboration plays an important part. It reinforces every advance.

Do you hear Me? I am speaking of collaboration! Every transgression against it serves darkness. Hear Me! All cooperation with darkness serves destruction. Remember Our Towers, where the Hearth of Collaboration shines.

The Thinker said, "Each of you is surrounded by universal collaboration."

448. Urusvati knows that the Tower of Chun is the center of the three worlds. This unity is possible because some of the Masters, although still in their physical bodies, can manifest in their subtle bodies, whereas others, in their subtle bodies, have the power to approach the physical world. One should be aware of the importance of maintaining harmonious vibrations in order to make this communication possible between the Subtle World and the physical world. It is most important to safeguard the surrounding atmosphere so that nothing harmful can increase the disturbance of currents. People strive to make contact with the Towers, not understanding that such an intrusion can be disastrous.

It is essential to preserve unity under ordinary, earthly conditions in order to attain at least an approximation of Our unity. May people rejoice, knowing that somewhere there exists the Ladder of the Worlds! This very idea will serve as a bridge for evolution. It is the ignorant preacher who teaches indifference towards the highest unification, but such limiting advice will certainly not help anyone on the earthly plane, for every limitation closes doors and deprives one of fresh air.

Even in the poorest environments people dream about the expansion of possibilities, yet man often lives without raising his eyes towards the stars or thinking once about Infinity. How can this be possible? Let the misguided preacher deprive only himself of the higher achievements, for the day will come when he will be asked what right he has to deprive his brethren of the Higher Realms. If people already know of the Subtle Worlds, they will inevitably think of the Supreme Goal, and no one has the right to deprive others of what they already sense within themselves. Indeed, it is pointless to lock a door when the key is already in the hand of the guest!

The Thinker indicated that man should strive towards the Divine Realms.

449. Urusvati knows the apparatuses that We use for the concentration of currents that are to be transmitted. These apparatuses are used whenever possible to preserve psychic energy. Of course, transmission can be accomplished without instruments, but the principle of frugality should always be applied. Indeed, there can be moments of such tension that it is necessary to project a current of energy with urgency. People can sometimes sense such tension, but cannot often determine its source.

We always advise unity as the basic requirement for collaboration, but if sometimes you notice that We place particular stress upon it, there can be many reasons. The most likely is a special need for consciously united energy—when a poisonous spider attacks, all attention is needed. A crafty enemy demands concentrated, united effort.

People often lose their equilibrium when they hear about danger, and fearing one danger, they evoke ten others. But with experience people will learn that danger, first of all, must be faced with equilibrium. When travelers are warned about danger, only a few accept the warning intelligently. The timid traveler will enumerate all the possible dangers and conjure up insurmountable difficulties, while the true warrior will collect his strength to overcome the obstacles. He knows that danger can appear from below, from above, and from every side, but this does not frighten him. On the contrary, the intensification of his forces fills him with joy.

Great is the feeling of joyous readiness! Such a

radiant feeling is without limit; it illumines the entire aura and multiplies the physical strength. The mother who saves her child is imbued with strength. Equally strong is the one who is ready to repel all attacks, and in such full readiness is manifested the unification of his various energies. We are speaking specifically about extraordinary combinations of energy, but people ignore signs of extreme danger. If the feeling of constant readiness is cultivated in childhood, it will provide victory over egoism.

The Thinker shared long journeys with His disciples. He used to ask them if they had taken their best weapon. They were puzzled and asked, "Which one?" And he would answer, "The most suitable for traveling—absolute readiness."

450. Urusvati knows that ancient proverbs were often scientific statements that in the course of time lost their inner meaning and were later repeated as superficial formulas. For example, it is said, "Sleep is like death," but no one believes that this saying contains any great truth. In fact, so-called death leads one into the Subtle World, and sleep is also a contact with the Subtle World.

Physicians correctly state that sleep is rest, but an aspirant should know that every contact with the subtle spheres is rest for the dense body. One could cite many similar examples in which people make contact with the Subtle World. Some project their subtle bodies into the far-off realms, whereas others touch lightly the domains of the Subtle World. Thus, physicians are right in stressing the outward importance of sleep, but the external does not illuminate the inner, most important meaning. People should realize that sleep brings them into contact with the Subtle World, that very world in which they refuse to believe.

We are not referring to materialization and mediumistic tricks, but to a condition that is natural to everyone. When people come to accept the real meaning of sleep, they will be able to notice many details.

Some people misunderstand Us completely when We discuss the importance of sleep, and even think that it is not at all necessary. It is true that in certain illnesses one cannot sleep, but such a state is tormenting and ruinous. In the highest mountains one's need for sleep is diminished, but even there it is never entirely lost.

It must be understood that when visiting the Subtle World one may encounter the subtle bodies of others who are still alive on Earth. When people think that they have dreamt of others, they may have actually made contact with their subtle bodies. Here it would be appropriate to mention that such meetings can be understood properly if one has fully comprehended the conditions of the Subtle World.

The most intemperate people can be quite reasonable and pleasant in their exchange of thoughts in the Subtle World, whereas in their earthly life they would never be so open-minded! They remember fragments of their experiences in the Subtle World, which, even though very small, convey some new understanding in their essential being. Such lessons brought from the Subtle World are of great benefit to people in the various situations of their lives.

These benefits could be considerably increased if before falling asleep people would realize that they are about to make contact with the great Subtle World. If they perceive even to a small degree the importance of these contacts, they will begin to approach this realm. One is often amazed at having dreamt at the same time of people both living and dead; but there is nothing astonishing in this, because for the subtle body there is neither time nor space.

Thus, We advise that sleep be transformed into an exquisite communication with the higher realms, but without straining one's subtle energies. At times the memory cannot retain the impressions of the Subtle World, and this should be accepted as natural. Even without this memory, it should be understood that contact with the Subtle World is made during sleep.

The Thinker used to say, "We are given the opportunity every night to follow beautiful paths."

451. Urusvati knows that people use various methods for developing the memory, and some have even invented a particular technique called mnemonics. They categorize memory into different types, and believe that the physical brain can be strengthened and developed by so-called "cramming." But they ignore the most important possibility, which transforms the human consciousness. They forget that continuous, concentrated thought about what one reveres most is the surest way to develop the memory. There is no need to burden the consciousness with petty details. One must first of all concentrate upon what has been chosen as the principal concept. Such concentration will increase the sensitivity of the nerve centers. When people learn to keep their ultimate goal continuously in mind they will acquire a better kind of memory, one that may be called synthesized.

This might seem like very simple advice—one need only concentrate! But it is most important that one know how to choose the object of one's concentration. We can mention Our Sister, who one-pointedly carries within Herself the memory of the most sacred and beloved; such an achievement is possible even amidst earthly tribulations. People should consider that a strong anchor can save a ship even during a storm. No one is forced to such concentration, but human nature itself directs one toward the surest means.

The Thinker constantly thought about His chosen Muse. He did not hide the fact that in days of turmoil He remained firm only because of Her; She was His source of strength and ultimately His salvation.

452. Urusvati knows that every newcomer brings with him many dwellers of the Subtle World. This is not obsession, but simply an affinity of auras. We are all surrounded by dwellers of the Subtle World, and each arrival brings his own retinue. These new guests should not be allowed to cause conflict. It is beneficial to create an atmosphere in which all are fused into a harmonious choir. Such increases of harmony will immediately attract higher visitors.

Let us not think of this as a new fairy-tale, but rather apply our scientific understanding to these facts. Even if the rule of contraries is applied, no one can prove that the information known about the Subtle World is invalid. Let doubters find proof before trying to invalidate the knowledge accumulated over thousands of years.

We do not expect blind faith and are therefore ready to accept any challenge from negators, but We ask them to use scientific methods. They should not categorically deny without scientific proof. Let them provide the data to prove that Our information about the Subtle World is untrue.

Such dialogues need not descend to arguments about whether the far-off worlds are inhabited. No one will be satisfied with the flat assertion that Earth alone is populated. But the proponents of the idea of the population, or rather the fullness, of space can cite physical laws. They can demonstrate that microorganisms exist there, and from that the thread of proof can be extended even to the Macrocosm.

Do not think that this is a primitive comparison. Remember that most people have never looked into a microscope or a telescope. We are referring not to the uneducated, but to the educated classes. It is amazing to find such great ignorance, not in poor villages, but in the marketplaces and towers of the city. These environments are true breeders of ignorance. Indeed, one might prefer conversing with farmers to encountering the hopelessly ignorant judgments of some city-dwellers! Thus, let the negators develop a scientific approach.

The Thinker often suggested that His fellow-citizens find a scientific basis for every decision.

453. Urusvati knows that people will always attempt to dissever concepts that are complete and integral. This form of violence demonstrates their ignorance. They try to separate the concept of evolution into materialistic and idealistic, but the majestic concept of evolution cannot be so easily distorted and separated from its application to life.

Do you hear Our grief when unity is disrupted? Can a physician imagine a person made up only of muscles or only of nerves? Such an organism cannot exist. And can one imagine only a materialistic or idealistic evolution? Neither is possible. Only a complete evolution comprising all concepts can transform life. We do not call this synthesis, for synthesis assumes a joining of parts, and in evolution there is no such joining. The muscles and the nerves are of but one organism, and an organism will function inadequately when deprived of any one of its motive powers. One can trace through the history of nations, how brief were their periods of great achievement, and until the fundamental forces of evolution are brought into harmony, humanity will continue to limp along.

If we ask ourselves whether the concepts of materialism and idealism are understood correctly, we shall discover that they are not. People should know that matter is also spirit. Each of these states is but a manifestation of the one Primary Energy, and every attempt to separate them will fail. Materialism alone is a customary standard for the ignorant, and idealism alone is an equally meaningless banner in the hands of fools.

The great evolution must not be demeaned. All the sciences should be summoned to a reasoning based upon solid foundations. Only by applying scientific methods will the significance of evolution be understood.

The Thinker used to say, "Citizen, why did you bind one foot? One-legged, you will be unfit for a long journey!"

454. Urusvati knows that every human action can be turned to evil. Ancient physicians, after performing a cure, added, "Let this good not be turned into evil." One can cite many instances of calamities that have resulted from the best intentions. For example, a farm worker who has been advised to arm himself against impending danger will think only about his own safety, and will neglect his land and crops.

The teacher should explain that there are many degrees of good. A man should not perform a good action if he knows it will result in evil, but what can he do to avoid the subtler degrees of evil? Again we must turn to straight-knowledge.

We know that the dark ones can to a certain degree distort the best intentions, but We do not weep when Our good has at times been distorted. We weigh the good that produces the best yield, for only in co-measurement can be found the justification for an action.

One should not forget that though darkness can diminish even the brightest light, the setting sun will always rise again. Thus each cosmic event illuminates human labor. It is not conceivable that an end will come, for there is no end. Joy is born from Infinity.

The Thinker comforted His disciples, saying that joy is infinite.

455. Urusvati knows how many misunderstandings there are about the concept of sudden illumination. In their conceit people often think that they are already illumined when they have only experienced the most fleeting moment of exaltation. True illumination results only from lengthy, inner work. Such inner work builds upon past accumulations and is sometimes unconscious, yet it does exist and makes illumination possible.

Illumination must be understood not as a fortuitous flash, but as a new degree of consciousness. Often people do not realize that this advance can come unexpectedly, as if it were the result of an accidental event. Certainly an outer event may provide the impetus for the opening of the "lotus," but this flower was already beginning to bloom in the depths of the consciousness. The wonderful "lotus" opens only after much laborious effort, but people seldom realize that they themselves have cultivated this beautiful garden! Only after long and dedicated sowing does one come to a flash of illumination. Without cause there is no effect.

Likewise, the meaning of solemnity is rarely understood. One may think that such an exalted state occurs by chance, but in fact it is achieved as the result of profound and penetrating reflection, and when it grows stronger one finds oneself well established in a new state of consciousness. We do not value ephemeral flashes, but do value the inextinguishable flame.

The Thinker taught that to everyone a lantern is given.

456. Urusvati knows that psychic energy unites and directs even the birds in their migrations, just as it aids human unity. But one should remember that cultivation of the will is the best aid for the attainment of illumination which, bursting into flame, shines like a torch and reveals the path. But how does one develop the will? Perhaps with the aid of concentration, or pranayama? Every aid is useful, but the strongest will is shaped by the lessons of life.

One need not wait for some extraordinary event in order to exercise the will. The most indomitable will grows amidst the events of daily life. It is not enough to simply repeat about the quality of will; it must be acquired inwardly as a psychic impulse. The will is strengthened by labor. People reveal the degree of their will power in every encounter.

The human mind flows by command of will, and awareness of this should be like an opening of the gates, not enslavement. The true education of the will accompanies the first awakening of consciousness. Although man is able to feel the advantage of the disciplined will in the earliest days of his life, not everyone can easily overcome an uncontrolled will. Chaos is conquered only through the realization that this crude matter must be transformed. But one has to pass through many incarnations before realizing independently the need to conquer chaos, and as long as one lacks spiritual experience, he should listen to advice concerning the will. He will then understand that the will must be both strengthened and disciplined. He will understand that the will can restrain him from offending his neighbor. The will indicates when one must offer help. By the will of the disciple Our guidance is accelerated. The will is a purifier when it is directed toward good.

The Thinker often pointed to the migrating birds and exclaimed, "What a beautiful force guides these travelers!"

457. Urusvati knows that the voice of consciousness is sometimes called "the still, small voice," but this is not precise. It is also called the voice of profoundness, which is somewhat closer to the truth. But why avoid the most simple, namely, The Voice of Consciousness? Only thus can we understand that the command of the consciousness has its own insights, and reflects the link with the Supermundane World.

One should know that the consciousness cannot be suppressed from without. On the contrary, it is nurtured from without by all the energies of space. Our Guidance is never imposed, and can nourish the best aspects of consciousness. He who knows the significance of cooperation can understand that one can help without imposing.

What do people do when the voice of consciousness begins to be heard? Usually they try to suppress it by every means; finding it disturbing, they reject it. Yet, if man does not recognize his own gift, how can he advance?

People often fear the so-called conscience, believing that it speaks only after bad deeds. What an error! Conscience, or consciousness, prompts one to good. But having committed a wrongdoing a person becomes tense and nervous, and can become so alert that the voice of conscience rings out for him.

One should never think that cooperation lies in

mutual condemnation! If only people would listen to warnings, they could avoid many dangers. The voice of consciousness is neither small, nor muted, and takes no pride in its independence. The true collaborator cares not to notice the source of success, and gratefully accepts the gift of Good.

The Thinker accepted these gifts as food for the spirit.

458. Urusvati knows how people misuse and pervert most new inventions. For example, there are new films that can be usefully applied in photographing subtle entities, yet few attempts are made to apply these opportunities. Sometimes old-fashioned snapshots were more successful in achieving results. Undoubtedly, in those times the researchers were using greater care and patience than is used now, and were not so easily discouraged.

It is impossible to foresee all the cosmic conditions surrounding subtle experiments. For example, the chemistry of the sun's direct rays is not favorable for them, and hurricanes or earth tremors are also disruptive. Quiet and soft light are especially helpful, as are the harmonized auras of those present and the sound of music. However, these conditions are simply fundamental necessities for the recording of phenomena; there may be subtle entities present that can be useful or hostile. They may be in disagreement about the usefulness of certain manifestations, and will try to stop them. There may also be hostile attempts to cut off the communication, but patience and striving can overcome all obstacles.

In addition, keep in mind that the participation of a woman is particularly helpful in subtle experiments. It has been observed during attempts at photography that when a woman participated, either physically or from the subtle sphere, the results were more successful. We have already spoken about the desirability of participation by women in scientific experiments. Ancient alchemists understood the full value of the feminine contribution, but today many scientists reject it. Because of this, the participation of women is frequently indirect, rather than direct.

Nevertheless, the fundamental nature of things will attract women, and they will leave their mark in new discoveries. For this reason it is essential to change the status of women. The subtlety and refinement of women's nature must be understood, so that they may achieve equal rights and the desired balance. It would be a sad mistake for women to replace soldiers on the battlefield, or perform heavy labor. When we are aware of the presence of valuable subtle energy we ought to be able to apply it accordingly. Thus, we once again come to the notion of true cooperation.

We must find the right use for every ability. The era of the Mother of the World is not a return of the age of Amazons. A far greater, loftier, and more refined task is before us. One can observe that machines often function better, and plants can live longer, in the hands of women. Of course, I do not speak of all women, but of those exceptional ones who manifest the subtlest energy. Their abilities glorify the age of the Mother of the World, and relate closely to the realm of healing.

And another quality belongs to woman—she manifests the highest degree of devotion. The greatest truths are revealed by her. Reality confirms this. Woman can ensure that new knowledge is properly applied.

The Thinker used to address His Muse, thus expressing His reverence for the subtlest force.

459. Urusvati knows how much people prefer to strive toward the far-off worlds rather than attend to their earthly problems. The reason is clear—Earth-dwellers bear no responsibility for the far-off worlds, but the duties of everyday life impose many burdens. Few people want to understand that the reality of the far-off worlds will be revealed only to those who deal successfully with earthly conditions.

Without a realization of one's purpose on Earth, it is not possible to venture into the supermundane spheres. Only through earthly self-improvement can we become worthy travelers to the far-off worlds. Thus, when We speak about the Supermundane we must, first of all, comprehend our earthly state. I repeat again that those who cannot successfully deal with the earthly cannot correctly strive toward the Supermundane.

Not even those who strive to follow the Instructions sent to them can always know how to apply them in life. But this should not upset us. Those who have passed through many earthly journeys know how their experience was accumulated, and the one who has experienced and learned much will be compassionate to those who stumble.

It must not be forgotten that in each incarnation we improve certain qualities in ourselves, whereas many other qualities remain dormant. That is why people often wonder when they see someone who is successful in some ways and weak in others. Only in the Subtle World are the former accumulations awakened, and, of course, so are the errors.

Thus the Thinker often defended a person by saying, "Do we know what is in his heart?"

460. Urusvati knows that the over-saturation of space can have dangerous consequences. We must take this reminder scientifically. The interference of radio waves creates spatial confusion, and even greater disturbance is caused by human clamor.

Psychiatrists must pay attention to epidemics of psychic distress. The effects of mass psychic manifestations should be investigated. It would be wrong to attribute psychic disease only to obsession, although an organism subject to spatial poisoning is also more susceptible to obsession.

Pay special attention to the term "poisoned." It describes the true nature of epidemics. Physicians have to understand how the chemistry that affects an organism is generated. It is very important to study mass movements, and to learn how some of them increase psychic disease.

Often a great explosion is less dangerous than human turmoil. Let us not forget that there can be conditions even worse than war. When We remind you about this We have in mind the poisoning of space. All ferment produces gases, but human unrest can create a very strong poison. Yet, no one believes that the resulting destruction is caused by the people themselves.

The time has passed when psychology was seen as abstract. Now it is understood that the psyche is a real laboratory in which poisons can be produced. Of course, beneficent remedies can also be created there, but for this thought must be directed only to the good.

The Thinker urged His fellow-citizens to turn to the good. In this way the activities of life would become a panacea.

461. Urusvati knows that the quality of action depends upon one's enthusiasm. Now we must ask whether there is a clear understanding of what is meant by enthusiasm. We are not speaking about desire, or striving, or inspiration.

We know that enthusiasm affects and ignites the aura, but scientists still do not know which nerve centers become most active during such bursts. This state of enlightened tension can arise during any labor. The ancients called it a divine greeting, for it alone could endow every task with the radiance of perfection.

One could say that striving toward perfection is a form of the highest creativity. But striving alone is insufficient, and We emphasize that each task must be performed with enthusiasm. The finest craftsman knows that the quality of all levels of work can be continually improved. We can say the same about Our labors. But without enthusiasm, the rhythms of Our work would be disrupted.

Urusvati knows how such a disruption of rhythm occurs. One need not expect the interference of dark forces. For instance, it is enough for participants in a discourse to be out of harmony for the rhythm to be disturbed. The restoration of rhythm is not easy, and requires a careful activation of certain centers, which, if too hastily activated, can provoke negative reactions. Thus We return to the fact that it is time to study this function of the nervous system. The study of reflexes gives impetus to further research, but without considering psychic energy, there can be no accurate results.

The Thinker's advice was to observe the various disturbances of rhythm and to record the physical symptoms that they cause.

462. Urusvati knows how painful the effect of disharmonious currents can be. And the effort to reestablish balance by oneself can provoke many painful sensations. We can recall the suffering of Our Brother K., when He was attacked by ignorant and malicious sendings. He would not have felt those influences so strongly if the currents of space had not been so heavy at that time.

We have already spoken about the epidemic inflammation of mucous membranes, an event that could be attributed to the influence of spatial currents aggravated by earthly confusion; We say earthly in order to point out the main cause.

It is not easy to restore balance when one is being attacked from all directions by a blizzard of malice. First of all, the cure requires calm, which is not easily achieved. Our Brother suffered for a long time, because, even under the most favorable conditions, calmness could not be restored quickly.

These attacks of earthly confusion are well-known in Our Abode. Each of Us, at one time or another, has experienced such tension. In fact, even ordinary currents are excessive under such conditions, and We try to hold off the harmful vibrations as much as possible. It is not surprising that at such times there can be no harmonious manifestations. The organism must be protected. We advise you not to tire yourselves, and if you feel an onset of drowsiness, do not force yourselves to stay awake.

The fierce collision of the currents will affect the sensitive organism. In earlier times one could retreat into the desert to avoid earthly turmoil, but now people have conquered even the air, and the currents are strained. Thus, when We speak about the oversaturation of space, We have in mind not an abstraction, but an earthly reality.

The Thinker used to speak about the "invisible battle."

463. Urusvati knows how dreary life can be without a Teacher. People have a curious understanding about this. Even those who deny the importance of the

Teacher are, by their denial, affirming it. Every denier is a teacher to his own followers; thus the concept of the teacher is affirmed, and even the opponents of this principle strengthen it. Let us not insist that all people think alike, but let each recognize the same fundamentals of life in his own way.

You also know that life without heroes is no life at all. Ask all who dwell on Earth if there was ever a time in which they had no heroic image before them. Every schoolchild will acknowledge that he has always cherished in his heart a chosen ideal. Great deeds inspire the best impulses. Children will also acknowledge that although no one taught them to revere a hero, this feeling developed from within. In this way the foundations of existence are born independently, emerging from the repository of the Chalice. They are preserved within as lessons from the Subtle World. Frequently people cannot express them in words, yet they are alive, and at the destined hour will transform one's life.

Do not tire of speaking about the Teacher and the Hero. Both concepts are essentially the same. They lead to achievement. They help one to endure the burden of life, and will be a source of courage.

The Thinker used to say, "The Teacher is the best Hero. His weapons neither rust nor wear out. An army may turn and flee, but a Teacher will not retreat. We bestow upon Him the wreath of the Hero."

464. Urusvati knows that spatial currents reach Earth in various rhythms. For this reason cosmic vibrations create unique designs. One should not think that supermundane influence descends like a huge cloud, enveloping the planet. Rather, one could compare the rhythms of the currents with the designs made in sand by the vibrations of sound. This explains why some people do not feel the influence continuously, but cyclically, and others not at all. Because of this the study of spatial influences is more difficult.

The waves of earthly gases are good examples of this. Some people suffer from these gases, whereas others who are near them experience no ill effects. In addition, each spatial wave is felt differently, depending upon the condition of the nerve centers. For example, tense centers can attract these waves because the tension itself acts as a kind of magnet.

When We speak about the need for calmness, We are also insisting upon goalfitness. For example, someone who has violated the principle of equilibrium will attract many peculiar influences and become a focus for invisible, conflicting currents. Of course, We can help with Our vibrations to some extent, but let us not forget that the destructive onslaught can be very strong, requiring a powerful defense. It is not easy when one becomes the center of a raging battle! For this reason We often advise you not to become too despondent. People may think that something irreversible has occurred, when in reality it was only a passing cloud. Thus each of Our Indications is at the same time medical advice.

The Thinker asked, "How can we thank our Invisible Physicians?"

465. Urusvati knows that true devotion to the Good is born in the heart, not in the mind. The heart's striving must be understood not as an abstraction, but as a reality. But how can one instill in the consciousness the principle that devotion to the Good is the foundation of life? Man must realize that Good is beneficial not only for the world, but also for himself.

People should recall various deviations from Good and look for their causes. First of all they will find that those who stray do not believe in the continuity of life and expect that their misdeeds will die with them. They fear death, and in their fear look for ways to prolong their earthly lives. But if they could peer into the Subtle World, they would learn to value the benefit of Good. However, they would rather pay scientists to prolong their lives on Earth, where they can immerse themselves in amusement and dissipation, than concern themselves with the phantoms of the Subtle World!

Let us see what one brings from the Subtle World. One brings a triple inheritance—first the karmic, which is one's individual inheritance; then the influence of one's ancestors; and finally, what one acquired while in the Subtle World. These inheritances may be good or evil, and determine how one's existence is shaped. Those who strive to Good are troubled and concerned as to how to help those who have turned from Good, yet, if all three aspects are unfavorable, change for the better will be difficult. We must also examine the causes, and will see that the defectors from Good are in danger of becoming cosmic debris!

The Thinker said, "Let Zeus gather all his lightning bolts, and rid Earth of its debris!"

466. Urusvati knows how often even the simplest of Our Indications are distorted. For example, We spoke about the need to carefully attend to the protection of our friends, and to provide help when necessary. It would seem that such advice is quite clear, but people often will see in this an opportunity to criticize their friends. Wherever the worm of condemnation breeds, one cannot expect a harvest.

Now let us understand the difference between condemnation and fair judgment. Everyone knows that there are crimes for which a severe judgment is deserved, but ordinary, everyday criticism is superficial and harmful. Often, when criticizing others, people attempt to compel them to act as they would wish them to. They do not want to understand that each bird has its own song and that it is wrong to force it to sing an alien tune. One can even kill the singer, but nothing will be gained.

It is regrettable to see how people impose their will on others, and it is even worse when these violations are committed in the name of Good. When We speak about concern for the protection of our friends, We have in mind the most solicitous care, and not tactless criticism. It is time to understand that it is wrong to poison the atmosphere with thoughtless criticism, which is akin to slander. All imposition of the will is an obstacle in communion with Us.

We have spoken about supermundane feelings, which, in their subtlety, can be transmitted to great distances. Can one admit coarseness into the Subtle Abode? Mutual help must be built upon the foundation of the loving heart. When people understand the power of the welcoming heart, they will learn one more path to Us.

The Thinker always distinguished the truly loving heart from the hypocritical one.

467. Urusvati knows how the free will is transformed in higher spheres into cooperation with Cosmic Mind. It is difficult for people to understand this process. Some think that the free will is suppressed, while others think that it simply disappears. There are various explanations, but it is quite rare to find an understanding of the harmony that occurs in which the power of thought is consolidated. There can be no slavery or force in this process—only attunement with Infinity.

Similarly, it is difficult for people to understand that the free will also exists in the Subtle World. They do not want to acknowledge that the Subtle World is like the physical one, but of another dimension. Those who have already achieved discipline in the earthly life and understand the meaning of harmony, can apply these achievements in the Subtle World immediately after their passing. Such a consciousness is called blessed wings, for it accelerates one's evolution.

But people do not often provide themselves with such wings when still on Earth; they usually enter the Subtle World with an undisciplined will, and with their frustrations and unsatisfied desires. During their earthly life, they do not think about the path ahead. They are content to live by other people's rules, which have in the course of time turned into dogma. One does not hear about the future life either in the family or in schools. On the contrary, such conversations are considered inappropriate. Families do not consider it desirable to speak about the passing into the Subtle World, and in schools such a subject may even lead to the dismissal of the teacher. Thus, because of ignorance and bigotry people prefer to remain in darkness.

How few there are who can speak about the lofty destiny of man! From the first days of his earthly life, because of worldly pressure, man is made to forget his glimpses of the Subtle World.

One can easily imagine how life would be transformed if the purpose of existence were rightly understood. Many seemingly unsolvable problems would be easily resolved if people understood the true goal of life.

The Thinker pointed out that humanity will wander a long time in darkness, ignorant of the meaning of existence.

468. Urusvati knows that while studying the Teaching one should pay attention not only to its content, but also to the language in which it is given. The Teaching is given in a particular language for good reason. All teachings, of all times, indicate to the sensitive student which nation was meant to manifest the next step of evolution.

It is sometimes thought that the Teaching is given in the language of the one who receives it, but this explanation is incomplete. One must study the causes in their entirety. Nothing is accidental. The one who first receives a Teaching is chosen, and the language is determined according to necessity. One can observe that the Teachings were given in different languages, each of which related to circumstances of world importance. Thus, the language chosen for a Teaching is, in a sense, a gift to a particular nation. Do not think that, because of this, the Teaching loses its importance to the world as a whole. Every truth applies to the whole of humanity, yet each period has its own task, and every nation has its duty.

Much time is required for a nation to develop the crystal of its essential nature. When amidst a population it is difficult to discern the true nature of a nation. An inexperienced observer will see only superficial traits, rather than the essence. Therefore We advise patience and intelligent observation in order not to regret later one's lightminded judgments.

People customarily judge lightmindedly, for they believe that it will never be too late to revise their opinions. But lightminded changeability is close to betrayal, which is a quality particularly abhorrent to Us. There can be no lightmindedness where the psychology of an entire nation or the significance of an entire era is under consideration.

An objection could be made that it is not easy to perceive the depth of a river when the waves are high. But this is why the Teachings are given! They concern themselves with the most diverse aspects of life, and are not just random collections of sayings but the mosaics of all of life. Let the pilgrim select the stones upon which to cross the river.

The Thinker said, "The river has many fords. Help us, O Muse, to find them."

469. Urusvati knows that the imagination is fed by impressions of reality. When man's flexibility and ability to observe have become sufficiently developed, he will gather in his Chalice the treasures of life, which will transform his future existence.

But let us not forget that other manifestations can also be called imagination. For example, some people may be able to describe aspects of the Subtle World that appeared to them at a particular moment, yet are reluctant to do so, believing them to be a product of their imagination. Thus the endless variety of the Subtle World is forgotten. Yet, it continuously influences man. Sensitive organisms may perceive, according to their degree of development, much of what occurs in the supermundane spheres. But people should not ascribe to themselves all their perceptions, for they may be influenced by invisible helpers. The imagination is therefore stimulated by a complex combination of conditions.

You already know how important it is to develop the imagination while in the earthly state, but many do not understand at all the nature of imagination. They claim that they do not experience the forming of images in their minds, and will say that only artists can have fantasies. Beware of such simplistic explanations.

These people do not understand that the imagination is an open window to the Beautiful that improves life.

When science finally helps humanity to develop sound judgment, knowledge will be placed upon a new foundation. Every manifestation must be subject to scientific investigation, but if the scientists themselves lack imagination, how can they use scientific apparatuses to the fullest?

Daily life is composed of a sequence of remarkable manifestations that should be recognized scientifically. It is good that the influence of micro-organisms is now understood, yet the psychic aspects, whether beneficial or destructive, have been ignored. This side of life must also be scientifically understood. Our Towers stand firm on the knowledge of nature.

The Thinker knew that evolution will be accelerated when knowledge is widespread, and the power of imagination is understood to be based upon scientific fact.

470. Urusvati knows about the scientific significance of so-called talismans. We have already spoken about these magnetized objects which, under favorable conditions, can retain their power for a long time. But some may ask about the fate of talismans that fall into unworthy hands. Just as a magnet loses power under negative conditions, a talisman in unworthy hands loses its power.

In the past many people were burned and tortured because their use of talismans was misinterpreted, but today science understands the magnetization of objects. People often ask which method of magnetization is the best. There are various techniques—one person may pass his hands over an object, another may put it near his head at night, and another may wear it close to his heart, or merely touch or look at it. There can also be magnetization at a distance, but one must know the object well in order to visualize it clearly.

Such methods of magnetization require that the object should not be moved or touched with the naked hand; an insulating material will be useful in this. These are not forms of sorcery, but the simplest scientific preventive measures. People do not often have sufficient patience for magnetization experiments, but the successful transmittance of energy to an object is its own proof. Such experiments help one to understand the precious gift of mastering psychic energy.

This gift is affected by surrounding conditions, but regrettably people do not know how to control their surroundings. No more than five out of one hundred families live in harmony. Much energy is wasted on domestic squabbles. The improvement of home life will teach goalfitness.

All those who possess a reserve of psychic energy should be treated with great care, but humanity does not even think about this. If dowsers are so valued, then those who preserve great stores of psychic energy should be valued even more! Every plant has its healing property, but its proper use must be found. The same can be said about the energy of each individual.

The effect of herbal mixtures can be extremely complex. What then can one say about the mixing of human energies? Have their combinations been studied? A medical certificate is sometimes required for marriage, and the time will come when a certificate will also be required for the quality of one's psychic energy. Thus will be solved the problem of disharmony between people.

The Thinker said, "Why do people hang millstones

on their necks and upon the necks of others? It is far better to work to grow wings."

471. Urusvati knows about the various degrees of cooperation. Usually people prefer the lesser degrees, because they involve less responsibility, less exertion, and less diligence.

The higher degrees are difficult because they require one to act on one's own initiative and to be able to discern the words of the Guide. Each one must find the courage to accept many arrows into his shield. Thus, the higher, the more difficult. Moreover, most people are not aware of how and where their psychic energy acts. It may often seem that nothing has been achieved, whereas in reality much is already occurring because of the action of psychic energy.

Man is usually not able to evaluate the full range of his mental world. One cannot trace all the currents of one's psychic energy, which, when linked to the energy of the Teacher, acts beneficially. Let the devoted co-worker put his psychic energy at the disposal of his Guide. One must trust the ways of the Guide, which may be complex. During a battle one cannot question the intentions of the commander. One should intensify one's striving to serve in the best way. Thus, the higher degrees of cooperation require an understanding that psychic energy can be applied more broadly than one might think.

We have an example of a famous commander who won a victory yet was unaware of it. He thought that his forces had been defeated when, in fact, the great distance prevented him from seeing that it was the enemy that was destroyed.

The Thinker said, "Listen, listen attentively. Do you know where your real power lies? The destined victory may already be yours, but your eye is unable to perceive it."

472. Urusvati knows of those moments when one is unable to discern the boundary between the personal good and the Common Good. The mind whispers that personal gain is in conflict with general welfare, but the heart says otherwise. Disharmony will cause a contradiction between the personal good and the Common Good, but it is possible to imagine a point at which the Common Good becomes the personal. It is a harmonious state that requires an equal harmony of all surrounding conditions.

Some may object that such a state is unattainable during earthly life. But who can tell what is attainable and what is not? Such an arbitrary distinction may relate only to a fleeting moment in the present but is of no value for the future. If, in the course of a single human life one can observe how much the conditions of life change, what then can one say about centuries?

Of course, those who like contradictions will point out that in many respects human character does not change at all, but more discriminating observers realize that human psychology changes, and that in this flexibility is hidden the guarantee of future achievements. The time will come when people will understand that Good is one and cannot be divided into the personal and the common.

There is great perplexity about thought and the concept of the cementing of space. People think wrongly that all personal thoughts are selfish ones, and wonder how good thoughts can emerge from the darkness of selfishness. Of course, if someone prays for something harmful to humanity, those prayers will pollute space. But every benevolent thought is good, both for the one who sends it and for all others. These are the thoughts that should "cement" space.

The Thinker said, "Let everybody find thoughts that are good both for himself and for humanity, because then his ego will be equal to the heart of humanity."

473. Urusvati knows that the length of time one spends in the Subtle World depends on many things. Among the karmic conditions, two examples should be noted. It is usually said that karmic dates do not change, but in reality everything is in motion, and the wheels of life are affected by varying circumstances.

First, there must be an ardent approach to learning. There are some experiments in the Subtle World that should not be interrupted, and the law regulating one's return will be modified as necessary for their completion. But also, there may be such a strong desire while in the Subtle World to send help to those on Earth that this striving will lengthen one's time there.

As you see, in both cases it is the element of self-sacrifice that is of significance—it is not easy to help those on Earth, for they fear such help and are always ready to faint at the first sign from the Subtle World! Similarly, experiments in the Subtle World require great discipline, for the conditions are not easy.

There are some who remain much longer in the Subtle World, where they labor in a way that is not possible on Earth. Because of the unselfish nature of their work, they cannot be suspected of avoiding service. The law is alive, and evaluates justly one's true motives. Thus, although some strive to reincarnate as quickly as possible—and their *podvig* is valuable—extended work in the Subtle World also has its reasons.

One can imagine how much certain workers are needed in the Subtle World. For some, bringing their knowledge to Earth would be premature, and they can apply their knowledge usefully in the Subtle World by helping to prevent pollution of the subtle spheres by ugliness. The abilities of man are indeed rarely evaluated accurately on Earth, but in the Subtle World the judgment is always goalfitting.

The Thinker knew that a true talent will always be valued, if not on Earth, then in the Supermundane.

474. Urusvati knows that earthly longevity itself has no particular significance. Besides hereditary causes, there are three reasons for a prolongation of life on Earth. First, when a person must complete some beneficial work; second, when he must help someone or something; third, and not the least important, when he can provide true testimony about events that were incorrectly reported. However, in all three examples there must be a conscious, irrepressible striving, free from destructive influences. The foremost of these is fear. There can be no fervent striving if it is weakened by fear. It can be chemically demonstrated to what extent fear kills life. Of course, malice, envy, and all other dark emotions also destroy the life energy. Therefore, one cannot think that he is self-sacrificing if that self-sacrifice is not already in the depths of the Chalice.

People may assure you that they fear nothing, but will tremble at the first test. Courage should be tested in schools. An entire course could be dedicated to a study of how to act in the face of various dangers. Children should not be expected to manifest immediate resourcefulness, but they can be taught to understand life and develop the ability to make courageous decisions. A competition in resourcefulness would be a good exercise. In time, the students would understand how the best people were able to manifest the greatest striving.

The Thinker demanded from His disciples that they dedicate at least one day a week to the exercise of resourcefulness. He knew that this skill would often provide valuable protection in life.

475. Urusvati knows how even the strongest minds can become weakened. There are numerous examples of this in history. Many people cannot understand that even a great mind can somehow simply exhaust itself. Physicians may ascribe such a deterioration to illness or fatigue because of excessive work, but, as is often the case, the basic cause is not understood.

Any particularly valuable person will be subject to fierce attacks that inflict psychic wounds and penetrate his aura, producing unbearable vibrations. Defensive counter blows provoke terrible battles, but the center remains calm, like the eye of a hurricane. If possible, We advise you to change your location during such assaults. It may seem strange, but moving one's place of work will delay the renewal of hostile attacks. There are events in history that would have been changed if the leaders had moved their location. Yet it is not easy to move and abandon a battle that is being fought for the general welfare. No one wants to assume the appearance of defeat, or allow the enemy to triumph. And those witnessing the event would not understand the wisdom of such a decision, and might attribute it to cowardice. For example, when Apollonius of Tyana had to travel abroad to recover his strength, he was often accused of betrayal and trickery.

The Thinker said, "The great father of the people, Pericles, was attacked with poisoned arrows. He did not protect himself with a shield, although the shield is an essential part of one's armor."

476. Urusvati knows that earthly existence can be transformed only through the force of a clear visualization of the future life. Some fear the future and thus lose strength; others imagine the Subtle World only mentally, and thus project false images; still others behave as if they were already dead and think of nothing but the marketplace. Few realize that even a life of one hundred years is only a moment in Infinity.

One should contemplate the future on three levels. First, as expressed in words; second, in images that are beyond verbal expression—borne, as it were, on the waves of deep, tidal currents. Finally, in thought so profound that it is inexpressible by word or image, and only psychic energy and the solar plexus can remind us of it!

And so, one must visualize the future with the help of these three levels of contemplation. Such visualization is like casting an anchor—the ship is then held steady. Thus the sensible thinker will secure himself, and be able to draw himself toward the desired goal. The wise one knows where he can express himself most usefully. Only a fool dreams about life's transitory trinkets. Those who already have achieved much will no longer be enticed by outward appearance, and will think about the grandeur of the task ahead.

One should learn to think about the future as if preparing to venture on a distant journey, while continuing to manage all earthly tasks. This is goalfitness, this is balance. We have spoken often about goalfitness. One must realize that this quality is demanded in all activities of life. We repeat this for We know how people distort this concept, and think that goalfitness need only be applied in special cases.

It must be repeated that each circumstance in life has its causes. To think of deeds as great or small is an illusion. The measure of a deed is not revealed immediately, and the wise one will remember his guideposts and apply them goalfittingly to his future life. He knows that good is inexhaustible, and that evil is finite. You have correctly noticed that at times We do not confront an evil manifestation. The reason is twofold—sometimes tactica adversa should be applied, and one should also remember that evil is temporal. Evildoers cannot be nourished forever by evil; what a repugnant spectacle it is when they begin to devour themselves by their earthly actions!

The Thinker urged His disciples to base their lives upon good. He said, "Good is inexhaustible, but evil is limited."

477. Urusvati knows that the ability to teach should be developed in people from their early years. Everyone can teach someone something, and should know how to do it. We approve of schoolchildren tutoring their younger brothers and sisters.

It is not easy to choose the best method of instruction. It will be individual, and the teacher must sense how best to approach the consciousness of the pupil. It is impossible without much practice to be a convincing educator, and only the ignorant would think that a simple reciting of information imparts it to the student.

It is regrettable that the art of teaching does not attract more attention. Yet everyone will remember how differently various subjects were assimilated during their school years. Success in learning does not depend solely on the abilities of the pupil; it depends primarily upon the influence of the teacher.

Thus, let teaching be practiced in all spheres of life. Let the teacher himself be mindful of the dignity of his calling. Thoughts about great Teachers will develop more easily when the concept of teaching has been firmly realized.

Teaching must be freed from egoism. The good teacher transmits knowledge accumulated by him, but he will not claim it as his own. He should be able to accept the gift of knowledge in order to impart it joyously to the next generation. The work of the teacher must be compensated, not only materially, but also with universal respect. Teaching is one of the highest callings in a nation. It is not so much the teacher himself, but his gift of passing on knowledge that will open the higher culture to people. Thus, not personal ambition, but service to the general welfare, should be the reason for teaching.

Such a concept of service does not come at once, it must be cultivated. Thus, let every student consider himself to be a teacher to the younger ones. There should be classes led by the older students, who could then have the opportunity to share their knowledge.

Such service should not be regarded as onerous. On the contrary, let everyone learn to give joyously, for only in such giving is born true joy.

The Thinker taught, "Everyone can serve his neighbor, and everyone can give, even when there seems to be nothing to give. How glorious is that inexhaustible giving!"

478. Urusvati knows that one must be able not only to gaze into the Heights, but also to look into the depths of his own nature. The latter is just as difficult as the former. The age-old serpent lies ready in the depths of the Chalice, and will awaken and stir with any misstep. He fills one with malice, he saps one's strength, and obscures good intentions. Only with great striving can one rid oneself of this ancient companion.

Yet a determined person can develop within himself one quality that can resist the stratagems of this monster. With purity of heart one can sense the borderline that defines the influence of the creature and, sensing this boundary, correct an intended mistake. Later other danger signs will appear. The most important thing is to abstain from acts of questionable rightfulness. One should develop within oneself this sense of right action and thus not waken the monster. It is far better to discriminate in one's actions than later regret the deeds.

We have spoken about questionable actions. One should think about this issue with caution. A lazy person will be glad to categorize most of his actions as questionable. He ignores the voice of the heart, and cloaks himself with hypocrisy rather than take the trouble to act. Everybody knows those hypocrites who hide their laziness and selfhood behind lofty words. One cannot imagine the depths of cunning that reside under the coils of this snake! Yet these hypocrites are not fit for real labor. It was said long ago that the pronouncing of lofty words is of no value if truth does not dwell in the heart.

An ancient story tells about the serpent that sucked the blood of humanity—an eloquent symbol for the awakened serpent that is indeed nourished by human blood. Let us not forget that such ancient symbols have a basis in truth; for in this way the monstrous bloodsucker devours his victim.

Another story tells of a sleeping dragon that was awakened by a small pebble thrown by a fool. Truly the smallest stone can cause the monster to stir.

The Thinker said, "Step cautiously. You may be walking amidst sleeping vipers."

479. Urusvati knows that the most insignificant action is interwoven with many surrounding conditions; the same can be said about great actions. Psychic activity, too, depends on many conditions, but this fact is not accepted in the field of medicine.

People neglect their illnesses. Moreover, they surround the sick with unpleasant conditions, and then expect an immediate cure. But healing must take place in harmonious conditions.

People are ever ready to summon a physician with demands and ill will. They do not know that the most powerful healing energy can be poisoned and cut off by them. Frequently people call a physician and at the same time whisper words of mistrust behind his back. Scientists should investigate the healing that takes place when there is trust in the physician, and the illnesses that worsen because of distrust.

We have said many times that every action must be accompanied by good will. Even ordinary housework will produce good results if it is performed with good thoughts. Many good deeds were destroyed because of irritation and unkind thoughts.

The Thinker particularly stressed to the disciples that they not permit their good intentions to sour.

480. Urusvati knows how We grieve at each new sowing of evil. One could ask, "Why lament? Is it not better to just stop the spreading of evil?" Thus speak the foolish ones who do not know how cautiously one must confront evil. Only a physician who has studied many illnesses knows how to diagnose the various conditions, not only in the sick organism itself, but also in the surroundings.

Evil can be compared to some forms of cancer. The physician knows that in certain organs cancer is incurable. He also knows that one must choose the best moment for surgery and properly prepare the organism for such a shock. The same situation, but to a greater degree, can be seen in a psychic battle.

The people involved do not want to admit that an evil monster has been born within themselves, and instead will attempt to conceal their disease.

But how can one intrude upon the inner core of someone who in every possible way resists such help? It is correctly said, "Investigate everything!" But how many are ready for such investigation? People do not like to think about their inner processes, and will angrily oppose every attempt to direct their thinking to a better understanding of their essential nature. All Teachings say that goodwill is necessary for advancement. It is equally true that for the eradication of evil, the consent of the sufferer himself is needed.

This is why We are saddened to see the conceiving of such evil monsters, because We foresee the scope and complexity of the coming battle. It is not possible to remove all the heads of a hydra with one blow of the sword. It is said that each drop of its blood begets new offspring! Therefore, one must find the way to cause the monster to die of hunger. Remove the monster's nourishment and it will disappear, crumbling into a handful of ashes.

But such total destruction requires time and favorable conditions; people can easily help to promote such conditions.

The Thinker said, "We are all physicians, and each of us can perform some kind of healing."

481. Urusvati knows that the Cosmos is a unified structure, held together by Primary Energy. An ancient philosopher declared that the heavenly firmament is more saturated than the earthly firmament. One may not fully agree with such a statement, but it is not far from the truth.

Generally speaking, people do not clearly differentiate between the worlds. When they speak about the

Subtle World they use imagery from the earthly world. And when they try to elevate the physical world, they compare it to aspects of the Subtle World. Truly, it is impossible to set boundaries between the three worlds. This fundamental idea should be embedded in the people's consciousness. No one can limit himself only to the physical world. Even those who deny the Supermundane are unable to rid themselves of a sensation of something beyond the earthly world.

Many expressions are used incorrectly by people. They speak of the hereafter and in doing so break apart the concept of a seamless unity. Yet, how can one imagine what people call the hereafter? Such thinking would return us to the tale of Charon who ferried the souls of the dead to the far shore of the river Styx. Primitive people invented symbols of crossing into another world, but symbols can be harmful, because by their vividness they impress themselves upon the consciousness and are not easily dislodged by an explanation closer to the truth.

As you have already noticed, We avoid the overuse of symbols. There are, however, many schools of thought based only upon symbols, and one can easily see how the old symbols have hindered the development of an understanding of the universe. All is alive, all is in motion, and the Primary Energy reveals itself in new and unexpected ways. People must not restrict their consciousness with antiquated symbols.

The Thinker asked, "Must we speak in the same ways as our grandfathers?"

482. Urusvati knows that symbolism, incorrectly understood, has brought much harm to the way in which people think of Us. For example, the symbolism of rays has in a way been distorted, and, by limiting the understanding of Our activities, has undermined the idea of synthesis and unity. Each one of Us can have His beloved domain, but it cannot be said that He acts mainly in accordance with one ray.

Further, the very names given to these rays are arbitrary. You know the source of these labels. You also know how they found their way into the literature and confused so many. It is impossible to stop these distortions, but in time they will give way to a more correct understanding.

Rays do, of course, exist, but each ray is nothing but psychic energy and therefore cannot be limited in its possibilities. Otherwise this could be taken to such an extreme that one would be permitted to save a man only by seizing his left arm, and not the right! This way of thinking could reach such a level of perversity that instead of an increase of possibilities there would be a diminishing of them.

Sometimes, for a purpose that seems good to them, people succeed in driving their consciousness into a labyrinth. Let these categorizers ponder whether they cause harm or benefit. The invention of limiting concepts is not useful. The most precise Teachings have suffered from all kinds of misinterpretations that dissevered their truths. We wish Our labor to be understood in its entirety and its unity. Only thus can one picture the cooperation that lies at the foundation of Brotherhood.

The Thinker pointed out that Truth should never be divided lightmindedly. He said, "Cutting up an idea is like dissecting a living organism."

483. Urusvati knows that each proclamation of truth draws out its enemies. Chaos attacks whatever is revealed in truth. One must not deplore this battle, for it is not only natural but also beneficial. Imagine a teaching that is proclaimed but attracts no enemies.

This could only be because it lacks importance and is unconvincing. Enemies are tests, and the degree of their fury indicates the significance of the teaching.

Much energy is generated in Us precisely by the actions of Our enemies. A famous Ruler used to say, "Today I become considerably stronger, for I face a new and powerful enemy." One should view enemies as steps of ascent. Each of Us has kept such thoughts during Our many long lives.

Where then are the descriptions of the Brotherhood? First of all, in the descriptions of Our experiences. We tell about Our labors, through which We gather strength for future construction. The essence is not in ceremonies, but in labor. It would be demeaning to others not to let them participate in the labors that fill Our whole existence. The life of the Brotherhood is the life of the Supermundane, because it is founded on thought. What can be more supermundane than thought?

People could elevate their earthly life into the Supermundane simply by basing their existence on thought. Our Teaching could properly be called The Proclamation of Thought. Great is the festival of the one whose realm is thought! And We can transmit more easily to those in whom thought reigns. But responses will not always come in expected ways. A response may often come in the very development of the thought, and the book will open by itself, and the strings will resound. The more varied the signs, the broader the field of thought.

The Thinker said, "Show me that dungeon into which the light of thought does not penetrate. The flowers of thought are more beautiful than all earthly flowers."

484. Urusvati knows that some countries are

alarmed by the decline in their birth rates. Regarding this, it can generally be seen that the living conditions in these countries are better than in those in which the birth rate is on the increase. There are many earthly reasons for this, but the main cause is overlooked—that there are dwellers in the Subtle World who do not wish to be incarnated in certain countries. True, there may be karmic conditions that compel them to be born in a particular nation, but aside from these conditions, their will is free to act.

The dwellers of the Subtle World know little more than those on Earth, but in certain respects they are able to learn about the future, and thus can choose better conditions for themselves. There are not many who would wish to come back to a heap of ashes! Why should one endure a karma not his own when he can prepare himself for more constructive activity by associating with a strong nation and participating in its great decisions? He will sense where is growth and where decline.

No task can be fulfilled only by earthly considerations. If people would ponder upon the Supermundane, they would be able to find solutions to the most difficult problems. Yet, even with great scientific attainments, people are far behind in their knowledge of supermundane tasks. It is impossible to think about the problems of humanity while still bound by earthly limitations. One does not have to indulge in fantastic dreams. It is time to think about the realities of both the past and the future. No one thinks seriously about the important fact that many dwellers of the Subtle World do not want to come to outworn places, and no one will compel them to choose an undesirable destiny if their karma does not require it. People must begin to examine existence in its entirety, and to pass their important observations on to future generations.

The Thinker said, "We do not think for ourselves alone, but for our unknown successors."

485. Urusvati knows that it is especially difficult for people to reconcile the seemingly contradictory concepts of free will and guidance. Some cry for the elimination of the idea of leaders, and others object to freedom of the will, but life itself reveals that only equilibrium permits progress and advances evolution.

In daily life one can see how both concepts can coexist harmoniously. The teacher presents a certain task and adds, "Apply all your abilities in order to make better decisions." This simple example illustrates how peacefully both concepts can exist together. Guidance simply develops the free will and, in turn, the free will, in its development, accepts the role of guidance. But everyone will have to return to this question many times.

People, it seems, divide themselves into two irreconcilable camps. The lovers of free will call those who follow teachers regressive, and those who adhere to the principle of guidance call the lovers of free will destroyers! Such is the misunderstanding that deprives people of the best possibilities. One should seek the unifying concept that can reconcile these extremes, and contemplate life in infinity, under whose dome all concepts are united. In this way measures will be revealed that can eradicate arbitrary divisions.

It is essential that a real teacher should encourage the free will, and a prudent pupil, while exercising his free will, will learn to value the importance of the teacher. You may note how often We return to discussing the seeming opposition of guidance and the free will. People must learn to reconcile these inseparable concepts. A better future depends upon the harmony of opposites. Those who do not want to understand this salutary doctrine expose themselves to much suffering. The teacher cannot change the stubbornness of the pupil if there is no room for the exercise of good will. Good will is free will.

The Thinker pointed out that goodness, freedom, and beauty live under one roof.

486. Urusvati knows that the arbitrary application of labels and names impedes and distorts the direction of thought. For example, a scientist discovered an aspect of man that he labeled "electric architect." The concept of man as architect has been used in certain philosophical schools and has a real meaning, but it is wrong in this context to talk about electricity. People have mastered one aspect of primary energy and lightmindedly use the term "electricity" as an all-encompassing metaphor.

If scientists do not understand the true nature of the primary energy they can designate it as some kind of special energy, but should not limit this great, fundamental manifestation by calling it electricity. It is hard to believe that scientists would not pay more attention to the unique qualities of this energy instead of limiting their interest just to its electrical activity. The attention paid to it is praiseworthy, but the inappropriate labeling will lead to new errors.

It is understandable when timid investigators attempt to protect themselves from attacks by the ignorant by using conventional nomenclature, but in doing so they bring upon themselves the criticism of future generations. They must weigh what is more honorable, to suffer the derision of the ignorant, or to be censured by future generations.

One can observe that this is true in all aspects of

life. People demean the unifying concepts and replace them with arbitrary and meaningless labels. One should pay attention to this tendency, the basis of which is cowardice.

How long will mankind continue to dissect the one body of the Universe? One may study isolated blades of grass yet must never forget the great organism to which they belong. One should examine isolated manifestations without forgetting that they are but links of one great chain. He whose thinking is without synthesis cannot approach the life of the Universe.

The Thinker taught the beauty of Unity, out of which pour the currents of energy.

487. Urusvati knows that the education of thought must proceed step by step, in proper sequence. One can easily imagine how dreadful it is when evil people master the power of thought. Therefore, the study of the power of thought must be preceded by ethical and moral education, else we shall succeed only in producing evil sorcerers.

Ages ago the teachings warned against permitting evil people to have access to yogic disciplines. And indeed, over the course of time, with the decline in ethical behavior, there appeared some who had mastered certain physical techniques without prior purification of the consciousness. Of course, concentration of thought is needed for the purification of the consciousness, but such concentration is inner and needs no external physical effort.

People do not realize that one cannot undertake pure work with dirty hands. It would seem that this precept would be understood by everyone, but it is rarely observed in life. Many people do not care whether their hands are clean or not, and can produce the most harmful chemical reactions. People give themselves high-sounding names and titles while hiding the lowest intentions. How many corrupt practices take place! The most prudent measures are needed to ensure that the means of power does not pass into the hands of such hypocrites.

Think how much even Our labors are hindered by the interference of evil people who are skilled in certain yogic practices.

The Thinker used to say, "First, let us understand the good, and then send it in thought into the world."

488. Urusvati knows that the concept of good must be taught in special ways. Schools teach courses on many subjects, but if they were to announce a course about good the students would try to avoid it! The good must be taught unobtrusively by infusing it into all subjects.

Some may argue that the concept of general good does not exist, because what is good for one is bad for someone else. Those who judge superficially will speak this way, for they only scratch the surface of events and are unable to look into the depths of things. The idea of good is unalterable in its essence. The heart will point out the essence of good.

One can see how even the criminal can be changed by suddenly perceiving the essence of good. Such a transformation may be seen as a miracle, but it is no miracle when one can touch the string of a vina and become enchanted by its sound. Everyone can be affected by different influences, some of which may stupefy, while others enlighten. Thus it is wrong to assert that something is beyond one's reach. It is more correct to say that at a particular moment one was unable to grasp a certain kind of knowledge; but the very next moment could provide that understanding.

Sensitive people are aware of how speedily the currents change, for they cannot remain unchanged for even a day. Even during the shortest intervals one can sense acute changes, not only psychic but also physiological. For example, one easily senses quick changes of heat and cold, feels passing pain, or any change in surrounding aromas. One may sense a slowing or acceleration of thinking, or may observe fluctuations in sensitivity. Many feelings of joy or anguish can result from these waves. The teacher must know how to prepare the student for a conscious recognition of many manifestations from the Laboratory of the World.

The Thinker taught, "We should learn to constantly sense the surrounding currents of the Divine Force. They may at times restrain us, but often will give us wings. The Grandeur of the World envelops us with veils of beauty."

489. Urusvati is aware of the independent and penetrating work that always continues in the consciousness of man. I will illustrate this by an ancient parable. There once lived a venerable Teacher who not only provided instruction in the practical subjects, but also helped his students in many other ways. The Teacher possessed, among other abilities, an intense and deep insight. The pupils were confident that their Teacher would always come to their help, even without being asked.

Once the Teacher said to the closest disciple, "Listen to what is being said by your inmost self," and smiling, he added, "It says, help!" The disciple became embarrassed and tried to assure the Teacher that he never wanted to burden Him with requests. The Teacher calmed him and explained, "My friend, I am confident that neither your heart nor your mind asked for help. They know that My help will come at the right time, but the depth of the consciousness directs the voice toward the Teacher in one call—Help!

"Do not be disturbed by this cry from your inner being, for therein is contained a unique link with Hierarchy. You did not ask for riches or honors. Your being, expressing itself in that one word, said, 'Guide me!' You did not make any conditions, but simply wanted to say, 'Do what is best.' You are confident that all will be done for the good, and if you do not recognize at once which is the right way, you are nevertheless confident that the best measures will be taken.

"You have heard about the three kinds of thinking—by the brain, the heart, and the consciousness. The brain is reasonable, the heart is sensitive, and the consciousness is wise. Your consciousness calls out to the Guide, 'Help!' and My consciousness says the same thing, and My Guide's consciousness will speak so also. There is no burdening in this call. The arm is stretched upwards, knowing that the Hand of Help will be extended during this dangerous ascent. And it is not for us to judge where the danger lies."

Such is the parable, and the Thinker knew it. He added, "A special beauty lies in the fact that our consciousness is a temple of wisdom."

490. Urusvati is familiar with the error that many of today's philosophers make when they separate man from Cosmos. To them, a man is a thinking being without a past or a future and with no link to the Universe. This explains why such thinking cannot reach into the future and is so removed from real life.

Man should not think of himself as alone, as if lost in a desert, knowing only that there exist other creatures like him, who come from the unknown and disappear into the unknown. Why should man's thinking be so limited? This leads to a very depressing existence!

Some abstract thinking is even more harmful than this kind of limited, materialistic philosophy, and must be changed. Materialism can lead to progress, but these abstract philosophies cannot aid man in his evolution. It is no wonder that many modern philosophers remain outside of life! Thinkers must first of all strive to understand the problems of Existence and the proper role that man plays in them. It is not useful to dismember a healthy organism. One should rejoice in every thought that is directed toward the unity of the Universe. It is regrettable that the practical scientists rarely can find unity with the philosophers. Here again we see divisiveness and errors caused by enmity.

It will be said that one cannot be a person of encyclopedic knowledge in today's scientific world. But it is not omniscience that is the goal. A respect for knowledge is possible that will free people from skepticism and negation. In each subject there is something that deserves attention. A true thinker can recognize this spark of truth.

The true thinker also will treat fairly all manifestations of progress. But, as a rule, people pay attention to only the final results of scientific work, and ignore the previous groundwork. This is a great injustice because it is in the preparatory stages that many unrealized discoveries lie, and great treasures can be uncovered by studying them. But people cavalierly dismiss the preparatory work and many desirable achievements are lost.

It is necessary to treat everything with respect. Do not think that My words apply only to the physical sciences—they apply also to the humanitarian ones. The most important thing is to free thinking from all kinds of prejudice.

The Thinker said, "Look at this self-important, supposedly liberal one! See how he hastens to cross to the other side of the street in order to avoid mingling with workmen, even though he has just now given a speech declaring his love for the common people!"

491. Urusvati knows that without supermundane perceptions one's life cannot be transformed. No labor can be uplifted without imagination. Pay attention to that good word—imagination. It is not fantasy, or cunning invention, but the discovery of higher images and the realization of lofty concepts. Imagination must be always real and truthful. We cannot always know where this truth is, but it does exist.

Such imagination is impossible among those of ill will, since benevolent striving is required, and evil can create only distorted images. Just as a beautiful kaleidoscopic image requires a harmonious combination of colors, the contemplation of lofty images needs an open heart. Any obscurity will distort one's imagination. Thus physical laws are once again shown to be linked with psychic foundations.

Yet even the highest achievements must begin here on Earth, often amidst the most oppressive need. The wealthy may wonder why their contributions are so easily made. But they so often believe that an offering need only be of money, and forget that they are entrusted with the wonderful task of combining their funds with high purpose! However, this requires imagination, and how many strive to cultivate this quality within themselves?

The Thinker taught, "It is given to everyone to glimpse the Divine Mansion, but the eye must first grow accustomed to gazing at the Celestial Radiance and perceiving the life of space in all its fullness. He to whom the Heavens are empty has an empty heart."

492. Urusvati knows that devotion is of greatest

value when it is manifested in the fullest measure possible. Only then is created a powerful, beneficent effect, salutary even over great distances. The kind of devotion that only goes halfway belongs to the realm of hypocrisy. Man deceives himself and others in this way and generates powerful poisons. Man ought to be able to say that he is devoted, even when it is of no benefit to him. But what ugly devotion it is when people choose to be devoted only when it is profitable to them! Everyone will agree that such covetous devotion deserves a very different name.

Our Brotherhood is based upon a mutual devotion that no circumstance can disturb. One may think that such intense devotion is the result of long collaboration. This is true, but people often collaborate in ways that do not necessarily encourage their devotion to grow. Thus, one's devotion should be tested in the smallest details. True devotion will point out the right conduct, and will teach a careful, loving, and simple attitude.

Devotion is not slavery, it is a smile of understanding and sympathy. Ponder upon this beautiful word, sympathy, for it expresses harmony based upon the consonance of feelings. Everyone longs for sympathy, but so often it is demanded for oneself only, without regard for reciprocal feelings. Many misfortunes have their root in this misconception.

The Thinker used to say, "Man demands sympathy, but where is his reciprocal feeling? He considers himself to be most unhappy, yet does he consider the misfortunes of others?"

493. Urusvati knows how much most people dread loneliness. This is not so much fear as it is a kind of oppressive feeling, which is quite natural for anyone who is unaware of the Subtle World and the continuity of life. But at times the same feeling is experienced by those who are familiar with the foundations of Be-ness. We should explore the causes of such overwhelming feelings.

It is quite possible that unpleasant premonitions or negative entities cause these depressed moods, but there can also be cosmic influences. The effect of the heavy currents can envelop one and produce an isolated condition and a sense of great loneliness. However, there is a panacea available to everyone. Such feelings can be dispersed by reaching out in thought to friends. One has friends on Earth, but also has many faithful co-workers in the Subtle World. Therefore, know about Us; appeals directed to Us will not go unanswered. The response may come in an unexpected form, but the oppressive influence will certainly be dispersed.

Many scientific discoveries lie ahead, but the awareness of the foundations of Be-ness will always be the keystone. Thus, you observe that the concept of the transmission of thought at a distance is only slowly being accepted among scientists because of their lack of supermundane feelings and their rejection of the fundamentals of Be-ness.

The Thinker felt pity for those who limit not only their life, but also their thought.

494. Urusvati knows that at the time of danger people forget the most helpful advice. Even an imagined danger deprives people of common sense. Many nations have instructive stories similar to the one about the head of a family who taught his near ones how to behave in case of fire. Nevertheless, when a fire occurred, none of them acted as they had been told.

In the schools of Sparta children were trained to face all kinds of danger in order to develop resourcefulness. This should also be done now, when dangers have multiplied. There are those people who continue to invent nonexistent dangers, concerned more about their own existence and caring little about dangers to the planet. It is impossible to explain to them that Earth faces many more dangers than those they imagine for their homes, which would be swept away by such planetary calamities.

Most people are reluctant to discuss dangers of a planetary scale, believing that some kind of official or priest is needed for such deliberations. But when the era of understanding universal goalfitness arrives, all people will know how to gather the information needed to deal with even the most difficult hardships.

Children in schools should also learn to face all kinds of dangers, yet this knowledge should not deprive humanity of the ability to rejoice in life. Then, having completed a long life of experience, everyone will be able to say that in danger itself lies the source of joy.

The Thinker knew that every danger carries the seed of joy.

495. Urusvati knows that, although the symptoms are similar, there is a difference between the process of the discharge of psychic energy and its unexpected disturbance. In the first instance, irritation of the mucous membranes is linked to the increased discharge of psychic energy, which occurs during an intensification of mental activity. Likewise, a long-distance sending of energy causes tension in the glands and tissues, which are particularly affected when the cosmic currents are unfavorable.

However, the disruption of psychic energy is not always caused by mental overwork; it may also be the result of emotional shocks or grief, or even unexpected fortunate or unfortunate events. Threatening world events may thus cause epidemics, whose diverse symptoms may be ascribed to heart disease, colds, and stomach disorders, but whose true cause—the disruption of psychic energy—is overlooked. An increase in nervous ailments may also be noted during such epidemics, but people do not realize that ultimately all illnesses are related to the nervous system. And the treatment in all cases must be not only physical, but also spiritual. A calm striving toward lofty ideals is needed, and the quiet repetition of Solomon's saying, "And this too shall pass." If this kind of internal suggestion is not sufficient, outside suggestion can also be applied.

In addition, you already know some useful remedies, such as nux vomica, arsenium, ferrum, and, of course, our old friend, valerian, and, in cases of fatigue, musk. Warm baths are always beneficial. There are other remedies that depend on the particular bodily system that is affected. One can relieve the symptoms of psychic disturbance in all its phases.

Such increases in disease deserve immediate attention, since all illness connected with the nerve centers can spread quickly and should be checked. Ignorance of causes always leads to bad results. And if one adds to all this the various kinds of self-poisoning, a sad picture emerges.

One may grumble, "Again you want to frighten us!" But if this were so, all medical advice would seem just as frightening. If We see a new danger, We must warn you of it.

Some will mock the notion of striving toward lofty ideals. For them music and all arts are but idleness. They do not understand the word "ecstasy" and see it only as a harmful bent.

The Thinker knew such scoffers. He used to say, "The nation should expel such chronic ignoramuses. Let them find some island for themselves. But then the sea would protest and engulf such an island of ignorance! There are limits to how far the laws of nature can be violated."

496. Urusvati knows that everyone who acts wrongfully will, when challenged, claim that he was misunderstood. The more one learns about human motivation, the more one will be accused of such misunderstanding, and be blamed for the transgressions of others. But let us not try to point out all the varieties of human cunning—these would fill not just a book but an entire library!

It is amazing that people usually wait until it is too late to call for Our help. It may appear that they act this way because of shyness or timidity, but more often the true reason is quite different. Such people do not have faith, or even imagine, that there is a Source from which help can come. Only when their misfortune has taken them by the throat are they ready to remember the forgotten Towers. It is not only the uneducated but even the most learned who will ignore the highest concepts.

It is difficult to understand the human psyche that cannot distinguish between the beneficial and the harmful. Remember that people at times are so overwhelmed by all kinds of undisciplined desires that they themselves cannot even discern where desire ends and action begins.

The Thinker constantly taught the disciples to keep their store of desires in order.

497. Urusvati knows that the guiding inner voice does not always express itself in verbal formulas, and often is manifested just as an impulse. The inner voice acts as a tuning-fork, which evokes a harmonious response. It is to be noted that such responsive harmonies can be evoked in different ways. The tuning-fork calls forth and inspires, but the resultant action is shaped by the individual's present situation and previous thinking.

People are unaccustomed to heeding the inner voice. They prefer to suppress this Voice of the Silence, hiding it in the depths of consciousness, and thus lose the opportunity to make use of the offered impulse.

A boy once complained that he could not see his reflection in a well because his brother was throwing stones in it. Many can use the same argument, and blame their near ones for their own obscuring of consciousness. Truly, for all observations and conclusions a calm consciousness is needed, otherwise the perception will be distorted. But such calmness does not come from a renunciation of action. On the contrary, one can participate in all the best aspects of life while the consciousness remains calm. This is possible when man knows his future path.

The Thinker used to say, "Imagine yourselves as a millstone. It receives water power from above and works to make food for man. The wheel does not know who will be nourished by this food, nor does it know who will bring the grain for grinding. It does not know the component parts of the water in whose flow many energies are united. The Teaching should not isolate you from the perpetual course of labor, for the blessed current flows unceasingly."

498. Urusvati knows that people are especially attracted to the forbidden. It is told that a certain Ruler desired to introduce an enlightening, useful measure into life, yet everywhere met with opposition. He turned for help to a wise counselor, who asked,

"Have you tried every available means to declare your offer?" Receiving an affirmative answer, the counselor said, "Then you must issue a law that forbids the very things you are advocating. You will see how people will then desire the forbidden, and if the law is sufficiently strict, there will be an even greater desire to break it."

This old parable has equal meaning today. It can be shown how entire movements grow stronger and become purified because of prohibition. Throughout the entire world the unique tactica adversa sometimes proves to be the best way. It is amazing that humanity must go through such labyrinths when the simplest ways are available. But the spiral of evolution is complex. It even demands a temporary lowering in order to rotate higher later.

We know these earthly peculiarities and accept them as unavoidable. Even supermundane thoughts must follow a complicated human path. We must patiently observe how the travelers struggle up a difficult route instead of taking the shortest way. But if one is in the middle of crossing a stream, his movement cannot be disturbed. We can only lightly touch the one who walks, so carefully that he will not notice it and will not stumble and fall. Even the most well-meaning touch must be full of caution. One must learn this in earthly life too, amidst one's daily labor.

The Thinker used to say, "We must all sense where help can be applied. The less noticeable it is, the more perfect it is."

499. Urusvati knows the great importance of readiness for action. We have spoken of devotion, goalfitness, and containment. True readiness is demanded in everything. This quality should be remembered, because it is not easily attained.

People imagine that they are ready for action, but at the last moment they can be overwhelmed with doubt and self-pity. But readiness requires an increase of energy. A person who is about to jump cannot slow down before his leap, and must even accelerate to gather the most energy. Such an example is applicable to all actions.

Let people examine history to learn how many brilliant achievements were thwarted because of doubt that arose at the last moment. Let us not forget that the lowest impulse in people is to take no action, which facilitates the opposition by the dark forces to all useful action. They always choose the last moment to stop acts of bravery.

The Teacher should stress that courage must grow in harmony with readiness. There is a kind of still-born courage that is never ready and always finds excuses in the petty circumstances of daily life.

Thus remember that the best Forces will be with you, but only when your readiness has been developed in full measure.

The Thinker said, "Let us be ready, by day and by night, then the darkness itself will disappear."

500. Urusvati knows the irresistible longing to act for Good. This striving cannot be evoked by artificial measures, and can only be formed in the depths of the consciousness in the course of many lives. Such attainments must be treasured. Selfless action is not only good for the one who acts; it also creates an atmosphere that inspires others to useful work.

Majestic hymns and lofty treatises have been written in honor of labor. This is of course proper and good, but imagine the hard-working laborer who is chained for life to an unchanging task. Old stories tell us about oarsmen shackled to their ships and slaves bound to the turning millstone. Nowadays the chains are gone, but new kinds of shackles have been invented.

Hymns to labor sound quite different when sung under such unchanging conditions, under which workers can never advance. Leisure time for these workers continues with the same monotony, from which escape is often found in the horrors of drunkenness. It is easy to say that people should not drug themselves, but they should then be offered a higher alternative. They should be taught about the continuity of life and about supermundane processes. They should hear about the power of thought and the highest concepts. But they must also receive something else that will teach them to heighten the quality of labor—a craft must be provided to each one, for in one's craft one attains continual perfectment.

Under any conditions it is possible to learn some craft that will preserve youthful thinking, and transform one's home into a beautiful abode. Independence is gained by free creativeness! The development of crafts can be traced throughout the centuries. Such voluntary labor will resound forcefully, and much progress will result.

We have said that the rhythm of labor is a particular yoga. In every yoga is needed striving and exaltation. These flowers bloom in the garden of craftsmanship. Loving his craft, man will learn to love all labor, and will thus be closer to Us.

The Thinker taught that labor instilled with beauty will lead to perfectment.

501. Urusvati knows how often people complain that their efforts at self-betterment bring down upon them all kinds of misfortunes. Such a misconception is appalling. Certainly, a person who is truly committed to self-betterment will never utter such an absurdity.

He knows that with the refinement of the senses much becomes clearer than before. He does not wonder at being entrusted with participation in the battle for the welfare of the world.

Can such a battle be called a calamity? Only a coward would think that lifeless stagnation is preferable to life-giving activity. Yet one often meets with those who retreat because of fear and choose purposeless vegetation. They support their choice with examples from the lives of great saints, who, according to their interpretation, led a simple life, without complicating it with excessive philosophizing or challenging activity. But they forget that such hermits could project cosmic power with a single thought.

Who can measure the power of thought? Who can prove that the meek but enduring words ascribed to these thinkers are really authentic? After only a hundred years the sayings of outstanding individuals become distorted. What then can one expect after thousands of years? Nor can we know who distorted the most—their friends or their enemies. Often, the so-called friends, for their own personal reasons, distort the true meaning of the sayings. Let us not forget that the copyists also contributed their share. And you know how many printers' errors there are! Thus it was in all ages.

The Thinker said, "I would like to know in what form My writings will live."

502. Urusvati knows that the far-reaching embrace of the consciousness, or containment, must be clearly understood. Many think that containment means the acceptance of opposing arguments, but in fact containment is the understanding of true motives. One can understand with compassion the motives that guide one's interlocutor, but it is impermissible to

immediately give up one's own long-established and carefully-considered principles.

Containment has much in common with compassion. A compassionate person can clearly see how others err and act against themselves. But how careful one must be in trying to influence them! One should remember the ancient saying, "One does not argue about taste." There may be karmic reasons for one's tastes and inclinations, but often they can be traced to cultural conditioning. It is not possible to quickly help someone to eliminate such ingrained tendencies. Nor is it easy to persuade someone to question his own tastes when they differ from those of people around him, especially if his tastes cause no harm. The disharmony can be pointed out, but not everyone is capable of recognizing it.

Do not think that I am speaking about those strong habits that dominate people. Right now I refer to inclinations that are much deeper than habits.

The Thinker instructed, "If you learn to open your heart so that it can embrace another's pain, you will then be able to find the needed words of comfort."

503. Urusvati knows that unoccupied dwellings, without human psychic energy, quickly deteriorate. We have already spoken about machines that work differently depending upon the hands that operate them. This idea can be applied to more than the conditions in factories. Now we can point out an experiment that can be very easily conducted. Imagine three houses, all built in the same way. One remains unoccupied, the second is lived in by disharmonious people, and the third is the home of a harmonious family. It is instructive to observe how differently these buildings will react to these different conditions. The success of an entire state depends upon the quality of the psychic energy of its leader.

It is not education alone, or experience, but the inherent quality of one's psychic energy that enables one to overcome the most difficult obstacles. People often wonder how a particular individual can govern successfully without following accepted customs. If his personal physician had the necessary understanding of psychic energy, he would be able to point out the special qualities of the individual's psychic energy that explain his success.

Experiments with psychic energy do not require any unusual conditions. The primary energy flows everywhere, and it should be observed in all manifestations of life. And one can say that the simpler the way of observing it, the more valuable the experiment will be. Yet one special quality of this energy must be noted. You already know that the projection of psychic energy affects the glands of the sender. We have noticed that when We send energy to certain nations, the effect on Our glands is greatly intensified. This is explained by the difference in the psychology of nations. The energy cannot be assimilated harmoniously everywhere, and is sometimes even opposed. This may result in a reverse blow, which increases the irritation of the glands.

Try to understand that even people who are not hostile can possess a consciousness so peculiar that Our sendings of energy cannot be assimilated by them. That is why We consider the sending of energy to be a sacrifice. But humanity will not soon understand what sacrifice is meant.

The Thinker taught, "Do not expect that your thoughts will be welcome guests everywhere. Your best thought will bring you much sorrow. Like a beggar it will knock at all doors, but it will be rejected and, returning to you, will wound your heart. Do not grieve about this, for it is inevitable."

504. Urusvati knows that Hierarchy transforms even the smallest into the most valuable. It should be evident that this statement refers first of all to spiritual values, but people are so taken with the search for material wealth that even in such a spiritual context they will look only for a material meaning.

It would be instructive to see how many followers of Hierarchy would remain if We stated that Hierarchy cares only about spiritual values. One can observe how people try to search the Teaching for every hint that, in their opinion, refers to earthly wealth. Let us not blame such people too much, for most of them live in poverty. Yet, one can also meet quite well-to-do people who strive to Hierarchy only for the purpose of multiplying their earthly goods. These people do not understand that earthly goods are not given while on the path if the striving is only for the material.

Beware of those who approach out of a desire for earthly goods. They are glaring examples of the degree to which spiritual Teaching can be distorted. Even the smallest selfless contact with Hierarchy can solve many of life's problems. But higher knowledge cannot be sold for a pottage of lentils.

We grieve that the basis of much so-called spiritual striving is the pursuit of earthly goods. It is precisely then that such goods are beyond reach. Only by the realization of sacrifice can the true Treasure of the World be found. Examples of this should be offered, for people often avoid the most simple.

The Thinker requested His disciples not to think about earthly goods—at least for a few days! In this way, positive thinking was forged.

505. Urusvati knows that at times We deplore earthly success, and even sometimes rejoice at so-called earthly misfortune. Earthly successes and misfortunes are seen quite differently when observed from a supermundane level. In the Subtle World earthly adversity is quickly forgotten, but the effects of these forgotten calamities are not lost.

The refined spirit, while on Earth, longs for struggle and progress. For such a spirit, any pain or shock is but an impetus for achievement. The refined nature does not seek personal well-being, for it strives toward perfection.

Do not think that suffering is ordained for those on Earth. Perfection is ordained. It is disharmony on Earth that causes pain. As if in a narrow cave, one struggles to reach the distant light. How many scars and wounds will be inflicted by the sharp rocks? What slippery ascents await? There is nothing to grasp for safety if the concept of Hierarchy is not alive in the consciousness. We hasten to offer support whenever there is danger, which often appears just at those times of earthly success.

The measures of success and failure are quite idiosyncratic. The immediate surroundings of Earth prevent proper examination of what lies ahead, and without a supermundane understanding it is not possible to judge the earthly equilibrium. You know how varied Our help can be. It may be unrecognized, or perceived as misfortune. So many cannot understand what is happening to them, but in order to save the most valuable one must learn to give up the less important.

Later on it will not be understood why these words were said, and even the concept of Armageddon will be forgotten once again. But you know We are speaking at a time of great tension. Only supermundane measures can provide inner equilibrium.

The Thinker, seeing His fellow citizens preparing for war, said, "Friends, offer your best thoughts to your country."

506. Urusvati knows that science is the foundation for the future success of humanity. But this statement must be understood correctly. Scientists regard themselves as bearers of knowledge, but we must recognize that few of them understand the significance of the knowledge that will exist in the future.

We should not divide science into materialistic and idealistic, or supermundane and mundane. The key requirement for scientific progress must be known. Psychic energy must be applied in all realms of life. The acquiring of knowledge cannot move forward without the inspiration of the primary force. Thus, one can observe diligent scientists who skillfully collect significant materials but do not know how to assemble them into a beautiful discovery. On the other hand, one can see scientists who even with limited means are able to succeed and introduce useful innovations. Consciously or not, they know how to apply psychic energy, and do not reject it.

If you compile a list of those outstanding scientists who are already working with subtle energies, you will see that they exist in many countries, but are not united. Each of them approaches the understanding of psychic energy in his own way. All see the energy in different ways, as if some force compels them to avoid the simplest, essential way. Imagine how much strength would be gained if they were to unite their isolated efforts! They would learn to respect one another's research. Unfortunately, such respect is not sufficiently in evidence.

An open-minded researcher will attract sensitive co-workers. He must not be blamed for insufficient specialization, for psychic energy demands a broad scope of observation. Information should be collected from all sources, even the most ancient. Ancient writings must not be thought of as fiction. On the contrary, an unprejudiced mind will find in them many scientific indications, and will understand that there were entire eras in which the supermundane and the earthly were not seen as contradictory. Psychic energy will attract researchers only when it is understood as a bond between all worlds. The science of the future will be the source of the loftiest solutions.

The Thinker instructed His followers that science must be beautiful, for then it will know no limits.

507. Urusvati knows that the idea of intuition is often misinterpreted, or even abused. Even those who accept it do not understand it properly. They often suppose that intuition can be acquired without effort, and simply falls upon them from the sky. They do not think about the vast accumulations intuitive individuals must have and the enormous tensions they must endure.

We need not repeat to you about the existence of the subtle links between the worlds. You will often have to remind people about treating intuition with care. It is hard to imagine how few there are in whom this quality is already developed. Even then, for some of them it manifests itself only in certain ways. For example, if someone has premonitions regarding his dear ones, or can foretell physical events, or receive insights about himself, that does not mean that such a person can also intuit other kinds of events. One can expect no more from people than they can give. It is a mistake to ask of people more insights than they are capable of. The sea of subtle vibrations is inexhaustible. It cannot be embraced by one person.

It is important to know that the development of intuition requires an understanding of the condition of those around one. Only in a state of mutual caring can the inner voice be made clear. It is possible to develop the inner voice until it becomes continuous, but because of the chaotic vibrations on Earth, We do not advise you to try to overcome the conditions of the dense world to such an extent. Imagine someone who, amidst earthly activities, unceasingly listens to his inner voice. He would become like one who abandons his work in order to listen to the radio! He would perish, without sleep or nourishment.

Therefore, let the inner voice ring only when it is struck by a consonant vibration. In this way one will not abandon the earthly path, and will be in contact with the Higher World without disrupting one's inner equilibrium.

Throughout the ages, teachers have advised that the earthly path should be lived in earthly conditions. Only temporarily may one leave one's earthly tasks, and then only for the purpose of bringing more help to humanity.

People should learn to safeguard all the treasures entrusted to them, most especially psychic energy. It must not be thought that because it is the primary energy, it requires no care. Every cosmic substance is in need of harmony. On this is the economy of the Universe built.

The Thinker declared, "Safeguard harmony, for it can be broken as easily as the finest vessel."

508. Urusvati knows that We work to develop hard-working individuals of strong character and dynamic will. There are many who labor, but among them it is not easy to find people whose higher perceptions have already been developed. Entire generations must be cultivated before the ranks of new co-workers are sufficiently increased. The new co-workers may be isolated by earthly conditions. They will therefore be unable to know one another, and cannot join forces. They may also be so different from those around them that their qualities will provoke envy, and from an early age they will be subject to mockery and persecution. No wonder that their lives are not easy. They are like birds in cages, but even golden cages are prisons to them. However, these daring ones should not give way to despair. We note each of their steps and help to remove many dangers on their way. Even so, everyone who senses the way of service must walk cautiously. Great service excludes imprudent action.

I say to them: Do not give way to confusion. Even when reflecting, do not permit confusion to enter your mind, and sternly compare the ideas that are offered to you with the truth. Remember that confusion is a worm of decomposition. We have already spoken much about doubt, but be able also to discern the vibrations of confusion.

For the shortsighted, fear, doubt, and confusion are all in the same bag, but those who see clearly must know how to distinguish the various vibrations of these states. Some see confusion as shyness, but these two are quite different. Confusion is a clouding of the feelings. Our co-workers must have feelings that are clear and vigilant. Only in such watchfulness will Our co-workers be able to notice the viper.

May we see in every country growing numbers of true aspirants and co-workers, active in the best sense of the word. We want to see the Supermundane joined in full measure with all earthly labors.

The Thinker untiringly pointed out that those who strive must serve the highest laws.

509. Urusvati knows that each grain of truth must be accepted. The source of the truth matters not. It can be uttered in any language, can be clothed in the garments of any century, and can be proclaimed under any circumstances. There is neither old nor new truth. Who can prove that a truth was not long ago proclaimed on some long-vanished continent? Some heralds may have been distinguished by high learning, while others may have been illiterate, yet they were all sowers of truth.

You may wonder why We are reminding you of this. It is always necessary to repeat that the path of truth is broad. There will always appear those who claim that truth can be revealed only through them, but how can such impostors assume that their structure is firm? The chief enemy of truth is intolerance, and the more tolerance and benevolence there is the stronger will be the foundation. Every step of truth is directed toward the common good—this is the defining criterion.

Some may ask, "Where then is the love that we know is the pillar of the world?" But can common good exist without love? There must always be less criticism and more thoughtful care. Let us examine the garments in which truth has appeared throughout the ages. There was nakedness, but there were also sumptuous garments. Regrettably, naked truth is not always accepted, and must be embellished. We say this so that you will understand the truth more broadly. An attitude of benevolence should be cultivated in such a way that its sincerity is preserved. Amid earthly turmoil, true benevolence is not easily found, but without it one cannot assimilate even the simplest teaching.

Therefore what We say now is not an abstraction, but a daily reality.

The Thinker taught, "Benevolence is the distinguishing quality of the one who advances on the way."

510. Urusvati knows that the more complicated the circumstances are, the more calmness is needed. Do not take this as moralizing, but as medical advice. One cannot imagine to what a degree complex currents can damage the organism. That is why developing a state of calmness is beneficial.

It is well-known that people poison themselves and their surroundings with irritation, and though the dangers of imperil have already been mentioned, people choose to ignore them. Moreover, even when irritated they often insist that they are calm. We must learn to be honest with ourselves. Also, let us not forget that a simple moment of silence can calm the waves of agitation.

Physicians should examine people during states of agitation and irritation. They will discover the roots of future illnesses. Researchers may be astonished to see how illnesses can originate during periods of disrupted equilibrium. In a state of calmness, the predispositions are obscured and cannot be noticed, but under the influence of negativity they reveal themselves. Physicians usually ask a patient to calm himself before an examination, but calmness is not the most revealing state. Of course it is not always easy to be with a patient at the most revealing moment of agitation. Complete observation is needed, and it will be most instructive to see how negative forces activate dormant ailments.

Thus in all existence negative qualities increase when provoked. The smallest malicious thought can cause great damage.

The Thinker said, "Be your own physicians. The application of goodness is an excellent poultice."

511. Urusvati knows the many qualities of psychic energy. Its essence remains unchanged, but around this kernel there are quite diverse qualities. As an example, examine the effect of the composition of blood. At present much attention is paid to the various characteristics of nations, whose distinctions can be observed not only in the composition of the blood of the people, but also in the particular properties of their psychic energy.

The influence of the thinking of some nations can often be sensed quite strongly, whereas the thinking of other nations has little effect. For this, karmic causes or atavistic tendencies may be responsible, but one must also consider the way in which the composition of blood affects the psychic energy. It is not possible to enumerate all the bonds that exist between people. It is mankind's shame that it does not study these bonds and learn about such human qualities. Psychology should embrace all those scientific domains that enlighten the future of earthly life.

The study of thought, or in other words, psychic energy, has at present no place among the traditional sciences, and psychology is the only haven for its study. Today it is especially important to put these matters on a scientific basis. But for this the cooperation is required of a full range of scientists who have at their disposal the needed laboratories.

Is it not appalling that even today the sciences are divided into separate camps, with little connection between them? It is as if some sciences are accepted as authentic, while others are considered to be questionable! Of course, such doubt is based upon ignorance and prejudice.

One cannot imagine how strong these prejudices are. This must be repeated, from the loftiest palaces down to the lowliest huts. It is most likely that the strongest prejudices reside in the palaces. Thus one must continually repeat about the true mission of science.

The Thinker taught, "Learn to open the door to science. It would be a shame for it to remain in rags, out in the cold. Do you hear the knocking of knowledge at your door?"

512. Urusvati knows that supermundane explosions surpass all earthly ones. No earthly ear can hear them, but the developed subtle hearing can feel the tensions they create.

Many believe that people in positions of mundane power are especially sensitive to the supermundane battle, but that is not true. Those with earthly power can be quite remote from supermundane contact, but there do exist others who are messengers, the true bearers of the burden of this world. It is they who deserve to be called leaders, for they endure the highest tensions of the Supermundane.

Ordinary people are not aware of the columns and springs that support and maintain equilibrium. But the destroyers sense whence comes the psychic energy, and their missiles are directed to the chosen ones. Most people pay no attention to such super-battles. There does not yet exist an apparatus like a seismograph that could indicate supermundane tensions. One can only imagine the psychic tornadoes that rise beyond the firmament and merge with higher energies. This special time has its special signs, but people continue to dwell within their earthly limits, living like locusts. The Teacher advises the maintaining of calm as an earthly shield.

The Thinker used to say, "We are guarded on all paths. The manifested protection descends from above, but let us also provide our own shield against earthly arrows."

513. Urusvati knows that We disapprove of fear and suspicion, and consider them to be derived from ignorance. At the same time We insist upon vigilance and caution, qualities that belong to an enlightened consciousness. For the unwise it is not easy to discern the boundary between different feelings. They will see caution as suspiciousness, and vigilance as fearfulness, thus lowering the best qualities to a shameful level. But the wise will understand where caution is needed, based upon clear insight.

In a world that is torn by confusion the careless one is a fool. The sensible one will weigh all causes to determine the true source of harm. He will do this not out of fear, but with courageous resolve. He will not overlook the viper at his threshold, knowing that the seed of evil yields poisonous fruit. He will not think it unnecessary to pay attention to a small scorpion, for even out of the smallest can spring the deadliest sting.

You have noticed that there are times when one's ordinary activities are pushed aside by higher concerns. Those concerns often cannot be expressed in words, but the consciousness senses the high degree of tension in space. The wise understand clearly that there can be cosmic tensions requiring that all one's attention be directed to planetary conditions. There may occur illnesses, for the organism is affected by the currents of highest tension. At such times one cannot decide not to pay attention. On the contrary, all vigilance is needed, and all fear should be rejected.

We speak about the mundane and the Supermundane, for We, being always on watch, are in a position to state that Our vigilance is ever-increasing. Fortunately, vigilance can be developed without limit, and one should not hesitate to repeat that at times of highest tension, the highest degree of vigilance must be manifested. It is not fear that compels one to such an affirmation, but a desire to serve in the best possible way. Heroes are born out of this desire. We have spoken about the qualities of the hero, who fortunately can exist in all walks of life.

The Thinker said to His disciples, "Think of yourselves as heroes, and sense what heroic deed you can perform today."

514. Urusvati knows that psychic energy will in the future be studied carefully. Right now people have only a primitive sense of its presence, but in the future it will be shown that all scientific achievements must be connected with the study of psychic energy. In this, two things will be studied—psychic energy that is activated by will, and energy that is revealed seemingly spontaneously. The latter will demonstrate a particularly significant cosmic manifestation of the primary energy.

People already understand the power of thought and try to apply it. Thought-projection is becoming more common, but the question of spontaneous action of the psychic energy is less familiar. Until now, people have not recognized that the outpourings of the energy can have spatial significance. Yet it can be seen that certain powerful individuals emanate a force without being aware of it, and that power is often projected to great distances.

Why then are these individuals not aware when they participate in what may be a great event? They cooperate with the will of Cosmos. They cannot avoid this cooperation, and, like a consonant string, vibrate to the great projection of power. Such leaders intensify the planetary currents, and their deeds as saviors or destroyers of mankind should be studied.

One can easily observe striking manifestations that take place near certain leaders, but people cannot yet understand these happenings, and cannot even describe what they sense. They should direct their attention to the link between the earthly and the Supermundane. Let this be studied in a way that is appropriate for free and open-minded scientists.

The Thinker taught, "It must not be forgotten that everyone can perceive higher manifestations, but they must first admit them into their minds."

515. Urusvati knows that evolution must be voluntary, and cannot be forced. People refuse to understand that this basic principle applies to all aspects of evolution, and that the development of the seemingly insignificant is also part of the great cosmic evolution.

Those who ignite wars should think about the abyss into which they thrust the planet. Even a war that afflicts only a few countries promotes the destruction of the entire planet. No one thinks of war as a planetary sickness, yet one can see what improvements in life are cut short everywhere in the world by even local wars. Such convulsions are not needed when steady progress is possible.

Earthly sensations of pain fill space. Explosions shake the laboratories that work on the healing of nations. Let people think—are they not destroying something that cannot be rebuilt, that may have been built over the centuries by the Wise Ones? It is easy to destroy when one does not think on a cosmic level. But it is time to think about the harm that is inflicted on the Subtle World, and to develop a deeper understanding of the link between the worlds.

We have just said that evolution must be voluntary. Understand this broadly. Evolution is advanced not by coercion, but by human good will. Some think that evolution is propelled only by forces so high that human participation is useless. That misconception leads to most harmful consequences. People must be participants in evolution. They must intensify good will in order to merge their accumulated power with the current of higher energies. Man cannot be indifferent to the betterment of life. Man must stay vigilant, as a guardian of progress.

It must be understood that criticism and condemnation are bad weapons. This can be seen by observing the karma of nations. Those that condemn gather heavy clouds above them. Evolution is the realization of good. Let each one think about what he regards as good. He will at first err, and mistake his excessive ego as good will, but if he deepens his thinking he will ultimately discover within himself the true sparks of the common good.

We must not demand complicated terms and philosophizing. Evolution is harmonious and simple in the beauty of goalfitness. Thus we will labor for the common good, knowing that every sincere striving for good is already an active contribution. Thus we will learn benevolence.

The Thinker used to say, "If we collect only bitter herbs, our soup will also be bitter."

516. Urusvati knows that any act of negligence toward higher manifestations is inadmissible. It would seem that this warning should be quite clear, but it is often misinterpreted. People argue about the nature of higher manifestations, and claim that such manifestations are so rare that one does not encounter them in earthly life. Thus, they attempt to free themselves from the obligation to pay attention to higher manifestations in the midst of earthly life.

But those who are wise know that higher manifestations do indeed occur in the very midst of earthly existence. They understand that everyone, during a moment of inspiration, is already in a supermundane state, and can experience precisely those sensations that are linked with it. Every such state is a supermundane experience. It makes possible clairvoyance and clairaudience, but only when one acknowledges these latent abilities.

Some thinkers recognize that constant communion with higher manifestations is more valuable than a single striking experience. It is desirable for people to learn to refine their organisms for constant communion, though even one powerful manifestation can demonstrate the infinity of Higher Power.

The state of vigilance refines the organism, but one must also experience the tension that occurs when one is before the fiery gates; only by this test does man prove his true courage. Wisdom is courageous, for it is based on this test. No one can make claims for himself until he has stood before the Fiery Forces. Thus, one must be ready for the possibility of higher manifestations and love them. Negligence about this is a retreat into darkness.

The Thinker advised the testing of one's courage in all ordinary, everyday events. He said, "The one who can resolve domestic problems will not fear the most threatening attack."

517. Urusvati knows that calmness is a relative state. We advise the need to preserve calm, but We know that even with the best intentions, one can attain it only to a limited degree. Nevertheless, if one repeats

to oneself the need for calmness, it will be attained at least to some extent.

Let us not blame those who do not understand the true significance of calmness. They sometimes understand it as a state of inaction and absence of thought, but it is really a state of rest, and must be understood as harmony of thought. If one were to ask hermits how they achieve their equilibrium, they would explain that thought about the goalfitness of the universe is the best conduit to calmness.

People may notice that after some time their past concerns seem less important. Thus the test of time is realized. It can then be seen that while many seemingly important events over time lose their significance, less-noticed events are often recognized later as having been important turning-points. They are preserved in the deep memory of humanity, whose consciousness has its own measures.

One physician stated that in certain cases of dark despondency he made use of tactica adversa. Thus, when a patient insisted that everybody was turned against him, the physician commented, "Do not ignore the possibility of an earthquake, against which no human response is possible."

One should ponder upon calmness. There can be two extremes—eternal calmness, or eternal agitation. It is not possible to advance during a state of agitation, and inspiration will not descend upon those who are possessed by it.

The Thinker used to say, "A restless one is like a sack full of nutshells."

518. Urusvati knows the inner significance of earthly successes and failures. Even over short periods of time, their karmic significance can be observed, and one can see how at times just one small action tipped

the scales, how failure opened the best gates to victory, and success turned into loss.

One can observe all kinds of events in life, but only a study of the past can provide any clue to their causes. Only one who knows the causes can perceive the higher justice. What people experience as a misfortune may be an unavoidable consequence of actions performed long before.

Events on Earth have not only earthly causes but also supermundane ones. The karmic entanglements resulting from human actions on Earth continue into the Subtle World. True, much can be resolved in the Subtle World, but such resolutions do not take place often, because so many dwellers of the Subtle World make poor use of their opportunities there and spend all their time struggling with the effects of their earthly lives. They do not have sufficient determination to resolve their past errors and thus renew their consciousness. But the Subtle World offers many opportunities for such renewal, for the loftiest supermundane instructions are provided there. Let people remember, and learn to apply them in their future earthly life.

The Thinker indicated, "Let people draw enrichment in their lives from the supermundane source."

519. Urusvati knows that the earthly and the Supermundane must be understood as an indivisible reality. People tend to oppose such a concept. Some demean the earthly, and others blaspheme the Supermundane. We continually send thoughts about the harmony of these realms, but it is difficult to explain that far-sightedness and near-sightedness are just different qualities, and it is impossible to prefer one or the other. The far-sighted one does not see nearby objects, whereas the near-sighted one cannot perceive distant beauties. But it must be acknowledged that both capacities have their advantages. Let us not glorify the Supermundane by demeaning the earthly. The wholeness of the Universe is Beauty, and one must love all creation, for only then can one's mission be fulfilled.

Yogis often take pride in their attainments and forget that the toiler who works in harmony is not less than they. Similarly should one view the desire for longevity. When longevity is not justified by a particular mission, it can even contradict the law of nature. All natural acts must flow in harmony, and man should harken to the conditions of the world. Thus he will understand the natural yoga, which is the true link with the Highest.

We have said much about the three worlds that must be cognized. One cannot expect evolutionary development when the foundations of Be-ness have not been realized. Without this there can be convulsive disruptions, in which the elements of evolution will be destroyed. Thus let us harken to the groans of space.

The Thinker said, "Harken attentively, does not your ear catch the wailing of space?"

520. Urusvati knows how the pace of earthly events is often accelerated, in a way beyond human understanding. One may wonder whether such processes have only an earthly cause, but they clearly demonstrate their supermundane origins.

Truly, one can see evidence of supermundane activity by observing events on Earth. People are inclined to regard earthly events as an accidental sequence because they refuse to admit the presence of the Supermundane Mind. The ancient wisdom, however, was already aware of the Great Intelligence, or Nous. Such thinking permitted a balanced understanding of earthly events, but at present, despite the advances in science, progress in philosophy has lagged, thus engendering many calamities for which people cannot find a wise solution.

One can recall how a certain Ruler, before making an urgent decision, used to retire into solitude for at least a day in order to escape the assault of worldly concerns. One can apply one's thought to a critical matter, but it is even better to free one's thought to soar into the Supermundane World, to then return fortified by the power of the Supermundane.

People must learn to turn to the Supermundane World. Earthly events prove that people, despite everything, do not recognize the possibility of communion with the Source of Power. Many misfortunes plunge multitudes into despair, but even amidst calamities people do not know how to accept Help.

The Thinker often pointed out, "Do not give in to despair, for by doing so you reject the Help."

521. Urusvati knows the subtlety of the supermundane energies. Even powerful currents can be interrupted by earthly influences. It is difficult for people to perceive such manifestations, but you yourselves have experienced the way in which earthly disturbances can interfere with Our healing currents.

Thoughts sent by Us can easily be interrupted by human clamor. Sendings from afar are easily blocked by human obstructions. All this means that on Earth all interactions are subject to earthly law. It should be understood that for the acceptance of Our currents the organism must first of all be made more subtle by mental refinement. The broadening of consciousness was stressed long ago, but it is still misunderstood. People often believe that the broadening of consciousness is simply the acceptance of everything, but then the consciousness would be turned into a cheap roadside inn! A true broadening of consciousness must increase one's receptivity and discrimination. Only deep thinking can assist in such purification. For communion with Us one must learn to think.

He who does not know how to think properly loses himself in a tangled thicket of contradictions, instead of discovering all-encompassing meanings. Only through untiring striving can one free oneself from the web of earthly ties. Without free will, one cannot move toward a broad understanding of the unique aspects of the Supermundane.

We have just spoken about the indivisibility of the Supermundane and the earthly. Will it not seem a contradiction that We speak now about supermundane uniqueness? But there is no contradiction in the fact that one breathes differently upon the summit of a mountain than at its foot. Some people are afraid of the air of the summits, and similarly some fear to think about the Supermundane. This fear may be so great that it can paralyze the mind.

You know people who cannot think about the Supermundane. Psychiatrists should study these individuals in whom certain brain centers are dormant. For the development of the imagination lengthy experience with the most varied conditions is needed. A properly developed imagination saves one from fear.

Earthly pundits will tell you differently. According to them, the imagination is illusion and must be banished by earthly logic. However, it is more correct to live not by earthly logic, but by the law of higher reason. The ancient Nous allowed for the acknowledgment of the Supermundane World.

The Thinker revered reason as the path to the Supermundane.

522. Urusvati knows the joy of Universal Justice. Various names were given to this concept in different nations. Each one in its own language called it Karma, Moira, Fatum, Kismet—thus did people name destiny. Some approached it with joy, others with gloom. But no one denied the existence of the Law that revealed itself throughout Cosmos. The wisdom of this dynamic power indicates the harmony of the Universe.

Certain creeds attempted to destroy the profound significance of Cosmic Justice, and by doing this they fell into great error. It can be seen how the creeds that rose against truth soon lost their significance, and how those who respected the Cosmic Law were able to succeed.

If we trace the history of nations and of individual leaders, we will see that the law of Universal Justice is one of Beauty. Let us not dwell on signs of revenge, for the Law excludes such violence. It is goalfitness that proceeds from karmic justice and is glorified on the scales of balance. Let us again take the blindfold from the eyes of Themis. Justice must be all-seeing.

Let us not be terrified by cosmic events, but accept them with dignity as consequences of a great law. With attentive consideration we will perceive their true causes.

The Thinker prevailed upon His fellow citizens to develop keenness of sight, to learn to perceive the causes of events.

523. Urusvati knows how highly We value spiritual progress, which must include renunciation of self, and also an understanding of earthly conditions. The one who renounces everything earthly cannot be a fair judge of this, and similarly, the one completely involved in earthly concerns cannot rise above them sufficiently to observe fully. It is rare to find the person in whom these two attitudes are harmoniously reconciled. Most people see them as contradictory, because they do not know that spiritual advancement can be accomplished in ordinary life.

Monasteries were established to help strengthen those who were weak in spirit. But those monks who were strong went out to spread their teaching far and wide. They could not remain long in their hermitage. Their spiritual vessels filled, they felt a need to return to the world. Thus, they not only brought spiritual help, but also themselves acquired a knowledge of life. This aspect is not usually understood, because people are unaware of the needed harmony between renunciation and acceptance of daily life.

Those who deny earthly conditions also deprive themselves of mercy and compassion, without which spiritual development is not possible. The teaching of the regenerated world cannot live with hard-heartedness. Humane science cannot flourish where the heart is numb. Our Brotherhood could not have existed without a full experience of earthly conditions.

The Thinker advised His disciples to learn to understand the human glance.

524. Urusvati knows that a disorganized crowd generates especially harmful emanations. A crowd impelled by one emotion is somewhat less discordant. When researchers are able to apply scientific methods to the study of the human aura, they will see what deadly processes are generated by discordant currents.

One should not think that general accord in a crowd is easily attainable. People in any crowd exhibit dissimilar motives, and new poisonous emanations are generated, precisely because of disparate striving. Scientists must take this factor into consideration.

Never have populations massed in such numbers as

at present. Previous eras did not know gigantic cities such as now exist. Rome, during its period of decline, reached a population of ten million, but this accumulation only contributed to its ruin. Thus it is now. There are limits beyond which a Leviathan begins to decay.

Many indications are given that people should settle outside the cities, but all advice is ignored, and people poison themselves in their Babylons. One can already see that events have taken a direction that was warned about long ago. Once begun, a process follows its own logic, and cannot be stopped. What is engendered must grow. The challenge is to see the blessing in a transmutation that others will see as the destruction of the New Atlantis. The joy of transformation can create better forms of society, but are many ready for this joy?

The Thinker pointed out that the best joys are unknown to people.

525. Urusvati knows that people are responsible for three aspects of health. First, their own health; second, the health of the planet; and finally, the health of the Supermundane World. The last is not an exaggeration, for earthly dwellers must realize that they have no right to violate the harmony of the Supermundane World. Similarly, the health of the planet depends upon a wise use of its forces. Finally, people must safeguard their own health, not only for themselves but also for those around them. The human organism, though seemingly small, is a powerful repository of energy, and truly dominates its earthly environment.

A right understanding of these three kinds of health can provide true progress. When I speak about the individual's health, I naturally have in mind not only the bodily but also the spiritual health. The history of mankind demonstrates that evolution proceeds brilliantly when both conditions are in harmony. It can be seen that ancient Greece progressed when equal concern was given to the health of the athletes and the wisdom of the philosophers.

On the other hand, one can point to countries where sport became an obsession and the significance of the spirit was suppressed. It is easy to see to what such imbalance can lead. In such a society, those who speak about spiritual health will be accused of hypocrisy. We can point out how lofty knowledge and true service for the Common Good create the foundations for the health of the spirit.

One should not advocate renunciation of life, for the natural health of the spirit is forged in the furnace of life. Also, the health of the body must be understood sensibly. The gift of physical life must be safeguarded, but that should not be done at the expense of selflessness. It is difficult to find balance amidst life's contradictions, but a healthy spirit will pronounce its wise decision. A person can plunge into a dangerous current to save a dear one, but will not succumb to fever if he is carried by the wings of spirit.

Humanity can become the guardian of the planet if harmony of the spirit and body is attained. Humanity can send pure thoughts into supermundane worlds if the spirit is strong.

The Thinker asked, "Do you not think that we can help all the Muses by our thought?"

526. Urusvati knows how often, during transmission of thought, only some words reach their destination. There are several reasons for this. First, the words may not have been sent with equal strength. Also, there can be interfering currents that interrupt the transmission, or intrude with irrelevant information. Such currents are often the cause of insomnia.

If people could comprehend the storms that rage around them, they would learn to be cautious in all their actions. But they do not even admit that the words they hear can have a spatial origin. These storms are especially strong during earthly battles. This alone should remind one how closely linked are the clashes in the earthly and supermundane spheres. People should pay close attention to what they hear internally. There can be tensions that physicians would attribute to earthly causes, but they do not know that supermundane causes surpass earthly ones a hundredfold. People believe that the blue sky is empty, but science already knows about the filling of space. Is this idea so difficult?

You may hear cries of terror, but you also hear exclamations of joy. The wailing of terror reaches you more often, because in such outcries people put their greatest energy. People are weaker in their ability to express joy. At present, when so many horrors darken Earth, one can readily observe the emanations of despair. Scientists could conclude that if a cry of terror penetrates far into space, it must have been sent with a powerful energy, and emanates noticeable rays. It is quite true that each human word has its own aura and pierces space to a great distance.

Also, during troublesome times one can see unwise people who continue to live as if nothing is happening. It is amazing to see such foolishness, as if during a conflagration someone were to start dancing! But to fall into despair would be equally unwise. We stress calmness, the special kind of calmness that is based on a full knowledge of all that is happening. A wise person understands what actions are appropriate during world turmoil.

You can notice that during these days of aggravated tension We do not pronounce the word Armageddon—the parrots have taken possession of it. They repeat important words in every possible variation, but at the same time they dance upon a volcano.

We call out—fire! fire! But few understand what fire it is and what tension permeates the world.

The Thinker taught, "Each moment is witness to the destruction of heavenly bodies, and there are tensions so great that only a harmonious choir can prevent catastrophe."

527. Urusvati knows that Nirvana is a condition of high, harmonious intensification of energy. Paranirvana is a state of even higher tension. People believe that Nirvana is inaccessible to them, and for Samadhi lengthy bodily and spiritual exercises are needed. But let us remember that the human organism is a perfect microcosm, in which are contained infinite possibilities.

Everyone can experience fleeting sensations of Nirvana and Samadhi, but these hints pass so quickly that the earthly consciousness is incapable of assimilating them. A person may feel that he is losing consciousness for no reason, or has been ignited by an unexplainable fire, or has lost all sense of having weight. There is much that can be noticed only by a broadened consciousness. Only the exceptional, who are few, can understand what is happening. There have been many achievements by science, but not one has affirmed that everyone is able to experience the higher sensations. In order to do so the spirit must be kept pure.

Who, then, can achieve spiritual purification? Some may say that for this one must become a great philosopher, like Anaxagoras, Plato, or Pythagoras. But besides philosophers, the world was directed by such leaders as Pericles and Akbar, who left us memories of great ages of well-being. In addition to magnanimity and compassion, they demonstrated firmness in leading their nations on the path of salvation. Everyone has heard of the shoemaker Boehme, and the chemist Vaughan. There have been many such examples throughout the ages, and people can understand that spiritual purification is achievable in all walks of life.

At present, too, there are those on Earth who are conscious co-workers for the cause of evolution. People may not know them, but the crowd has never recognized the great achievements of the lowly. On Earth the hand and the foot are co-workers of the spirit. Those who carry the burden of evolution are not distinguished by royal garments, and they go unnoticed. History will reveal their path. People should rejoice that there are always special souls on Earth, who bolster their faith in the coming of the New Era.

The Thinker, even when He was sold into slavery, said, "This is splendid proof of the diversity of the human path."

528. Urusvati knows that a garland made of flowers that are in themselves beautiful can be beautiful or unsightly, depending on the chosen combinations. We teach you to speak with everyone according to the level of their consciousness. This does not mean that We want you to belittle your interlocutor. We want only to indicate that each person is different. Languages are different, and knowledge differs still more.

In any treasury can be found things of great value, but to find them it may be necessary to search through everything. You may become dirty and dust-covered, and perhaps endure insults and blasphemy, but afterward you may have in hand a great treasure.

Thus, in order to speak according to the level of consciousness of your interlocutor, you must first listen to him, sense his emanations, and understand his intent. Remember, all people are different, separated by profession and specialization, because the salutary synthesis of earlier education has been lost. Sometimes people yearn for a universal spoken and written language, forgetting that one should first of all think about mutual spiritual understanding.

There is a kind of preacher who does not take into consideration the mentality of his listeners. Such arrogance causes irreparable harm. These narrow-minded individuals do not understand the needs of their flock; they demand unquestioning faith, forgetting that faith is earned through knowledge. Yet they themselves not only lack knowledge, they also often have no power of attraction. I speak not only about preachers, but also about school teachers.

Simple advice about speaking according to the consciousness of the listener evokes much criticism. Sadly, people most often speak according to their own consciousness. This comes mostly from their inability to listen. Friends, learn to listen, and you will more easily reach your interlocutor. True, with an expanded consciousness it is easy to understand the individual nature of your interlocutor, but such a degree of insight is rare. Therefore, utilize ordinary human means. Mutual respect is akin to compassion.

The Thinker taught His followers to make garlands, saying, "He who finds the beautiful combination of flowers will also know how to find a useful combination of people."

529. Urusvati knows how great is the joy of being

able to live in the future. Such a way of life is in harmony with evolution. One must learn not to belittle the past and to understand that the present does not exist—everything either was or will be.

It is not easy to perceive the future as reality. People are not able to think about the future because they are afraid of it. They fear that the future will not include them. They do not wish to think about the continuity of life and have no idea that they can cooperate with a Subtle World. Thus, they cut themselves off from the future, do not want to know the past, and remain in a present that does not exist. Remaining thus with nothing is a most dangerous state. But people could so easily connect themselves to the future, especially nowadays, when science is making such progress.

We rejoice when We see in others the ability to connect to the future. Such striving is like the hoisting of an anchor, which permits one to set sail to the salutary shore. Striving into the future is at the Foundation of the Brotherhood. Events follow a Plan, and one must cognize the structure of the Universe in order to become accustomed to Infinity. One cannot fall permanently in the Infinite, for an infinite future will always permit one to find progress. Try to imagine an earthly life with no past or future; how wearisome life would be as if on a tiny island in the midst of an ocean. True, one would always have the possibility of looking upward—but only if one were sufficiently farsighted.

The Thinker sorrowed for those who could not feel joy about the future and knew not how to look upward.

530. Urusvati knows about the appearance of new diseases. They are extraordinarily varied, but come mainly from inflammations of the glands. The inflamed glands discharge secretions to either an excessive or insufficient degree. The glands themselves may enlarge, or may shrink, even to the point of disappearing.

People could exchange helpful information about these ailments, but they fail to do this, and thus encourage the spread of epidemics. It can be observed that the pulse and the temperature fluctuate greatly, and there can be pains in the nerve centers.

These ailments are not caused by people themselves, but are rather the result of spatial reactions, which set up a kind of vicious circle. By their thoughts and actions people increase the intensity of the spatial reactions, but these, like a boomerang, strike back at them. Thus, a dangerous epidemic develops. Physicians do not recognize the new symptoms, and continue to resort to old diagnoses. Naturally, the spatial reactions affect the weaker organs, and provoke a great variety of new symptoms.

It can be said that humanity poisons itself, and that the more refined organisms suffer. Thus, with the advent of very dangerous events, new illnesses appear. Regrettably, history does not record this, but we have compiled records that reveal how mankind punishes itself.

The Thinker constantly conferred with physicians, to discover whether they could notice the waves of epidemics.

531. Urusvati knows that We call the new epidemic "the yellow sickness," for it causes a yellow pigmentation, not only of the secretions but also of all the mucous membranes. This sickness should not be allowed to spread.

It is important to maintain a calm mood. This needs to be explained. Bad moods should not be blamed on indigestion or colds. People should understand that the causes will be found in the nerve centers, which receive impulses from spatial reactions. The time will come when physicians will be able to discern which center is afflicted, but as yet they only speak of weak nerves and treat them with drugs.

It is time to come to an understanding of the importance of the nervous system, which connects man to the Supermundane. The important matter is not that someone suffers from weak nerves, but rather what centers are affected, and what spatial reactions are afflicting them. Thus science can uncover evidence from the highest realms for further research. It must be recognized that the psychic energy of space can be studied, and that earthly life can be improved during just one generation.

The Thinker taught, "Every drop of water contains a world, just as every particle of air is a microcosm."

532. Urusvati knows that We advise a realistic, scientific approach to everything. Even the loftiest inspiration must be confirmed by scientific investigation. One should not think that such an approach is belittling. Many beautiful ideas lose their support because of an illogical attitude. Faith without reason must be replaced by the light of real knowledge.

Even the best adherents of the great religions turned to science in order to find support for their beliefs. But let us not forget that knowledge must be gained without prejudice. There are many scientists who in reality are hypocrites, and undermine the beautiful freedom of science. The Supermundane provides broad possibilities for scientific work. You yourselves can see how constrained is today's human thinking.

It can be demonstrated that even in antiquity exceptional minds were not afraid to think about living space. Sometimes they peopled it strangely, influenced by the ideas of their time, but still the daring of their thought was great. We gained our knowledge through both experimental and theoretical ways, because both ways, in their highest state, achieve the same results. It should not be thought that We want to impose Our ideas upon you. We want only to remove the fetters that impede the progress of humanity.

The Thinker taught, "Leave your fetters behind, for they prevent you from thinking freely."

533. Urusvati knows that under certain conditions blood transfusions are permissible. There can also be transfusions of psychic energy. It will take a long time for physicians to discover techniques for accomplishing this, but it can happen spontaneously when the emanations of individuals come into contact.

In the future the process of transfusing psychic energy will be a common event. The harmony of humanity can be augmented when the distribution of psychic energy has been mastered. If blood can be given to others without harm, the same can be done with psychic energy. For transfusions of blood the physical health of the organism and hereditary factors should be taken into account, but for the exchange of psychic energy more subtle conditions must be considered—it is essential that the energies involved be compatible. This can be determined by scientific methods. For example, certain residual precipitates of energy are discharged during exhalation, and they can be caught on a highly-polished metallic plate.

To be fair, it should be acknowledged that this method was used in antiquity. The alloy, of which the plate was made, and of which We already have spoken, was particularly valued, but scientists today pay no attention to ancient knowledge. Thus, they did not study the recent approach of Mars from the point of view of psychic energy. People repeatedly spoke at that time about the approach of war, but they never thought of observing the condition of the human brain, which had been poisoned by the influence of Mars.

It is regrettable that people do not make use of all the information provided by nature. For example, people know long in advance about an eclipse, but do not examine evidence of its influence on the human psyche.

The Thinker taught, "Do not lose those moments when Nature offers Her revelations."

534. Urusvati knows that vampirism of energy is the complete opposite of the true, harmonious, mutual exchange of energy. It must not be forgotten that this kind of vampirism is widespread and science does not know how to oppose it. Physical means are of no use where psychic energy is abused.

Poorly-informed people know nothing about the borderline between vampirism and a beneficial transfusion of energy. They judge according to their own limited measures, and suppose that any acceptance of energy must be an act of egoism. They cannot imagine that in some instances it is urgent to manifest a special outpouring of energy. Such an act of giving is not performed for oneself, but for the Common Welfare.

One ought not be surprised that the refined energy has its own unique properties. Manifestations of the primary energy are as varied as are all cosmic manifestations. For the ignorant all nature is uniform, but for those who think, the incalculable and varied bounty of the Universe is clear. There is no point in arguing with those who do not accept a scientific approach to cosmic manifestations.

It is astonishing that man customarily refuses

to gain knowledge of the very laws of existence that would be of most benefit to him. In these conflicts one can see the eternal battle of chaos with the manifested order. Do not be too disturbed when you see how difficult it is for people to assimilate the simplest foundations of life.

The Thinker at times admonished those who argued, pointing out that the simplest is always assimilated with particular difficulty.

535. Urusvati knows that the emanations of psychic energy can be seen as a slight vapor, or as a radiance. But the inexperienced eye cannot see these manifestations. Generally, people cannot understand why many unexpected psychic manifestations are visible, whereas tensely awaited ones are not. People should simply remember that many exterior energies surround them and act upon them.

There are many times when people do not acknowledge even obvious phenomena, and explain them away as being caused from within themselves. The reason for these errors lies in the fact that people do not think about external influences, and if they do, they see them only as an interference. Such thinking leaves no room for cooperation.

Any cooperation for a good purpose is of value, but of greatest value is psychic cooperation. Until now no attention has been given to the deep significance of such cooperation. During certain gatherings of philosophers it was customary to become immersed in deep contemplation, but this custom usually led to a tendency to preoccupation with the self, and mental collaboration became impossible.

Many orators can testify that at times their speeches are particularly convincing and vivid, as if some powerful energy is driving them. Certainly, there may be supermundane influences, but there can also be the helpful influence of the thoughts of co-workers and listeners. On the other hand, some orators can testify that sometimes there are complete disruptions in the flow of their thoughts. Words fail them and they cannot utter even their already prepared texts. This is caused by the disorderly thinking of their audience. We are not aware of any scientists who investigate such occurrences. If the influence of thought is not studied, it is no wonder that supermundane influences are not recognized.

The Thinker taught, "Let us not forget about the invisible friends and enemies."

536. Urusvati knows that every human touch has a magnetic effect. Because of this some people refuse to shake hands. The time has come for science to explore the conditions necessary for therapeutic massage. Generally, more attention is paid to the physical aspects of massage, and the many beneficial substances that medical science prescribes for rubbing into the skin. People see these methods as very important, and of all the many available approaches to healing, the great benefit of such massage is recognized. However, it has been forgotten that the role of the therapist must be understood, for this is more important than the massage itself.

Only when there is a harmonious blending of psychic energies is healing possible. Observe that massage can have different effects on people with identical ailments. There are many cases when the light touch of a sympathetic hand acts as the best remedy, but it is also possible that even the best physical massage can sometimes cause harm. Physicians and nurses should be tested for the quality of their psychic energy. Not only faith in the physician is needed, but also the beneficence of his energy.

Such preliminary preventive studies will permit an improvement in the health of people. It should not be thought that an inharmonious energy is bad energy. It is simply not in harmony with the energy of the patient, and the harm it causes can be considerable.

The Thinker insisted that people learn to accept and understand the importance of harmony, otherwise any dog would be in a better situation.

537. Urusvati knows how manifold are the qualities of psychic energy. They can be explored by studying vibrations and emanations. In the future, this will be made possible by the use of more sensitive apparatuses that will become available. But there is one method that can be utilized now. We have already spoken about the magnetization of water. You yourselves observed to what extent, and how quickly, water takes on the properties of the psychic energy of the one who magnetizes it.

It can be observed how individual is the effect of a person's psychic energy on water placed near his head. One can also note which minerals added to the water aid in these observations. Iron is useful, but sulfurs are not.

These tests were frequently performed in earlier times. Sometimes a few drops of wood oil were poured upon the surface of the water. This was thought to aid the action of the currents of energy. Attention was also given to the vessel, a copper one being preferable to pottery. The walls of the vessel had to be polished, and the vessel was not used in the household, but was kept closed, with a copper cover. All this indicates how much thought was given to these tests.

It is probable that there were other ways of observing the various qualities of psychic energy. Of course, the ancients called their observations divination. That is why these observations were dismissed as non-scientific. We are again pointing out to you the thinking spirit of man, which always recognized the immutability of the foundations. One can smile at the way in which most people are satisfied with superficial terminology, but the essential is unchangeable, and among the ancient customs there can be found true scientific knowledge.

The Thinker instructed, "Do not think that your ancestors were fools. You have forgotten much that was achieved by them."

538. Urusvati knows about the transmittance of sensations and feelings at a distance. This confirms even more the presence of the psychic energy that permeates all of space. Let us not forget that teraphim can be used to facilitate such transmissions, but there is no need to hold any kind of image if the energy is being sent by command of the will. Teraphim can serve to help the transmittance, but a strong will has no need for such assistance.

In life, transmissions of sensations occur as often as do thought transmissions, but they are overlooked by people. Sensations can be transmitted consciously and intentionally, but also unconsciously. The unconscious transmissions are far more frequent than conscious ones, and can cause painful sensations and moods.

In the future humanity will be able to integrate the entire vast realm of thought. Even governments will recognize to what extent life is permeated with such powerful energies. One should not think that this aspect of life can be ignored, for it is as material as the physical body.

The Teaching of Life must, first of all, point out

the true essence of human existence. One should not think that only wizards or magicians can control the forces of nature. Everyone lives in contact with this powerful energy, but unfortunately many do not wish to learn about this advantage. Countless books have been written about aspects of the sacred knowledge, but they will be of no use until man becomes aware of his own capabilities.

All teachings, even those containing the most urgent counsels, are read casually, as if they were just curious stories. People do not understand that these writings are given to them for immediate application.

The Thinker urged His fellow-citizens to recognize the World that, though invisible, can be sensed.

539. Urusvati knows the many warnings and instructions that have been sent to humanity. Compare the teachings of Pythagoras, the letters of Prester John, the activities of St. Germain, and the letters of the Mahatmas. You will find in all of them a concern for the purifying of humanity.

It matters not in which languages they were given or how they were adapted to each era. The fundamental ideas underlying all of them can be traced. Sometimes the writings were considered to be forgeries, but is it not obvious that the same thoughts lived throughout the ages? Many of the writings were attributed to particular individuals, but far more of them were anonymous. One can see how all of them found their following in various countries. This vast literature should be studied; it has never been fully collected, and the inner meanings of the many writings have not been adequately compared.

People often complain that they have no guidance, but the library shelves are stuffed with these manuscripts and printed works. You need only examine them, and you will see how many authors, known and unknown, labored for the evolution of humanity. Some of them wrote under various pseudonyms, and it is therefore not possible to collect the works according to the authors, but only according to the variations in their inner meaning.

We do not see Our names as being of great importance. These names change often in Our long lives. We value the labor itself, and do not pay attention to whether the author's name can be found on the top or the bottom shelf.

Let us not forget how many manuscripts have been destroyed by the hands of enemies.

The Thinker used to say, "Can We be certain that Our writings will be preserved under Our names? Let us not concern ourselves about it, for such thoughts are but a waste of time."

540. Urusvati knows that many important writings can be found not in state libraries, but in family archives. State repositories do not contain all the manuscripts that exist, and it would be a mistake to think that even the vast numbers of published books encompass all the important problems of life. On the contrary, We can assure you that the most important writings remain unpublished, and may be disintegrating in family cellars.

It is horrifying to think that so many unique achievements that can never be repeated are perishing. The safeguarding of private archives must be undertaken, but this is not an easy task.

Nor should one assume that material by well-known people will always be of great interest. Remarkable materials may have been written down by unknown, ordinary people. They could have been witnesses to significant events, or have recorded important statements from older generations that were later never repeated and could now be lost because no one has thought of publishing them.

Likewise, many chronicles are languishing in the monasteries and temples of various faiths. A great quantity has already been lost, but much still lies buried in the dust. It should not be thought that information on various questions does not exist. People should be aware that much was carefully written down but remains hidden in dark corners. Let everyone pay close attention whenever they hear that manuscripts are preserved somewhere. Brilliant ideas were left buried because of timidity or indifference, and many bundles of manuscripts lie unexamined in the storehouses of libraries.

The Thinker encouraged in His pupils a commitment to preserve family archives.

541. Urusvati knows how great a task is the study of family archives. In them important events may be mentioned only casually, and known names referred to only by initials, nicknames, or even code names. Entire accounts may have been written in an intentionally obscured way. This often happens because of a fear of persecution. Therefore, many archives, including some that have already been studied, actually contain much of importance that has gone undiscovered.

Archives such as those of the Duc de Choiseul, Goethe, and Stroganov contain valuable information, with many hints about the inner life of Our Brotherhood. We should be grateful to Madame Adhmar for the writings left by her. Without them much information about the activities of St. Germain would not have been known. One could wonder why the writings of Madame Adhmar were needed when We Ourselves could have made it all the clearer. But people value the testimony of contemporaries, and in the eyes of humanity such records are more substantial proof than Our anonymous information.

Arabian records, and also those of Iran, should be studied. In those archives can be found many travel memoirs that clearly reveal why We speak so often about cooperation between peoples. Similar narratives, repeated in different ages by historic personages, offer vivid testimony to this.

It is astonishing to see how the information about the Brotherhood was able to reach unexpected places. Such records can be found in Ireland, in Norway, and in Spain, where information was brought by seafarers from the East. Let the explorers not cease their quest, for unexpected discoveries await them!

The Thinker taught His disciples not to despair. "Seekers, there is no limit to discovery. Continue your search."

542. Urusvati knows that the training of the faculty of thinking is at the foundation of Our Inner Life. It is wrong to believe that after reaching a certain level one's thinking cannot be further developed. Thinking must be inculcated in early life, and continuously cultivated. Those who consider life to be an idle parade of events should be pitied; labor is necessary in everything, just as in the sharpening of thought.

We pity those who imagine that there is no need to think. A vast portion of humanity does not know how to think properly—one cannot consider disorderly fragments of vague thought as thinking. They are formed out of chaos and melt away as quickly as snowflakes under the sun. Many people will find an existence based on thinking to be extremely tedious.

You long to know more about Our Inner Life. The currents bring to Us a surfeit of earthly turmoil, but even in the midst of such chaos We find the time to think. Not much time is needed to create thought-forms, whose clarity is achieved through constant training. These exercises do not require a specific mood. When one's heart strives toward the Common Good, all of one's thoughts are attuned to it. The striving can be austere or joyous, or steadily compassionate; all can be the keynote of one's thinking.

But the precision and clarity of the thought-form also depends upon the reserve of psychic energy. Some people think that We do not have to worry about maintaining this reserve. They do not understand that the reserve of energy must be preserved. For some, the store of psychic energy is regained only slowly, while others can achieve it more quickly. For still others it is enough to close the eyes and take a deep breath, and the energy is regained. We too must replenish Our reserve; it would be unscientific to deny it.

Sometimes you do not receive a quick reply to your questions. Perhaps at that moment urgent events are taking place, or We are occupied with replenishing Our store of psychic energy. Let us think about everything in a human way and we will not err. Thus the microcosm will understand the condition of the Macrocosm. Think humanely about Our Inner Life, and in all your thoughts preserve the beauty of the thought-form and learn to love the idea of labor for the Common Good.

The Thinker said, "If we could apply all our power to love, we would always be successful."

543. Urusvati knows that a permanent state of vigilance is one of the foundations of Our Inner Life. Do not think that such watchfulness is something supernatural. There are many people who possess this particular sensitivity, and can sense unusual vibrations

and changes around them even during sleep. This state occurs without lengthy preparation, for the psychic energy works independently when outer conditions do not burden it. Therefore, if the energy functions freely, even unconsciously, how much more powerful it will be when it is consciously cultivated! If you also consider the longevity of Our souls, you will then be able to imagine how Our own qualities develop.

People think that this continuous vigilance must be unbearable, but such apprehension is unfounded. No active worker who is a master of his craft considers his work to be intolerable. He is so accustomed to it that he cannot live without it.

Likewise, a state of high sensitivity, consciously developed, will not be a burden. It becomes one's natural state, especially when one's level of development is such that less sleep is needed. Such sleep is more properly understood as a state of vigilant repose rather than slumber.

We do not always release the subtle body. In this way We can retain consciousness during Our repose. If any of Us wishes to enter the Subtle World, then a Friend assumes the state of vigilance. He also watches over the body, in order to prevent undesirable currents from approaching. Thus you can see that vigilance, with the help of certain apparatuses, is a necessary condition of Our Inner Life.

The Thinker taught, "Let everyone develop sensitivity; then success will follow a hundredfold."

544. Urusvati knows that some aspects of Our Inner Life are misinterpreted. For example, it is said that We favor those to whom We were close in previous lives. Because of their ignorance, people see this as unfair, yet they themselves prefer to work with people whom they have come to trust. No one would consider such a choice unjust. This is simply human nature.

Let us also not forget the harmony needed for collaboration. Much time is required to achieve a harmony of the nerve centers. We need harmonious strivings, in order not to waste Our energy. Who can better assist the common work if not those who were already associated with it at some time in the past? It is understandable that We choose trusted workers from those who have already labored for Common Good.

We help those who are entrusted with a special mission. And this is just, because around these messengers burdensome currents will collect. Many are those who would like to get rid of such workers. If they could, they would dispose of Us too! But it cannot be claimed that We will work only with old friends. The gates are open to all for cooperation, but only tested co-workers can understand the full meaning of trust—of great trust to the very end, in spite of all. Such conditions of cooperation are not forced on anyone, nor commanded, but learned through experience. Likewise, only experience reveals the way in which Our help comes, but the narrow-minded fail to recognize it, because they can judge only according to their own restricted field of vision.

The Thinker affirmed, "Higher Help is so beautiful that only a refined mind can grasp its beauty."

545. Urusvati knows that some people fall into negativity and even accuse Us of self-centeredness. They state that We offer help only where there is benefit to Us, that We deny help to those who ask for it, and, finally, that We do not provide help in the form that people expect. Such accusations are often spoken, but more often they are thought.

People refuse to understand that help is possible

only when based upon cosmic and karmic laws. They are reluctant to acknowledge that harmonious unification can be achieved only with much time and mutual effort. People shout for help, without concern about how they should prepare for it. In illnesses appeals are sent to Us only after the organism has been irreparably damaged.

Listen to all those unspoken and spoken accusations against Us, calling Us cruel idlers who are unwilling to offer even a part of Our inexhaustible energy! Thus, even people who have heard about Us and have heard about goalfitness and co-measurement, accuse Us, because these concepts remain abstract for them. Sometimes those who know nothing about Us cause less harm than those who do know, yet irresponsibly pollute space.

The Teaching clearly indicates how wisely the energy must be distributed. It must not be used in ways that can cause harm. Indeed, Our Inner Life has many facets that could be ameliorated with sensible human cooperation.

The Thinker begged His disciples to act goal-fittingly. He said, "Learn to send your arrow into the heart of the target."

546. Urusvati knows that the inner life of those who labor for Us is founded upon various forms of inner discipline. Independence of action, courage, goalfitness, tirelessness, compassion, reverence for Hierarchy, and many other qualities are developed diligently and consciously. One cannot imagine leading a sensible life if it is still subject to chaotic behavior.

Our workers know that each aspect of inner discipline is developed by them of their own free will. They do not regret the effort required to achieve it. They understand that self-reliance must be developed to the fullest. Before turning to the Guide, each student will first ask himself whether he has exhausted all possibilities on his own. Every aspect of discipline can be cultivated under any of life's conditions. People do not understand this; they think of Us and Ours as imperious and rich, and do not know that We endure all the difficulties of life and gain strength through them. Few people agree to experience to the fullest the chain of earthly lives, with their plethora of sorrows caused by human ignorance. It is best to accept the burden in full rather than to shuttle back and forth on the same path. Our co-workers know that all forms of discipline are necessary for progress.

The Teaching explains clearly the task of Our co-workers, and each one must decide in each life which aspects of inner discipline are needed. Our Inner Life is based on strict inner discipline.

The Thinker insisted that His disciples should learn to love discipline, for without it one cannot become strong in action.

547. Urusvati knows that everything in the world is unique and unrepeatable. The law is one, but it is expressed in matter in innumerable ways. There are two kinds of people, those who sense this unrepeatable abundance of Cosmos, and those for whom all is unchanging, uniform, with neither significance nor beauty. In the second group you will find people with inflated egos, who place themselves higher than all the great manifestations of nature.

Certain apparatuses used by Us reveal incalculable varieties of energy and matter. The pendulum of life is one of these apparatuses. It can be used for the analyzing of soil, for revealing the qualities of psychic energy, and for demonstrating thought transmission. In the last, it can be observed how thought impels the psychic energy and acts with great speed. Those to whom thoughts are sent sometimes think that the pendulum expresses their own thoughts. This may seem so because the thoughts sent were already impressed on their consciousness before being demonstrated by the pendulum. In any case, the pendulum shows how thought is transferred into physical energy.

Some apparatuses require the transmission of each letter separately, and need the participation of more than one person; thus they resemble the physical telegraph. But We are speaking now about mental transmission; the pendulum shows how thoughts are formed. Their diversity can be perceived according to the way the pendulum responds to the psychic energy. Only a sensitive eye can discern the individual details.

The Thinker pointed out in His writings the infinite variety of individual traits in the human soul.

548. Urusvati knows that cruelty, rudeness, hypocrisy, and falsehood impede the evolution of humanity. If science, proud in its achievements and successes, cannot help to promote humaneness, and art does not succeed in elevating the consciousness, then all is not happy in the world!

The social sciences point out the bases of human progress, and in none can one find praise for the above-mentioned vices. All of them speak about the same thing, the elevation of human consciousness. Even the most extreme teachings do not support falsehood. But neither science, art, nor religion can uproot those vices that constrain man like fetters.

Do not forget that science, art, and religion have at times been the excuse for the most wicked activities. Members of some philosophical societies devote their meetings to discourses about higher subjects, but immediately afterwards indulge in the most shameful behavior. One should search for the root of all social illnesses. Only the healing of the inner life will help to elevate the social life.

Besides scientific learning, besides the brief exaltation inspired by art, courage is fundamental to the betterment of the inner life. Patience and courage develop together. One who is patient will also have courage and endurance.

Chaos should be opposed by better traits that live within us. Only by individual effort can one continuously ascend. People fear the word "ethics," yet too easily talk about morality, as if these concepts did not have some foundation. But human moral character will not change except through the influence of the inner life.

The Thinker taught, "The character of the people will shape human history. Let these fires be resplendently aflame."

549. Urusvati knows the affinities and aversions that arise in human relations. Often people cannot understand the causes of such mounting feelings. Beyond the possible karmic and physical causes there must be something else that raises walls between people. These walls exist and only differences in psychic energy can be the cause.

It can be observed that people with insufficient psychic energy begin to hate those who possess it to a high degree. People do not understand this, and search elsewhere for the cause of this enmity. Envy also grows from the same root.

It is instructive to study the various human types. There are of course racial and class differences, but there is something beyond these that is universal. Differences in the characteristics of their psychic energy can often provoke animosity between people. Most do not know the true reasons for the hatred and envy in their hearts. The true cause is beyond their understanding, for they know nothing about psychic energy, which for them is an empty abstraction. Such people are spiritual paupers, whatever their race or class.

Every envier, slanderer, or hater is a spiritual pauper. He deprives himself of the higher accumulations by having no interest in learning about the foundations of Be-ness. It is painful for Us to see how such paupers harm themselves and others. It is even impossible to offer them relief, since those who offer are hated by them.

The Thinker knew such uncompromising deniers. He said about them, "Look how the burden of hatred bends their backs."

550. Urusvati knows that those who attempt possession cannot tolerate large stores of psychic energy in others. They are repelled, just as arrows are deflected by a sturdy shield. Their malice is then intensified, and their hatred increased, even to their own detriment. One can often observe that the obsessed act irrationally, driven only by the urge to commit evil.

It should be understood that many villainies are committed in order to placate some invisible evildoers. People usually call them demons, but it is simpler to call them dregs. However, a powerful demon is not needed for the development of obsession. Everyone on Earth with a criminal nature is driven to become an obsessor and thus feed his unsatisfied hatred.

It should be acknowledged that not only the fainthearted, but also those who give in to doubt become easy prey to possessors. When this illness occurs, the possessed one loses awareness of what he does, and those around him are astonished by the sudden change in his personality. But the time will come when scientific apparatuses will exist that will be able to reveal the dual personality of these dangerously ill people. Many terrible events in history happened because of possessed people. Let us not forget this.

The Thinker said, "At times it seems that not archons, but ghosts, craving blood-drenched food, are speaking."

551. Urusvati knows that certain apparently progressive leaders actually live retrogressive lives. They are not true leaders, but transitory corrupters. In spreading the higher Truth, just as in any walk of life, setting a personal example is necessary.

One can talk about ideas of patience, valor, or mercy, but only if one has the courage to manifest these qualities. We should search our own past to determine whether we were able to be heroes or martyrs—if we were, we then have a right to proclaim these fundamentals of earthly existence. But in the search through one's past, one must not limit oneself to seeking evidence of some great deed, glorified throughout the nation! There is wonderful evidence also to be found amidst the daily routines of life, in which inner chaos can be overcome and the wild beast tamed. Every good deed must be valued. It is not only the great deed for the sake of the nation, but also the small, barely-noticed achievement that can lead to mastering a higher step.

I have already told you that it is hard to discern the boundary between great and small deeds. Truly, a so-called small deed can be an excellent seed for future germination. We know whereof We speak. People call these tests, but is it not better to call them perfectment? Why lament tests when one can rejoice at perfectment and progress?

The Thinker urged His disciples to have successes every day, even if in ordinary pursuits.

552. Urusvati knows that the inception of an illness is of greater significance than what follows. We warn about the inception, because later no help is possible. The inception easily permits treatment through the mind. I am speaking here about both psychic and physical illnesses. It is especially beneficial when several thoughts are united in one direction. The one who is falling ill often does not even suspect the possibility of having an illness. It is helpful for his consciousness to be open, so as not to resist the beneficent sendings. That is why it is essential to be always attentive to the sendings from space.

There is no need to fall into self-deception and imagine what does not exist, but the consciousness must always be vigilant. It is sad to see how people remember that help is possible only when it is already too late. There are many examples of people who could have been cured, but their consciousness resisted and pushed away the helping hand.

There are people who, though unacquainted with the laws of psychic energy, are sometimes able to admit beneficial sendings. We rejoice when someone, even unconsciously, comes to the right path. Such unknowing people should be treated with care. They can easily be lost to Us, but a light, friendly touch can open their sealed treasury. Great patience is needed, and also great tolerance. These attitudes are of help in everything, including mental healing. A good physician knows the ways of caring for his patient.

The Thinker urged physicians to understand that the heart and the will are the best remedies.

553. Urusvati knows that tolerance is totally misunderstood. It is often seen either as condescension or as overindulgence of others. Since both of these are considered to be wrong, it is clear that the very idea of tolerance is not perceived in a proper way. But We see it as one of the basic qualities of humaneness. In human relations it must be reciprocal. All earthly life should be based on tolerance and compassion. Sometimes people manifest these benevolent attitudes consciously, but more often their tolerance and compassion are simply the result of an inherent goodness, and they themselves do not always recognize the value of these acts of kindness.

In everyday life, there is always someone who knows more than others, but because of kindness does not condescend or reproach others for their ignorance. On the contrary he will do his best to offer his knowledge without offense. We have often told you about speaking according to the level of consciousness of one's listener. This is the humane way.

We are often asked about Our Inner Life. Indeed, it is humane and based upon great patience. Do not think of Us as boastful when I speak about Our great patience. It must be great, well-tested, and based upon love for humanity.

It is not possible in daily life to easily develop patience. The crowding currents of space do not help in its cultivation. Many currents impede people who are totally unaware of them. We know how difficult the earthly life is. He who, in his ignorance, thinks of life as easy, is in great error. But this transitory earthly life is structured wisely; in it one forges the blade of spirit. The seed of the spirit is indestructible, but it is clothed in garments that are woven by man himself. This weaving is not easy!

Planting the seeds of humaneness must be done with forethought, for this garden is cultivated for a higher beauty. Thus do We point out the foundations of Our Inner Life. If someone has the desire and steadfastness to apply them, let it be so. The more tense the hour, the greater the merit of an accomplished deed. We do not hide the complexity of the foundations of life. In this mutual trust is humaneness strengthened.

The Thinker understood how many are the obstacles on the path. When encountering an obstacle, He would whisper, "Let us walk around this stone."

554. Urusvati knows that within man is contained all that exists. He can evoke anything in himself, from the beginnings of all illnesses to the highest transcendental possibilities. He can allow himself to develop any illness, but he can just as easily join the Higher Forces. Man needs only to understand that he is an inseparable part of the Universe. Misfortunes occur when people forget their possibilities, something they do far too often—that is why there are so many calamities.

No narrow reasoning can replace a true understanding of man's role. Man is the uniting bridge between the worlds. He must not forget his mission. His task is great, in all realms of labor. He cannot avoid the gifts reserved for him without becoming a source of calamity. Especially during the days of Armageddon, man must ponder over the meaning of his stay here. He cannot withdraw from preordained possibilities.

No religions will save man if he limits himself to their superficial conventionalities. The study of cosmic phenomena must not be overlooked. Scientists must look beyond seeing them as chance occurrences. Someone should trace the correlation between humanity's moods and nature's phenomena. Let science learn to judge even the subtlest combinations and correlations. Let us not force, but simply express the wish that science explore the true essence of man more broadly.

The Thinker knew that the time will come when science will look beyond the limits of earthly existence.

555. Urusvati knows well that most people are quite incapable of telepathic thought. They cannot even begin to understand what mental concentration is. Their thoughts are like moths around a flame. They do not care that when sustained thinking is fragmented by countless petty, everyday thoughts, a great cacophony results. They would become quite indignant if a telegraph operator in the middle of sending a message inserted his own words. They would be exasperated if in the middle of a virtuoso's playing someone were to touch the strings. From the point of view of the listeners it would be impermissible. But when thoughts are interrupted by some foolish exclamation, there is no criticism because the significance of thought is simply not understood. But it must be recognized that thought is at the very foundation of our being.

Some will insist that special schools are required for learning concentration of thought. Not at all–everyone can practice thought-concentration, beginning with the most simple ways. If one compels oneself to think clearly at least one quarter of an hour daily, there will be good results.

Let us not forget that every thought is heard by someone. Is it not shameful to let loose shaggy thinking into space? We are saddened when instead of clear thoughts such coarse fragments reach Us. Often, even when somebody calls out to Us, in the Name itself some broken fragments are injected. One must be considerate of the one who receives, and try to communicate briefly, clearly, and without extraneous details. Decide for yourself what is the most important and find the best way to express it.

The Thinker taught, "If you can express the most lofty in a brief way, do so."

556. Urusvati knows that air travel was known to the Atlanteans. Does it not seem strange that after the destruction of Atlantis this achievement was lost? After all, some Atlanteans who were left alive could have known the secret of flight. Yet, instead of this there remained in the chronicles only brief hints about airships, and later these were forgotten for a long time. Information about Solomon and his flying ship remained only as a fairy tale, just like the fairy tale about the flying carpet. For a long time humanity has dreamt about wings; this quest has continued for thousands of years.

Why should humanity have been deprived of this advantage for so long? This is not the only achievement that was forgotten, as if taken from us. But it could not have been otherwise; people ignored the true purpose of these accomplishments.

It is no wonder that today also many discoveries are being delayed. One can learn about records of vital importance that have disappeared, causing a prepared discovery to be delayed.

People are ready to believe fairy tales rather than look at reality. Progress has its cycles, and it is time to pay attention to the waves of human attainment. It is right to say that history offers only fragmentary information, but even these brief hints will help the thoughtful researcher.

The Thinker acknowledged the great age of Earth and man. He affirmed that the planet has lived through many catastrophes. He also wrote about Atlantis, but people for a long time have regarded it as just a myth.

For the ignorant the most obvious reality can become a fairy tale.

557. Urusvati knows how the subtle body is nurtured by good deeds. Many will think that this idea is foolish or even absurd. For them a subtle body does not exist, and the concept of good deeds is a relative one. But in reality, the subtle body gains strength from all that is lofty; that is why good thoughts and deeds are so important.

Similarly, art brings moments of highest joy and thus provides the most nourishing sustenance to the subtle body. When the ancients taught about deriving nourishment from air, they had in mind the influence of its finer qualities upon the subtle body.

Some people think that the subtle body is indestructible, and that no earthly influence can do harm to it, but this idea is incorrect. The subtle body is a material body, and therefore can gain strength, or become sick, or even decompose. It has its own life, which at times may not be in accord with the physical body. The turmoil of outside influences can cause it to cease functioning, even before the end of the physical body.

We have already spoken about the so-called living dead, whose subtle bodies have died, although the physical ones are still living. In such cases the psychic energy is in an abnormal state. It has mostly left the physical body after the death of the subtle body, but as long as the heart continues to work, the energy remains bound to the decomposed subtle sheath.

It must be understood that such organisms cannot progress, and are rapidly sliding downhill. These organisms are empty shells. However, this condition is quite different from that of obsession, which also can occur when the subtle body is weak but can still be nourished and healed by lofty deeds.

The Thinker insisted that man should rekindle his heart with music, since music was linked to the realm of all the Muses.

558. Urusvati knows how multicolored Agni Yoga is. An attentive eye can distinguish many tints in its flame. Surrounding conditions do of course affect the colors of the flame. And at different times different kinds of yoga are needed. One can perceive the magnificence of Raja Yoga, the radiance of Bhakti Yoga, and the tension of Jnana Yoga, but one can also see the ever present need for the luminous Karma Yoga. Labor is a constant during these days of mankind's confusion. Thus, amidst the varied flowers of Agni Yoga we can find the stem of Karma Yoga, upon whose foundation humanity will find salvation.

Let us not wonder that preference was not always given to the austere Karma Yoga. At times it seemed to be forgotten before the other more appealing and benign yogas. We know that Karma Yoga cannot offer such rapid attainments as Bhakti Yoga, but labor will be the anchor of salvation of the planet. Let the purple of the Raja Yogi be grand and the blue radiance of the Bhakti Yogi beautiful, but no less beautiful are the combined blue and violet colors of the Karma Yogi. He receives, as it were, something from both the purple and the blue radiance. His labor is majestic and impelled by love. Thus, in the flame of Our Agni Yoga one can see the luminous colors of labor.

It is essential that man deeply apprehend the beauty of flourishing labor. He must learn to understand labor not as the means to daily bread, but as the way to salvation of the planet. Precisely, conscious labor creates the healing emanation that can combat the poisonous lower layers of the atmosphere.

We carefully observe those who toil. Among them are true Karma Yogis, but often they cannot call themselves this, because they have never even heard the term. The laboring multitudes do not know the word, but they do know the ultimate importance of labor.

The Thinker taught, "No history can point out the true toilers. Their names are preserved beyond the clouds."

559. Urusvati knows that all yogas demand profound discipline. This should be stressed, because some people think that there are yogas that do not require strictly disciplined conduct. They believe that some yogas are more difficult than others, and dream about following the easiest. But all require the same degree of inner discipline.

For the yogi, there must be a great degree of tension of the psychic energy, because it builds an immunity that is so needed during the opening of the centers. The yogi has been compared to a person with flayed skin. This is a crude analogy, but not without truth. If the yogi did not develop immunity, he would not be able to endure the contact with the spatial currents. Urusvati knows that certain currents cause painful scraping and prickly sensations. One can imagine what might happen without the building of immunity!

Some will be sure to smile when We say that the main factor in the acquiring of immunity is a good thought. But one cannot become a yogi without acknowledging the power of good thoughts. Such thoughts are the best gatekeepers at the entrance to the Subtle World.

So many people imagine themselves to be yogis, yet they are filled with malice! People assume that they will experience a sudden enlightenment that will by its own power carry them over all obstacles. It is true that enlightenment can be sudden, but for this to occur a great inner tension must be steadily accumulated. It is not the crossing of the legs, but the concentration of good thought that will be effective. Voluntary, daily discipline of thought brings the best results.

We return many times to this concept of voluntariness. It is the foremost condition of discipline. The least thought about forcing destroys all achievements. Not only does the Teacher not compel, but the disciple also must not force himself. The discipline of Good is a self-generated joy. What an indestructible immunity is created through joy! The calmness of a yogi is not due to detached imperturbability, but to an inner, flaming joy. Such is the path of discipline. Some will say: How easy! But they do not know that joy is a special wisdom.

The Thinker taught, "He who has learned joy has already stepped onto the path of wisdom."

560. Urusvati knows that psychic energy responds to even the smallest atmospheric change. This energy is different in each individual. It is therefore more difficult to study its qualities, for there is insufficient terminology to describe its manifestations. Yet it can be seen that psychic energy is responsive to everything connected with the person.

For example, one can hear fragmentary, chaotic words that may seem senseless, but each of them is directly or indirectly relevant. The individual cannot shut down his apparatus to cut off the distant simultaneous calls, but he can sense when something has a particular significance.

Often, it is difficult to determine the relative significance of what has been heard, but all communications are stored in the repository of consciousness. In time they emerge from the depths of the consciousness and reveal the true meaning of events.

Thus We observe the innumerable properties of psychic energy. It is impossible to apply one simple law to encompass them. There is a special beauty in the multiform manifestations of this energy. The generosity of Cosmos is expressed by these unrepeatable manifestations, which will always be beyond the grasp of the human mind. But this should not be an obstacle to the study of psychic energy. It is like an endless book of Nature. Therefore We summon all humanity to join in the study of the primary energy.

The Thinker foresaw that man could master his relationship with Nature, if he learned which gates must be opened for this achievement.

561. Urusvati knows that the teacher cannot force the will of the disciple, yet at the same time guidance must continue. This task is difficult, even for an experienced teacher. One can see that similar difficulties are found in every walk of life.

It is not by following a previously thought-out method, but by attending to the promptings of his heart, that the teacher finds the way toward the perfectment of the student's free will. It can be cultivated, but tender touches are needed so as not to cause distress. The teacher must know that the perfected will is the most precious victory. It is the will alone that brings one closer to the path of evolution. One should not trample this flower, which blossoms throughout one's many lives. The most delicate care must be taken in the education of the will!

I affirm that not only education is needed, but also enlightenment, for when the guidance touches such a sensitive apparatus as the student's will it is inevitably linked with psychic energy, which the will expresses in the manifestation of striving forward. The will vibrates continuously and must develop. A loss of will means decay. Without will, it is impossible to face the onslaughts of chaos.

The Thinker taught His disciples to use even everyday events to sharpen their will. He used to say, "The bow must not be left unused, lest it dry up and break."

562. Urusvati knows the chronicles of the ancient Mystical Brotherhoods which describe the many obstacles encountered by the initiates on their path. From these records one can see that the Brotherhoods were fully informed about the laws of Existence. The Teachers in the Brotherhoods warned the novices about the inevitable attacks by the forces of darkness. The Brothers were not disheartened by the horrors unleashed by those forces. On the contrary, they knew that with their gradual ascent the ferocity of the attacks would increase.

Much advice has been given about how to avoid confusion and doubt. There once was a solemn hymn that was intended to be sung at times of dire persecution. When injustices were inflicted upon the Brothers, it was joy that had to be expressed, and sympathy that was to surround the persecuted Ones, who were hailed in the same manner as those bestowed with the highest honors.

But one condition was not indicated–the chronicles did not mention wealth or money, for the reason that everyone who entered the Community renounced personal property. If a newcomer had money he declared it and then was designated a keeper of this common property, given to the community. Only with uplifted thinking could such unity, based upon fullest trust, exist.

One might wonder that such Communities could exist. From the modern point of view they seem impracticable, but in the remote past, although people had no "iron wings," they sometimes possessed wings of Light. People do not recognize that their ancestors might have had flights of thought that led them to a beautiful self-renunciation. Yet Earth did have such dwellers, and they were capable of thinking about the Common Good.

The Thinker suggested to the people, "If you have forgotten about self-sacrifice, let us then walk to the cemetery. Let the sarcophagi of your ancestors remind you of valor, of a time when life was given for your native land. The necropolis may at times be more alive than the Acropolis."

563. Urusvati knows that some people believe that nothing exists beyond their life on Earth. It is of no use to talk to these people about the Subtle World. Their consciousness is not able to contain and keep the reality of the Subtle World, and they therefore cannot bring any recollection of it to their new lives. With words alone it is impossible to instill in them any idea of the continuity of life. Only personal experience will gradually help them to understand the essence of things and learn to deepen their consciousness.

One can find such negators among those who are considered to be pragmatists. But both these labels, negator and pragmatist, are often misapplied. They must be tested against real evidence. A denial that is not confirmed by evidence is simply based on ignorance. The majority of people have their own ideas about the supermundane existence, and these ideas should be examined with similar care. They understand the Subtle World in varied ways, depending upon their own traditions and beliefs. Actually, the Subtle World is so varied that each notion about it does have some element of truth. Therefore, one should not attempt to persuade people that their ideas have no validity. Thought can create unlimited variations of reality. The substance of the Subtle World appears to be covered, as it were, by a web of human imaginings.

The dwellers of the Subtle World must learn by themselves to experience the beauty of the ascent. They cannot be forced to discover this beauty if their eyes are still unable to perceive reality. But care should be taken that people understand the continuity of life, that they accept this truth as immutable, and that they learn to love the path of ascent. Let us not dispute how best to impart this knowledge. It must be remembered that each wanderer will approach the truth, but only if he wishes to. Let people yearn for this, then nothing on Earth can impede their striving.

The Thinker used to say, "The will directed to good gains victory. Both the simple stonecutter and the great architect serve equally to build the temple."

564. Urusvati knows that religious strife is the cruelest of all. One should not interfere in religious disputes. People should not devour one another in the name of their Merciful God, and should work only to create good.

The Teaching is good only when it is in worthy hands. This can be said about all human institutions. It was observed long ago that the quality of life depends on the integrity of the leaders. Great tolerance is needed, so as not to intrude upon the beliefs of others.

With great care one can introduce knowledge about all creeds into education, but it must be taught wisely. We have spoken about the harm that is caused by coercing. Remember, coercion is the poisoning of consciousness. Everyone must be free to express his own beliefs, but it is difficult to do this without succumbing to the temptation to convert others. Let each state his beliefs simply as a means of self-expression, without creating the impression of a desire to influence others. Only a refined consciousness will indicate the beautiful line that leads one to freely chosen service. People are afraid of this word, service, because it implies obligation. But one should accept courageously all that is connected with duty for the sake of the General Good.

The Thinker commented, "Do you hear how noisy those people are in the public square? Once again they depose the old gods in order to populate their Olympus with new ones."

565. Urusvati knows that love for humanity does not exclude love for one's country. There is a mistaken notion that the concept of humanity is the loftier one, that it is a sign of broad thinking, and that it diminishes the importance of the individual nation. We have spoken often and enough about humanity and directed attention to it, but it is appropriate now to speak about the concept of the mother country.

It is not without reason that someone is born in a certain country and belongs to a certain people. Karmic conditions direct one to a particular place. Prior to incarnation, one learns the reasons for one's destiny and assents to it. Each incarnation takes place voluntarily. There may be a reluctance to return to Earth, but at some point it becomes unavoidable, and at the last moment is agreed to.

One may feel a particular attachment to, or alienation from, different nations, but weighty reasons impel the newcomer toward one particular nation. Knowing all this, one can understand the attraction one feels toward one's native land. In one's service to mankind, there is no doubt that the greater part of one's effort will be given to the land of one's birth.

One should not think that a special love for the mother country is a limiting or unworthy feeling. Even knowing the imperfections of the country will not diminish one's striving for it. Karma leads one not only to a particular place, but also to certain tasks to serve a certain people.

People frequently reject their motherland because of the intrusion of life's circumstances. They do not know the true essence of things and fail to fulfill their karmic task. Frequently they will repeat an old cynical saying, "Wherever life is good, there is my motherland." There is great error in such cynicism. Truly, he can best serve mankind who does so for the sake of his motherland.

Human dignity is becoming lost in the world's turbulence. Under the spell of conventional understanding, people lose true wisdom. This indicates that one should turn to the foundations–to the truly scientific foundations. Learning the laws of karma will help one to perceive man's destination.

With such knowledge, a person can never be deprived of freedom or happiness. Wings may carry him throughout the world, and he will love all mankind, but will also know that he serves his native country.

In the Teaching of Life, the destination of man must be explained clearly. There are many obstacles and confusions on the path. No one wants to be seen as backward, and in his desire for acceptance man is ready to care more about the population of the entire planet than about the needs of his country. Let man be reminded where his best forces must be applied.

The Thinker strove to develop a true understanding

of the concept of the motherland. He used to say, "Citizen, serve your motherland and know that you came here to fulfill a great duty."

566. Urusvati knows that while each one of Us was striving to the Supermundane, He never disregarded the earthly. Can one neglect this Earth, which nourishes mankind and where the attainment of perfection takes place? Man understands the value of Earth, but often expresses it wrongly.

Each one of Us labors for Earth, but even those of Us who prefer monastic ways do not sentence themselves to a hermit's life. They continue creating and offer labor for the benefit of mankind. They never weigh themselves down with gold. They commune with laymen and are known as peacemakers and builders.

However, we do not condemn hermits, who bring great help by the power of their thought. We see how these spiritual toilers are able to command the psychic forces. They purify their spiritual essence to such an extent that they are in advance of the rest of humanity. But Our work is devoted to more direct ways of help to people.

Our Inner Life can be expressed simply: We help. This labor is most difficult because people reject Our help in so many ways. They beg for it, but when it begins to take shape, they not only do not offer assistance, but, as it were, take up arms against it!

Many a time We have asked people not to oppose Our help. But they judge in their own way, and every higher concept is seen as a threat. Thus, We do not often receive cooperation, though it is of great urgency, for Earth desperately needs extraordinary efforts by human hands and feet. Thus the Supermundane compels one to think about the earthly.

The Thinker was a great philosopher, but he required His disciples to be active participants in the life of the nation.

567. Urusvati knows about the magnetic storms that influence the health and feelings of people and animals–indeed, of all that exists. But people are especially subject to the effects of psychic storms. Spatial currents are always present, and can be exceedingly difficult to bear, but their effect can be made even worse by psychic storms.

Magnetic storms take place independent of human participation, but psychic storms are actually generated by humanity's misdeeds. For example, during terrible wars and calamities, it can be seen that not only physical but also psychic illnesses increase.

It is strange that physicians do not recognize this. They will say that at such times it is field-surgeons who are needed, but they do not realize that psychiatrists are also needed, and not only on the battlefield. They overlook extraordinary conditions that are now far more prevalent than ever before.

Do not take this statement to mean that the situation is hopeless, or Armageddonal, but it is true that at present the clashes are so violent that healing actions are desperately needed, and not only on the battlefield. But we should not fall into pessimism, because even such global storms will inevitably lead to purification. For now, however, remember that man's inner state is under great stress.

The Thinker foresaw that with an ever-increasing population, the world's dangers, both visible and invisible, will continue to increase.

568. Urusvati knows that an undeveloped imagination is an impediment to the process of self-perfectment. People usually think of imagination as the creator of things that are unreal, but in fact a correctly developed imagination serves to broaden the consciousness, and adds to the flexibility of thinking.

When people hear a piece of information or an idea, they will usually interpret it according to their own ego's understanding, and instead of discerning the true meaning, they replace it with illusive interpretations. Because of their poorly developed imagination, their understanding is narrowed and distorted.

People think that the imagination tends to lead them away from what is real, but it is the developed imagination that permits a broader perception of reality. Let us not forget that the imagination derives mainly from the accumulation of experiences from one's past lives. Research based on such experiences cannot produce a mirage.

A widely educated person should possess a rich imagination. For such an individual the realm of the impossible is diminished, and possibilities multiply. Those who are endowed with imagination are not dreamers. The dream of the enlightened mind is true foresight.

The significance of imagination must be clearly understood, especially during this time of renewal in the world, with its reconsideration of values. The conventional understanding of all our concepts must be re-examined, for without this, humanity will wander forever in a phantom-world. May true knowledge lead people to the Supermundane! For this revision of one's way of life, bravery is needed.

The Thinker taught, "It may be that our vision is obscured by dust; let us rid our house of it."

569. Urusvati knows the joy that comes from feasting one's eyes on perfection: the grandeur of nature; a self-sacrificing deed; quality of craftsmanship or of engineering. High quality is always a feast, and a joy. This kind of admiration is without ego.

People are endowed with a beautiful gift–the ability not only to create, but also to recognize quality and rejoice in it. Whether rich or poor, ruler or beggar, all can do this. And from this, joy is born–a healing dome over our long-suffering Earth.

People are justly horrified by the abominations that poison our world. They ask how these ulcers of humanity can be healed. One of the truest remedies is joy. It is the best antidote for both the body and the soul. Fortunately, no one can be deprived of the ability to rejoice.

Joy as a response to quality is luminous. This kind of joy, without selfishness, adds to the Common Good. We live Our lives sustained by this joy. Both nature and creativeness offer inexhaustible joys, without which a devastating battle would cover everything with darkness. Our Inner Life is lived not only in toil, but also in joy.

The Thinker knew the healing property of joy. He taught, "Even the least of the slaves cannot be deprived of the joy of the Universe."

570. Urusvati knows that karma delayed is karma multiplied. It is necessary for everyone to understand to what extent they can assist in accelerating the actions of karma. Thinking excessively about the past is detrimental. It is better, much better, to think about one's future actions. Let them be perfect, let them be guided by the strongest striving. By striving for a better future, one will sooner be able to live through a considerable portion of one's karma.

What is commonly called repentance is usually misunderstood. It is thought of as continuing remorse for one's former misdeeds, but such an immersion in the past impedes one from the possibility for advancement. Is it not better to simply replace one's imperfection with something more perfect? People must be persuaded to think about the future. Let the ship rush to its destined harbor and not wander the ocean in search of lost cargo that has already sunk to the bottom! The ship must not waste time in futile searching. It is better for the ship to lose part of its cargo than to arrive late at the harbor, where new tasks await.

One could point out many examples from the past when striving to the future brought the best results. This applies on Earth as well as in the Subtle World. Thinking about the Supermundane must be accompanied by striving toward the future. This is a proper approach to the great law of karma.

The Thinker encouraged his disciples to develop a correct attitude to so-called destiny. He used to say, "The Great Moira will not hold you if you turn to the right path and race to the future."

571. Urusvati knows the difference between a *podvig*–a fiery achievement–and a prudent act. A *podvig* is beautiful, majestic, solemn, wise, and awe-inspiring. It can never be described as prudent.

When Joan of Arc addressed the elders of her village and spoke about *podvig*, they found her imprudent, and even reckless. Of course, a *podvig* is reckless, for it is performed not out of deliberation, but out of straight-knowledge.

There are many for whom the idea of *podvig* simply does not exist. For them, prudence is the highest ethical level. Their entire world outlook is defined by prudence. For the sake of it they would refuse help to their fellow man, they would be willing to betray their country, even to bring harm to humanity, and they are ready to justify all their crimes by repeating this dead word–prudence.

Do not interpret Our attitude toward prudence falsely. This word is based on good concepts; goodness is always good and a wise understanding is always useful. But the worldly misinterpreters manage to turn good ideas into shameful ways. If they could, they would eliminate the word *podvig*, which is so completely against their mentality.

Teachers must teach the differences between concepts, otherwise their pupils will repeat ideas senselessly, like parrots. The polluting of human speech is a public crime.

Here is one more page of Our Inner Life. We can confirm that each of Us performed acts of *podvig*, some of which were noted by historians, though most of them went unnoticed. One should not burden one's memory in thinking about one's own successful acts of *podvig*. But excessive prudence is not for Us. We may recommend caution and a careful weighing of possibilities, but if a fiery act of *podvig* is profound in its significance, the more We shall rejoice. We note every act of *podvig*, for it forges new evolutionary links.

The Thinker said, "Leave prudence to the shopkeepers, love the daring of the heroes."

572. Urusvati has been told, and knows, that Ajita–the personal name, meaning invincible, of the Bodhisattva Maitreya–has put on his coat of mail. Is it proper for a Peacemaker to clothe himself in a warrior's garb? We have discussed the general welfare sufficiently. We have stressed the need to protect the creative work of mankind. We have pointed out the horrors of fratricide. And We have also spoken about the dignity of one's native land. Thus, the most com-

mitted Peacemaker on the one hand indicated that all means should be used for establishing peace, and on the other sent armies to defend the frontiers of the land of His people.

People tend to see an unresolvable contradiction: How can Ajita the Peacemaker advocate battle? This is difficult to understand if one's thinking is based on false values. Man should accept the idea of protecting and saving his country, and reject entirely any idea of its enslavement. Let man discern in his own heart where enslavement begins, and where defense is necessary.

And now a few words about the coat of mail. For Us, steel coats of mail are not needed, for the armor of psychic energy is far stronger. Thus one can surround oneself with an impenetrable, invisible armor. People may notice the invulnerability of some heroes. To attain this, a powerful upsurge of the will is needed in order to face dangers without harm.

The Thinker taught the young people, "Sometimes the best armor is the invisible one. Learn to command yourself to produce such armor, and it will appear whenever you fight for the Common Good."

573. Urusvati knows that sensitivity must be cultivated. When We speak about a "sensitive ear," some people assume that We refer to physical hearing. Some also think that sensitivity is an inherent quality, and that attempting to develop it is futile. Indeed, sensitivity is an inherent quality, but it depends upon the purity of one's consciousness. Even in the best instances, it must be developed, or more precisely, called forth from the depths of consciousness.

One must first of all want to acquire sensitivity. A state of psychic alertness must be cultivated. This is not easy. Everyone will find within himself his own obstacles; some will be impeded by laziness, some by lack of faith, some by the bustle of daily life. Everyone is hindered by something, but the power of will can overcome anything.

Nor should one indulge in wishful thinking, for this encourages one to rely on illusions. Psychic hearing should be developed with the utmost honesty, and experiences truthfully recorded. Earthquakes and other cosmic agitations will serve as an opportunity to exercise one's psychic sensitivity.

Likewise, sensitivity to the auras of others opens a vast field for observation. Amidst the most ordinary routines of life, one can find opportunities for the sharpening of one's sensitivity equal to those available in the best laboratories. Let man make use of all possibilities, because everyone is affected equally by cosmic influences.

The Thinker taught, "Supermundane worlds send us the subtlest sensations; let us learn to be receptive to them."

574. Urusvati knows that the spreading of false information is an especially harmful manifestation of ignorance. But what can be done about school textbooks that propagate so many errors? The humanitarian and physical sciences progress, aspiring to new, verified achievements. Is it fair for the younger generations to be offered obsolete, meager misconceptions instead of real attainments? Much confusion is brought into young consciousnesses through false information.

If textbooks are not corrected, then teachers must speak to their pupils about the mistakes of the past. Is it not shameful that distortions are perpetuated and thus afflict the young consciousnesses? This is certainly the case with information about supermundane matters.

Let us not be too disturbed if we see that ancient texts were misunderstood or incorrectly translated. Different languages have their own peculiarities. In today's understanding, many customary terms have lost their true meaning, but scientists will eventually find their way through this labyrinth, and the true knowledge must be made available first of all to the young ones.

Scientists must be committed to affirming the foundations of truth, even if this forces them to discard their previous ideas. The humanitarian sciences must have access to improved translations of the ancient texts. It is astonishing that people speak much about new directions, while textbooks contrive to repeat their misconceptions. You know that cognizance of the Supermundane requires utmost honesty.

The Thinker used to say, "If people must approach the earthly with honesty, how much more honestly must they deal with the Supermundane!"

575. Urusvati knows that in the Supermundane World, time, in its earthly meaning, does not exist, although there are dates that relate to inevitable consequences of certain events. Valid prophecies never offer indications of earthly time. You already know that foreseen supermundane dates are given indirectly through descriptions of their related events. This shows that the supermundane worlds foresee the flow of events, without attention to so-called time. A sensitive consciousness will be able to remember the details of a future event, and accordingly discern the rest.

Even during his earthly life man can learn that time does not exist. For example, he loses his own sense of time when his aspirations are strong. This tension exists in the same way in the Supermundane World. When we become engrossed in our labor we do not think about time. Not without reason is it said that concentrated labor, full of striving, aids longevity. From it harmony is born. Because of it, the perception of supermundane knowledge becomes possible, and events are understood in their full logical and chemical significance. It must always be remembered that chemism is part of every manifestation.

This is one more page of Our Inner Life. We strive to be in harmony with the Supermundane World. We do not value time in its earthly sense. The essence of events, their flow, and their correlation are of utmost significance. We reveal the meaning of events in an accessible form. In everything the essence must be felt. Therein lies the ability for equanimity, about which We have already spoken.

The Thinker taught, "Strive to the essence of things, in it is revealed the justice of the Universe."

576. Urusvati knows that the times during which one has the experience of straight-knowledge were called by the Egyptians Sacred Sleep, by the Hellenes Divine Visitation, and by the Babylonians The Touch of the Unseen Visitor. Each nation in its own way wanted to note the special and unusual nature of such experiences of insight, when earthly man makes contact with the supermundane realms.

The ancient ones understood this state better than do people today. They lived with nature and were not endangered by poisonous emanations. But this is sufficiently known. I wish now to speak about another aspect of this condition. Our contemporaries are developing a right attitude to hypnotism and it is now being used with benefit in medical and other realms. But for achieving a hypnotic state, the assistance of another person is needed. However, even if this person's consciousness is lofty and refined, he will still introduce elements of his own personality.

In the future it will be desirable to go back to the practice of direct insight. But even the Delphic Prophetesses required the use of certain vaporous substances, mainly because the supplicants overburdened their primary energy. But the evolutionary process requires that people gain insight only through a purified consciousness. The proper striving of thought will lead to the development of insight in a right and natural way.

This too is one more indication about Our Inner Life. Our many lives of experience have led us to the most natural application of Our energies. Achieving such synthesis is not a simple matter, but once achieved, it leads to the most natural and simple ways.

The Thinker taught, "Let each one attempt to find within himself the simplest solutions. Friends cannot be of help when one must stand alone before the Supermundane Grandeur."

577. Urusvati knows that the unique and unrepeatable nature of events in the universe is characteristic of its special beauty. Even the simplest shepherd can see the individuality of each animal in his herd, but city dwellers too easily lose the ability to recognize what is individual. Generalizations are applied in addressing all issues, and recognition of the great generosity of nature is lost.

Because they cannot discern the multiformity in nature, people ask Us for instructions that can be applied to all. We can offer instructions in a general way, but beyond that, details for each individual are needed.

People ask about Our apparatuses, but they would be quite disappointed to learn that many of them are simply plates made of materials that function well together. Some are made from only one metal, and others from different alloys. There are also plates made of minerals, and some of certain kinds of wood. A wide variety of methods is used both for sending and receiving. Conductors can be found in all kingdoms of nature, but their application is quite specific.

Our implements are not chosen in haste, but only after lengthy testing. We have had ample time to study the properties of Nature, and have gathered this knowledge in different ages and climates, and under varied conditions. At first Our desire to know was strengthened; then a conviction was formed that observations can be conducted under almost any conditions. The matured will enabled Us to draw knowledge from the Supermundane. An awareness grew that time has no meaning in Infinity. Our many failures still did not cause doubt. An increased power of observation accelerated the gathering of knowledge. Along the way, We learned to see who are the helpers and who the hinderers.

Do not think that experiments and observations are easy. If one out of a hundred succeeds, that is success. We never regret failure, because it teaches more than success. It is regrettable when someone is too eager to achieve success immediately. One should not waste time, nor regret time spent. One should observe oneself, but without making oneself the center of the Universe. One can find success at all times and in all things. In such labors, one strengthens one's will.

You understand that it would be wrong to prescribe that everyone sleep on iron or keep a lithium plate nearby. Roses or apples are gifts of nature that may be beneficial to some, but not to all. Pay careful attention to effects. Although nature's crudest idiosyncrasies are the most evident, you know that everything that exists is distinct and individual. One should learn to be sensitive to the causes and effects of everything. Conducting such observations will be a worthy step on the path of yoga.

The Thinker taught, "It is said that some dwellers in heaven are all-powerful. Well, let us gather all our strength, perhaps a place has been prepared for us in heaven. But this Ladder is a tall one!"

578. Urusvati knows that thoughts about eternity need not be linked to thoughts about death. If a bee flies into the house the right response is to set it free. And this is the common expression–to set free, in order to fly to freedom. Cannot the same be said about man? If he is in bondage here on Earth, and free in eternity, then joy must surely be found there. But thought about eternity will cause joy here, too. One who thinks about the meaning of life, about soaring over earthly obstacles, knows how to feel joy.

The unknowing ones think that lofty thoughts are always filled with sadness and boredom, but the one who has tasted knowledge will be filled with joy in life. Even thinking about his past errors will bring him joy, because he knows that the realization of one's errors is the true way to leave one's misconceptions behind.

Some wonder how it is possible to speak of joy during times of hardship. But it is on the wings of joy that one flies over the abyss. When man has reached impassable rapids he cannot turn back and must fly over them in order to circumvent the danger. It is happiness that the wings of joy are always with him. The beauty of the universe helps to call forth from the depths of the consciousness sparks of joy. And this is one more page of Our Inner Life.

The Thinker referred to the stars as the sparks of Joy.

579. Urusvati knows that it is most difficult for man to gain control of his thoughts. By an effort of the will man can eject a thought, but this does not mean that he can free his consciousness from the roots of that thought; a deep psychological process is taking place. One may assume that his thinking has changed, but the smallest reminder will prove that the viper continues to live in the depths, ready to reawaken.

The ocean currents are a good example of this. What has the wave on the surface in common with the depths, where a monster stirs, but never rises to the surface? The same happens with human thinking. One speaks about the power of the will that can rule thought. But the question is, what kind of thought is meant? Man can know that he is free from a certain thought only when he is sure that it has been torn out, roots and all. But it is not easy to be certain of anything when we speak about depths of consciousness.

One can observe the fleeting circumstances that may evoke a thought. Sound, color, or chance surroundings can in a flash revive a thought that was assumed to have been driven away long ago. Man knows that it is unhealthy to wallow in past errors, but he nevertheless returns again and again to wander around in the useless ashes.

Man must learn to distinguish the many levels of thinking. He must not lightmindedly judge according to the superficial layer of thought, which is so vulnerable to strong disturbances. Let man test himself upon many of life's events. Frequently, it may seem that one has stopped thinking about something, when in fact, on another level, he is quite immersed in thought about it. When teaching about thinking, its many-layered diversity must be pointed out.

The Thinker insisted that the disciples should test themselves upon all the different strata of thinking. "Or else," He said, "an invisible dragon can take possession of a man."

580. Urusvati knows that many people will always refuse to accept the existence of Our Brotherhood. Even if they were to meet Us they would still be skeptical. There is no limit to skepticism. On the one hand, it springs from ignorance, and on the other it is based on erroneous thinking. The skeptics will never soar over an abyss. But there are those among them who are willing to accept the idea that We exist in subtle bodies.

The main thing is for people to acknowledge Our existence, and not to argue about forms. It is wrong to insist on a particular form, because co-workers from the Subtle World, in many forms, are also close to Us. Thus, people who can admit at least a part of the whole are already recognizing truth. If one accepts just a part of the truth, the rest will eventually follow.

Worst of all are the dogmatic ones who demand that everything be according to their own beliefs and reject everything else. Especially in the sphere of subtle energies, all ideas must be accepted as possible. We often sorrow over those preachers who repel more people than they attract. One should observe carefully, in order to determine the degree of receptivity of the listener. Even the avid denier can quickly turn into a supporter. Furious denial is sometimes like an abscess prior to opening; but if you should meet someone who denies Our existence, I advise you not to argue. Each vegetable ripens in its own time.

The Thinker said, "It is impermissible to coerce the

human consciousness. Those who are not ready must first mature."

581. Urusvati knows that Our friends in no way resemble those individuals who call themselves occultists and claim to be experts in the sacred knowledge, but exhibit traits that true occultists would not retain. They are often spiteful, rude, envious, intolerant, and without kindness. The sacred knowledge leaves no room for such shameful characteristics.

It is astonishing that people can study books that teach good, yet cannot part with their base habits. The teaching of good requires that the reader, at least to a small degree, will apply what he learns. But in life one can see precisely the opposite; the reader will shed tears of rapture, and immediately afterward do something shameful. Even so, such people love to boast about their self-proclaimed status.

Pay attention to those who are committed to true advancement. They do not impose their beliefs. They avoid claiming degrees of initiation. They always know that it is better not to speak about even their most sacred encounters. They are always kind and ready to offer help. The first task for the true seeker of the sacred knowledge is to cultivate goodness. In doing this he will attract good, like a magnet.

Study of the sacred knowledge requires calmness, and a harmony that enables the student to grasp the subtle vibrations that will purify his consciousness.

Our friends are never arrogant or pompous, because simplicity is their ideal. We value lofty striving, which not only draws Us closer, but also restores the health of the planet. We are saddened by pseudo-keepers of occultism. We do not care for the word itself, for every science is in its way a secret knowledge. Each day science resolves what had been a mystery the day before.

This is the most natural process of evolution; there is no reason to take pride in it.

The Thinker used to say, "Do not be proud of yourselves as thinkers, for everyone thinks."

582. Urusvati knows that human thought often circles around a destined discovery and does not know how to break the circle. People regularly study radio waves and do not realize that the very same methods can be used to study thought waves. Scientists know about magnetic storms, but do not realize that the same theories are applicable to psychic storms. People study the nervous system, but do not relate their study to the subtle energies. Sometimes what they find is at the very brink of the destined discovery, but they do not know how to take the necessary last step. Those who do not recognize the need to broaden the consciousness will circle around, without exit, for a long time.

We admire the nation that is not locked into a tight circle, as are other nations. Urusvati realizes correctly that seeking justice and striving to service makes a nation flexible. Such a nation is on the road to progress. Let it be judged for its many imperfections, but in these imperfections lie the seeds of possibility. Nothing is worse than a perfect little ball spinning forever in a perfect orbit. A nation learns from its misfortunes. Throughout the history of humanity there has been no advance during times of stagnant calm. Each nation that overcomes its misfortunes can also be flexible. The thinking of such a nation is open to new, bold discoveries. Austerity in daily life directs people to the future. It is a joy for Us to help where, amidst poverty, the aspiration toward service grows.

The Thinker spoke about the importance of motion.

"Let the people learn in motion, thus it is easier to find the best rhythms."

583. Urusvati knows that potential traitors are most indignant when treason is mentioned in their presence. Similarly, a criminal grows angry when hearing talk about fighting crime. In the history of every nation shocking examples of treason are cited. This is done not as a threat, but as a perfect illustration of ignorance.

A wise Lover of humanity once told His betrayer, "Do quickly what you have decided!" From the point of view of the Supermundane World this saying was very wise; the abscess of evil had already ripened; let it burst quickly.

Let us also remember the well-known example from the life of India. It would seem that the disciples of Ramakrishna revered him, but that did not prevent them from spying on him with improper motives. Ramakrishna gave all of himself to service. He suffered from an excessive outpouring of psychic energy. He departed before his time because of his self-sacrifice. The same thing happened with his disciple Vivekananda. But Ramakrishna was born to be a yogi. He labored for the higher good. One cannot deny that he was a perfect yogi.

On the other hand you know that there are sadhus who can perform pranayama in the morning, then murder someone in the evening. Their consciousness debases the ways that should serve only the good.

Thus let us bow before the good, whether great or small. Let us not, like merchants, weigh and measure everything, but rejoice when we meet with benevolence and good. These are especially needed in times of tension. The Teaching does not threaten, but warns out of concern. Let those who are not ready to serve at least refrain from ill will.

The Thinker begged his fellow citizens, "If one cannot volunteer to come to the defense of one's people, let him at least not succumb to ill will and spite."

584. Urusvati knows how difficult it is to talk with people who insist that what they cannot see does not exist. They think just as their ancestors did who lived before the discovery of the microscope and telescope. No reasoning can convince them. They call themselves realists, materialists, and skeptics, and call those who disagree idealists, and criticize them for what they see as superstition.

Yet in fact it is the other way around. These skeptics are the idealists, for they cling to ideas that they themselves have invented. And those whom they call idealists are the true realists, desiring only to learn and to gain knowledge from observation. These realists do not allow for superstition or prejudice, for they know about the endless abundance of the manifestations of nature. They trust only what is tested and true. It is they who should be called materialists, because they believe in the omnipresent reality of matter. Can those who are bound in limitation and ignorance claim to be true materialists? At every step you will meet many such people, militant in their ignorance. There is comfort in knowing that there are honest, probing observers who are engaged in studies of the highest realism. Their number is small and they are like the early Christians, forced to hide in catacombs. These researchers deserve respect, but they are harmed by those who are mired in dogmatic thinking. They are also harmed by those who cannot understand why certain levels of achievement are not accessible to them, and criticize everything except themselves.

The Thinker pointed to a dog, saying, "He sees much that is invisible to us. Man should certainly be no less capable than a dog."

585. Urusvati knows that loss of discipline destroys the best undertakings. Do not think that this worm is easily removed. Even the best co-workers can fall victim to this disorder.

It is difficult to talk to people about discipline. In many cases people take offense at the slightest hint about their destructive conduct. It is easier to speak about disorder, because people do not see much harm in it. But violation of discipline is a loss of harmony, a disorder of the most harmful kind.

People may read books that inspire discipline, but the small details of everyday life can intrude and disrupt, with a cacophony of disorder. Even institutions can be destroyed by a thoughtless act that causes disorder. People rarely admit that they can be guilty of such harm. They think they act for the good, when in fact they set up obstacles to the best and most significant undertakings. People usually believe that whatever pleases them constitutes good discipline, but what kind of discipline is it when people undermine useful work?

Harmony cannot be established at once, and one must guard all efforts directed toward the building of harmony. However, harmony is like an easily frightened bird, once lost, difficult to attract again. One should think how painful disharmony is to the Guides. This is something that is rarely considered.

The Thinker warned, "Do not inflict harm by thought or action; it is so easy to break a precious vessel. Think often about true harmony."

586. Urusvati knows that it is easier to see a dragon at one's door than a nest of worms. But who can say which is the more dangerous? Worms will come crawling, bringing with them suspicions and doubts. They will whisper, "We do not know the meaning of Agni Yoga, perhaps it is just an empty sound, leading to delusion. Would it not be better to express its essence in a simpler way that can be discussed and considered?"

All right, let it be as they wish: Agni Yoga is service to good. Understand this definition in its full meaning. Learn to serve good. Learn devotion to the Great Service. Find the fiery forces that will help to manifest courage on all difficult paths. Understand why these paths are difficult. Learn to accept naturally the fires of your nature. Understand all the great manifestations of the Universe. Do not become fatigued with daily labor, which is the best pranayama. Assist all seekers, on all paths.

Experience the greatness of thought that lives in the Infinite. Allow no fear in yourselves, and protect others from it. Immerse yourselves in knowledge, because ignorance is a terrible crime. Welcome the young ones with a smile, for you build the bridges and roads for them. Choose for yourself the heaviest labors, and be an example for all. In this way you will reveal to all the full meaning of service to good. Do not fear the whisperers of doubt, who will always be with you as your shadow. Let your shadow be a long one. Concentrate upon your work and your achievements, gained in a natural way.

The Thinker taught, "Only that which is achieved naturally will create the luminous future."

587. Urusvati knows how harmful undisciplined psychic energy can be. It is already known that the energy of one's thought acts in space, but no one can know the extent of its action. Most earthly thoughts are weak and diffuse, therefore they dissolve into space more readily than concentrated thoughts.

Now imagine what would happen if mankind, in its present condition, were able to produce strong thoughts that can survive in space. What a dangerous and harmful confusion of energy would result! Mankind must first purify itself and ensure the good quality of its thoughts. If that is done, the acceleration of evolution becomes possible.

You often hear complaints about the failed transmission of thoughts, but these complaints are really about the Law of Spatial Balance, which is always fair and just. People who complain should examine the quality of their own thoughts, among which there are assuredly many of bad quality. Keep in mind that thinking has many levels. Man would not object to some of his thoughts being revealed, but would want many of his disorderly and impure thoughts to be kept secret. But all thoughts, secret or revealed, enter space, and disorderly or impure thoughts pollute it. Man must apply himself to the purifying of thinking. This will be action for the good of humanity.

The Thinker advised that at all times, while inhaling and exhaling, man should maintain himself in a state of purity.

588. Urusvati knows the profound meaning of the ancient saying, "Search for Invisible Friends." The appearance of Friends from the Higher World, from the Supermundane, will be a strong support. Sometimes you will recognize Them, but generally They will remain concealed to you. Only the joy felt in your consciousness will indicate Their presence. Do not attempt to learn Their names, for They discarded earthly names long ago. Just as distinctions of time do not exist for Them, so also have earthly distinctions of identity dissolved for these Glorious Beings. The Benefactors! May Their numbers forever increase! They will value all luminous striving, and nothing will divert Their benevolent help when they recognize a developing achievement. They will help where trust is strong. May the benevolence of the Invisible Friends abide with you!

The seeker receives instruction, and then, on his way, awaits the indicated signs. But the way is long and he encounters signs that do not resemble the promised ones. Is there an error? Is he on the right path? Thus doubt intrudes, sapping his strength and weakening resolve. But then, the promised signs begin to shine and the seeker is awe-struck. "Has the preordained time come?" It is regrettable that doubt had affected his courage.

We do not speak only about supermundane Invisible Friends. There are invisible friends on Earth too. One must send them greetings! They can be more helpful than one's known friends. Learn to send a smile to these invisible earthly co-workers.

The Thinker used to say, "It is not only the visible friends who help, but even more, the Invisible ones. Let us not dream of having earthly meetings with Them; let us just send Them a greeting from the heart."

589. Urusvati knows that there are periods of extreme tension in the evolutionary process. There exists a misconception that evolution is inexorable, and that its law is absolute. But we know that everything lives and moves in its individual way. This means that coordination and discipline are needed so that harmony will not be disturbed.

There does exist an evolutionary logic, and this higher logic puts the Law into motion, but only when harmony is achieved in life and becomes a part of its foundation. Times of global change are especially difficult. The nations must clearly understand the path of progress, but for this some seeds of Truth must reach the people.

It is easy to see how many seeds are lost in this process of dissemination–not only lost but also distorted. Conflict is unavoidable where truth is twisted. People can be dissatisfied with all that is human, yet not know enough to turn to the Supermundane. Such discord can result in senseless fratricide. Never think that these cruel manifestations are necessary for evolution. One can only weep, seeing how humanity chooses such horrible ways.

We are astonished when, in spite of their many achievements, people still choose for themselves the crudest ways. This kind of confusion often occurs on the eve of great cosmic change. Knowing this, you can wisely interpret all that takes place.

The Thinker taught, "Besides the laws that are clear to us, there are others that the human mind cannot grasp."

AGNI YOGA SERIES

Leaves of Morya's Garden I (The Call)	1924
Leaves of Morya's Garden II (Illumination)	1925
New Era Community	1926

Signs of Agni Yoga

Agni Yoga	1929
Infinity I	1930
Infinity II	1930
Hierarchy	1931
Heart	1932
Fiery World I	1933
Fiery World II	1934
Fiery World III	1935
Aum	1936
Brotherhood	1937
Supermundane (in 3 volumes)	1938

Agni Yoga Society
www.agniyoga.org

www.ingramcontent.com/pod-product-compliance
Lightning Source LLC
Chambersburg PA
CBHW071557080526
44588CB00010B/939